MANAGING THE AMERICAN ECONOMY FROM ROOSEVELT TO REAGAN

NICOLAS SPULBER

Managing the American Economy from Roosevelt to Reagan

INDIANA UNIVERSITY PRESS
Bloomington and Indianapolis

Manufactured in the United States of America

Library of Congress
Library of Congress Cataloging-in-Publication Data

Spulber, Nicolas.
Managing the American economy, from Roosevelt to Reagan / Nicolas
Spulber.
p.   cm.
Bibliography: p.
Includes index.
ISBN 0-253-33669-4
1. United States—Economic policy.   2. United States—Economic
conditions—1918–1945.   3. United States—Economic conditions—1945–
4. Keynesian economics.   5. Macroeconomics.   I. Title.
HC106.S73   1989
338.973—dc19   88-8224
CIP
1   2   3   4   5   93   92   91   90   89

*For Rachelle and Aaron
for later reading*

CONTENTS

Acknowledgments

The research on which this book is based has been funded in part by two generous grants-in-aid extended to me by the Office of Research and Graduate Development of Indiana University. I am deeply grateful for this support.

I wish to thank Drs. Alice M. Rivlin and Charles L. Schultze, both of the Brookings Institution, for having reviewed parts of the manuscript and having made important and helpful criticisms.

I am also indebted to my colleagues in the Department of Economics at Indiana University: Professors Robert A. Becker, George M. von Furstenberg, Roy Gardner, H. Scott Gordon, Philip Saunders and Elmus Wicker, who have carefully read the manuscript in its different versions and have made numerous and valuable suggestions for its improvement. I also wish to express my thanks to my colleagues in the Department of History at Indiana University, Professors Robert Ferrell and Irving Katz, whose knowledge of American history provided me with very helpful comments. My thanks go to Virginia Ollis and to Stephen Cole for their editorial help, and to Linda Steinwachs who retyped several versions of the manuscript.

Any remaining errors are mine alone.

Introduction

The purpose of this book is to examine the impact of major economic events on the evolution of economists' thinking about macroeconomic policy and of the influence of this thinking on the policies themselves. The period considered is the half century 1932/33–1984. The assumption of major responsibilities by the federal government in the guidance of the American economy has increased substantially since the Great Depression of the 1930s. The ensuing vast technological, economic, and social transformations during and since that great economic contraction deepened and expanded the multiple obligations of the government in the economic domain. How did professional economists respond to major changes in the period considered? In what measure were their economic theories and interpretation of events, unambiguous and concordant? To what extent were the suggestions formulated on the basis of their theories effective guides to policy? How did the postwar United States presidents respond to the analyses and evaluations of their Council of Economic Advisers? Finally, in what specific ways did the government's use of instruments modify the economy's operations and its institutional framework? These are the questions on which this study focuses.

The book is an essay on economic policy making. I do not propose to present an exhaustive economic historical treatment of the period under review or any of its subperiods, nor to compete with the great merits of the outstanding extant studies that have explored and analyzed various critical problems or all the major issues that arose during the half-century considered. My approach is different. I center my attention on the views of those who were directly immersed in the problems and the economic policies of the time and on the discussions that they then engendered, trying to bring out their views and deliberately avoiding subsequent analyses. Of course, such an approach has its shortcomings as well as its merits. One runs the risk of imposing through this presentist angle one's own selection of facts and ideas and hence, albeit inadvertently, one's own interpretations. But, on the other hand, the advantage of this approach is that one can immediately perceive the interrelations between theories, policies, critiques, and policy course-corrections directly within their specific time frame.

I divide the period under study into five subperiods: the Great Depression (1932/33–1941); World War II (1941–1945); postwar countercyclical stabilization (1946–1960); competition with growth-accelerating countries (1961–1974); and the Great Stagflation (1974–1984). As subperiods the Great Depression and the war are, of course, standard; the others are not. I chose these divisions because I believe that the crucial economic concerns with stabilization, growth, and then stagflation were dominant during the indicated spans of time, whatever the changes in administration.

I start with the Great Depression because it eventually brought about a revolution in economic thought, a change in the federal government's influence upon each and every phase of economic activity, and a new public awareness of the importance of the interaction between the economists' analyses and the implementers' policies. It raised not only critical issues as to why calamitous economic contractions could come about, but also what the government could or would do to prevent such frightful wastes of human and material resources and to spur the expansion of output, employment, investment, and consumption. It thus generated new economic theories and new policy orientations that deeply influenced economic decision making in the ensuing decades.

World War II represented also a period of expansion of the government's involvement in the economy. I do not, however, directly address the war years although they had a significant impact on policy in the subsequent period. I decided to leave out the war subperiod because a mixed economy such as ours is in essence a nonwar economy, in which the government's actions are scrutinized, debated, and legislatively limited while they interact in specified ways with the operation of the private economy. Many of the stated limits are lifted only temporarily in a war situation: special circumstances are thus created in which the government's tutelage extends abnormally over certain activities usually discharged through market mechanisms.

The end of the war raised two major and conflicting problems. First, there was the imperative necessity to decrease government's direction of the economy and to reduce the size of the public sector. Second, the government felt the need to smooth out the transition from the war economy to a peace economy and to cope with the complex problems of demobilization, changes in the production structure, unemployment, and inflation. As might be expected, the size of the government sector fell sharply indeed during the postwar years. Federal expenditures as a percentage of GNP fell from a peak of over 45 percent in 1944 to less than 13 percent in 1947. Counter-cyclical policies aiming at *stabilization*—namely, at avoiding both unemployment and inflation—continued from 1945 to 1960, regardless of the changes of administration.

Eventually these concerns give way toward the end of the 1950s to a new major preoccupation, that of *accelerated economic growth*. By the beginning of the 1960s, economic growth became the dominant policy concept. The seemingly rapid growth of the Soviet Union and the apparent accelerated growth of the less developed countries made the question of growth fashionable throughout the world. Following the advice of the leading economists of the time, our policy makers believed that they could increase the GNP's rate of growth through government investment and careful manipulation of final demand. Federal expenditures as a percentage of GNP experienced a slow but steady rise from 1961 through 1974. At the same time the GNP almost doubled in constant dollars. Again the predominant concern with growth cut across political lines from Kennedy to Nixon.

The preoccupation with accelerated growth eventually yielded to other concerns as unemployment and inflation started to afflict the slowing economy at the beginning of the 1970s. By 1975, unemployment reached 8.5 percent of the labor force, roughly the same level as in 1930. Coincidentally, the GNP deflator rose by 3 points to 8.7 percent in 1974. Concerns with *stagnation* and *inflation*, which were to remain predominant during the second half of the 1970s, gave rise to lively debates among economists, policy makers, and the public. The conflict between the tendency to expand the government's intervention in the economy, advocated by some star economists of the 1960s like Professor James Tobin, and the opposite tendency, to limit the role of the federal government and to reassess its priorities (which was advanced by a variety of new protagonists), reached its climax by the beginning of the 1980s. Skepticism about the ability of the government to restore rapidly full employment with stable prices and steady growth finally ushered in a new administration which reshaped the national agenda and changed the priorities of the federal budget.

For a large part of the period considered, the dominant doctrine of macroeconomic management was the Keynesian one. John Maynard Keynes's *General Theory of Employment Interest and Money* (1936) helped to create the field of macroeconomics, clarified the economic objectives of "statecraft," and showed the interrelations between policy goals and the instruments needed to carry them out. Economic management under capitalism had, however, long preceded Keynes. Indeed, systematic interventions in the European economies had developed synchronously with the growth of money, the growth of the exchange economy, the spread of manufacturing, the rise of domestic and international competition, and the formation and consolidation of nations.

Historically, the doctrines concerning macroeconomic policy fall into two broad categories: *inward*-oriented policies and *outward*-oriented policies. *Inward*-oriented policies focus primarily on the level of domestic output and employment and on the allocation of output and labor across the sectors of the economy. Such policies are identified with the so-called mercantilist doctrine. *Outward*-oriented policies emphasize the essential role of foreign trade in the economic growth and development of the national economy and are identified with the classical economists' free-trade or laissez-faire doctrine. In their extreme form inward-oriented policies lead to systematic import-substitution and to high rates of protection, while outward-oriented policies are predicated on the absence of barriers to foreign trade and have no bias in favor of production for the domestic markets. The opposition between mercantilism and laissez faire, which has taken many forms during the history of modern capitalism, continues to reverberate through many contemporary policy debates.

Keynes's theory is inward-oriented. He posited that unless total effective demand for goods and services suffices to purchase the economy's full employment output, the economy will tend to operate below the rate permitted by its manpower resources and its capital capacity. If private consumption demand falls short of total output, private investment *and* government expenditure must make up the difference to avoid contraction in production and in employment. Keynes's emphasis on the role of government in securing full employment thus connects his theory with the basic orientations of mercantilism. But Keynes's theoretical apparatus came to be applied and extended in a variety of directions and combinations, giving in the process a great impetus to the post-World War II theoretical developments in economic science as a whole. His theories played a central role in the debates on policy and in the choice and implementation of economic policy. It is with respect to the Keynesian theories and to those that came in conflict with them that much of the theoretical discussions that follow is necessarily connected.

Notwithstanding an onrush of criticisms of modern economics' methods, analyses, and forecasts—particularly during and since the 1970s—and despite changes in the public mood concerning the public role of economists, the historical record of the contributions of economics to policy making is undoubtedly an important, creative, imaginative, and successful one. In the review of this record we encounter a galaxy of "pure theorists" as well as prominent "practitioners" in public service, and in particular in the presidents' Council of Economic Advisers, who have brilliantly demonstrated their ability to apply the investigative logic of economics and its tools to everyday policies.

The book is constructed as follows: Chapter 1 focuses on the anti-depression policies (1932/33–1941); chapter 2 on counter-cyclical policies (1945–1960); chapter 3 on growth-oriented policies (1961–1974); and chapter 4 on antistagflation policies (1974–1984). A fifth and last chapter examines the relation between the efforts of the economics profession to advise the policy makers, the ups and downs of these activities, and the conceptions that the economists finally developed about the effectiveness and the validity of their theories.

The first four chapters have an identical structure. The first section of each chapter sketches the economic scene; the second presents the economic theories generated in response to the given situation; the third examines the policy measures discussed or actually implemented; the fourth indicates the critique and debates generated by these decisions; and the fifth presents the economic legacy of each period. In sketching the economic scene, my purpose is to re-create in broad outline the environment within which economic theories and policies were debated. Next the focus is on the conflicting views and evaluations generated among the economists in response to their own perceptions of the major issues of the day. The impact of these views on the implementers of policy is then presented, pointing out that differences in presidents' outlooks and approaches necessarily placed in the limelight different issues and different schools of thought. These decisions in turn generated criticisms and debate involving alternative theories and conflicting assessments of their consequences. Interestingly and importantly, the entire period considered, from Roosevelt to Reagan, opens and closes symmetrically with a decisive shift in the country's priorities. It opens with a thrust toward larger government involvement in income redistribution, and it closes with a shift away from further income redistribution.

All the indicated sections are based on a detailed reading of the major books and articles published at the time, particularly in the major economic journals such as the *American Economic Review*. The exposition of the policy measures discussed or actually implemented is based on an extensive use of such policy documents as the *Economic Reports of the President* and the *Annual Reports* of that "outpost of academic economics," the Council of Economic Advisers. These later *Reports*, as James Tobin stated, exemplify "the parallels between intellectual trends within the economics profession and currents of public opinion and political sentiment," and it is on these parallels that I have centered my attention.

The book is addressed to students of economics and to practical men and women who wish to understand the complex issues and the vast range of economic management in a market-oriented economy. Our system and our policies evolve gradually in response to emerging problems. Though policies do change as a result of new experience, they also react in many ways to discussions and controversies which preceded them. Understanding the present and mapping the future requires a cogent investigation of the difficult questions and arguments which took place in the past.

Nicolas Spulber
Bloomington, Indiana

Managing the American Economy from Roosevelt to Reagan

CHAPTER
1
ANTIDEPRESSION
POLICIES

THE ECONOMIC SCENE, 1929–41

Depressions are calamitous contractions in aggregate output, sales, prices, profits, investment, and employment, accompanied by widespread bankruptcies and liquidations. Tightening its grip on business activities from the summer of 1929 on, the worst depression our economy has ever known, the Great Depression of the 1930s, brought in its wake steep declines in incomes, outputs, prices, and employment; a vast and swelling legion of the unemployed; and, finally, a menacing situation on the world scene where it accentuated the disintegration of international trade. Eventually, the debacle opened the way for a number of significant domestic institutional changes, brought about the expansion of the role of government, and conditioned appreciable modifications in the fiscal and monetary approaches to slumps and to the vagaries of the business cycle.

The downswing, which began in the summer, gained full momentum only after the astounding collapse of the stock market in the last week of October 1929. The dive of stock prices began on Thursday, October 24. It accelerated on Monday, October 28, and Tuesday, October 29, when it "literally swept everything before it." In what the *Commercial and Financial Chronicle* of that week called "the greatest stock market catastrophe of all ages," the declines in two days involved an aggregate depreciation of between $15 billion and $18 billion, equal to some 25 percent of the market value of the stocks covered by the index.[1] (See figure 1.) The stock market disaster, symptom of shifts in underlying forces making for a sharp economic decline, further worsened the contraction. Precipitous drops in prices, money supply, credits, investments, production, and employment, along with dramatic increases in bank failures, commercial and industrial bankruptcies, and farm mortgage foreclosures became

1

everyday occurrences. Problems that had been below the surface came into the open, forcing each sector and each plant, as well as most income groups, to grapple with increasing and often insuperable difficulties.

Reflecting both changing demand patterns and possibly wide distortions in the allocation of resources, the prices of commodities and groups of commodities fell rapidly at varying speeds. On the basis 1929 = 100, the wholesale price index for all commodities fell in 1933 to 69, for raw materials to 56, for semimanufactures to 70, and for manufactured goods to 75. The money supply and credit operations contracted spasmodically. Currency and demand deposits shrank from some $27 billion in 1929 to less than $20 billion in 1933. Loans and discounts of all banks dropped by one half. Regulations and/or general and local business conditions led to the immobilization or the nonuse of the funds that remained. Thus legal requirements prevented the Federal Reserve system from extending loans to failing banks except on short-term commercial paper and did not permit issuing of Federal Reserve notes except with this type of paper or gold as collateral. Paradoxically, while in the case of member banks, reserves accumulated in excess of the banks' legal requirements, in other cases bank failures multiplied because of poor credit control and the inability to collect loans outstanding.[2] Domestic investments to maintain inventories or to increase capacity contracted sharply in these conditions, from $16 billion in 1929 to less than $1 billion in 1932 and to less than $1.5 billion in 1933, reflecting business's gloomy evaluations of the economy's prospects. Moreover, the disturbed state of foreign markets further intensified the feeling of uncertainty about the future.

The disaster deeply affected every economic sector. Consider the case of farming. By 1919–1920, expansion in farm income, outputs, and exports during World War I had engendered a feverish speculation in farm land values. A series of painful readjustments in output, exports, and prices started in 1920, and net farm income fell at current prices from $9 billion in 1919 to less than $3.5 billion in 1933. (See figure 1d.) Concomitantly, the ratio of prices received to prices paid by farmers fell systematically, the value of all farm property sagged, and the average value per farm dropped to low levels.[3] Throughout the West the land and the livestock were mortgaged to the limit. After a succession of poor crops the land was bare, and the winds blew the topsoil into clouds of dust. The hard times in farming adversely affected not only the industries directly supplying agriculture with farm equipment but also transport carriers, banks, and marketing businesses, as well as the entire nonfarm population, by then also in the throes of the depression. In manufacturing, value added dropped from some $30 billion in 1929 to less than half its 1929 level in 1933. Compared to 1929, the number of both manufacturing establishments and of those gainfully employed in

Figure 1. Selected Indicators, 1929–1940

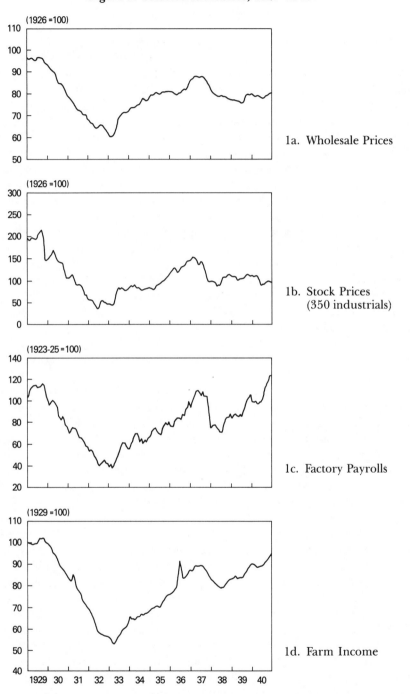

1a. Wholesale Prices

1b. Stock Prices
(350 industrials)

1c. Factory Payrolls

1d. Farm Income

SOURCE: *Excerpted from* Survey of Current Business, *February 1941*.

manufacturing declined by one third in 1933. The income originating in that latter year in all the goods-producing industries—agriculture, mining, construction, manufacturing, transport, communication, and utilities—contracted to less than one-half of the 1929 amount. In the economy as a whole the number of gainfully employed decreased sharply, while the percentage of the unemployed civilian labor force rose from 3 percent in 1929 to as much as 25 percent in 1933. Simultaneously, national income in current prices fell precipitously, from some $87 billion in 1929 to $40 billion in 1933.

A series of drastic and wide-ranging economic policy and institutional changes implemented from 1933 on under the new Roosevelt administration, which we shall examine further below, set the economy on a new course. From the beginning of the economic downswing in August 1929, to March 1933, when the trough of the decline was reached, the contraction had lasted forty-three months—longer than any other except one (which occurred between March 1879 and March 1882, namely, 65 months). The upswing started in March 1933 and continued until May 1937 when a new, severe recession set in and lasted until June 1938 (13 months). Afterwards the economy regained its upward drive and continued it through World War II, up to February 1945. We take herein 1941 as the cutoff point of the chapter—the last year of peace before the full onslaught of World War II, which the United States entered in December 1941.

Throughout the period considered, the share of government expenditures as a percent of GNP increased, at first steadily—from less than 10 percent (of which 2.5 percent was federal) in 1929 to 19 percent (7.0 percent federal) in 1933. It then oscillated around 19 percent (10 percent federal), except in 1937 when it fell to 16 percent (8 percent federal). It rose again rapidly afterwards up to 23 percent of the GNP (over 16 percent federal) by 1941. The public debt increased *pari passu* from $16 billion in 1929 to over $22 billion in 1933, $36 billion in 1937, and close to $49 billion in 1941. Public debt rose from a level equal to some 18 percent of the 1929 GNP to 45–55 percent of the GNP levels of the ensuing years. While in the big downswing the money supply had contracted by as much as 33.5 percent between 1929 and 1933, it expanded by not less than 55 percent through 1937 and then, after a slight contraction in 1938, increased again by over 50 percent through 1941 at a compound rate of 10 percent per annum for the period 1933–41. Commercial and finance company paper, which had fallen by over 200 percent between 1929 and 1933, also rose by an even higher percentage between 1933 and 1941. Simultaneously, business loan rates, which had fallen between 1929 and 1933 from about 6 percent to less than 2 percent, continued to fall through the balance of the 1930s to 0.5 percent in 1941. In the economy's big downswing, real GNP had contracted by as much as 8.6 percent per year; in the upswing, it expanded at a rate of 8.1 percent per year. Assuming that the 1929 income level could have been maintained in each of the following years up to 1937, the losses due to the depression would amount to a total larger than the income achieved in 1941.

Each economic sector participated in varying degrees in the upswing up to 1937 and then in the short but sharp recession of 1937–38. Agricultural income—including rising subsidies from 1933 on—rose at current prices from some $4 billion in 1933 to over $7 billion in 1937 and, after three less favorable years, finally reached the 1929 level of over $8 billion in 1941. For manufacturing, the Federal Reserve Board production index showed a steady expansion of output up to 1937 and then, after a sharp contraction, a renewed rapid increase. Income generated in this sector expanded steadily from 1933 to 1937 and, after a dip in 1938, rose to as much as $33 billion in 1941, over four times the 1933 level. The number of those gainfully employed in the economy as a whole followed the same pattern. It rose from 38 million persons in 1933 to the 1929 level of 46 million by 1937; after contracting in 1938, it rose to 50 million in 1941. Conversely, the percentage of the unemployed civilian population fell from the height of 25 percent in 1933 to some 15 percent in 1937; it fell to below two digits by 1941. In line with the overall expansion and contraction of world trade, U.S. exports also fell in 1933 to less than one-half of their 1929 volume; they expanded again but rather slowly, not reaching the 1929 level until 1941.

ECONOMISTS' RESPONSES TO THE DEPRESSION

What should the federal government do in the presence of an economic contraction of such magnitude? (a) Should it "let the storm blow over" or, rather, should it intervene decisively in the economic process? (b) If the mood of the country were for intervention, which instruments should the government use, monetary or fiscal? (c) Should there be *institutional* changes such as changes in the tax system or changes affecting the production framework, that is, labor-management relations?

These were the questions facing the country and its decision makers. As we shall see, there was no shortage of contradictory advice from business leaders, the press, the academic community. Let us consider the questions in turn.

a. **Should the government intervene in the economic process?** The prevailing attitude in leading political and business circles in the early 1930s was that such a crisis was inherent to the system, that it had to work itself out, and that the government had to keep its hands off "fundamental" operations of the economy. The influential *Commercial and Financial*

Chronicle, for instance, asserted in 1932—in the third year of the depression—that following the "speculative" push of 1929 the country's "adjustment to a lower level was inevitable and unavoidable." The *Chronicle* quoted with approval the "true diagnosis of the depression" given by Chicago banker Frederick H. Rawson, who asserted that the economy had "not been helped by the various attempts made to escape the inevitable liquidation which should have been allowed to continue its natural course."[4] Those opposed to the "apostles of inertia and of painful waiting," pointed out that already before the crash the economy had been hampered by an inflexible price structure that called for reforms. Jacob Viner of the University of Chicago noted that "our system rests upon the assumption of the existence of price flexibility . . . but in fact the price structure is shot through with rigidities, and even as in the case of tax rates and freight rates, with perverse flexibilities."[5]

Convinced that the depression was a passing phenomenon, President Herbert Hoover chose to follow the exhortatory approach. He tried to rely on the government's ability to advise and persuade both business and the public to "hold on" and the storm would blow away. The strategy of his administration ran along the following lines: (i) advise (and if possible persuade) employers to shun wage cuts in order to maintain "consumer power"; (ii) convince corporations to go ahead with capital expenditures; (iii) stabilize prices for agricultural products through the Federal Farm Board and orderly marketing; (iv) avoid cuts in the volume of public construction; (v) maintain easy conditions in the money markets; and (vi) propose the lowering of tax rates (under the assumption that there will be a budget surplus).[6] This policy, generally inefficient, could also be potentially damaging. It was pointed out that Hoover's attempt to maintain wages at predepression levels was unrealistic, and that his partisan efforts to "protect" the farmer (*inter alia* through the adoption of the Hawley-Smoot tariff) incited retaliatory and defensive measures abroad and deprived our farmers of their foreign markets.[7]

b. **Which instruments should the government use?** The professional economists were far from unanimous: monetarists or fiscalists, institutionalists and/or reformists, advocates of heavily directed state controls and of a variety of planning schemes, all disagreed as to what was to be done. One of the best known academic economists, Professor Irving Fisher of Yale, stressed the necessity for the government to use imaginatively its *monetary* instruments. He dismissed as absurd the idea that depressions could not be brought under immediate control through a "complete stabilization program." Stressing the ability of monetary management to cope with "all circumstances that could reasonably be expected to arise" in either booms or depressions, he pointed out that at least "nine cycle tendencies" contributed to the downswing of the depression: debt factor, volume of currency factor, price level factor, net worth factor, profit factor, production factor, psychological factor, turnover of currency factor, and the money interest-real interest factor. He added that the first three of these—debts (their liquidation), volume of currency (its contraction), and the price level (its falling, and its obverse, the "swelling" or appreciating dollar)—were locked together, the second factor serving as a link. Asserting that "the dollar disease—falling prices—is the main secret of great depressions," he declared that this "disease was needless." Stressing that the gold standard had afforded a safeguard against inflation but "no safeguard whatever against deflation," Fisher proposed a plan that would make the gold standard useful "against deflation and inflation alike." His "complete plan" of price stabilization involved issuing government bonds and actions by the Federal Reserve including open-market operations and adjustment of rediscount rates, buying and selling of gold certificates, rationing of credit, adjustment of gold reserves in the Federal Reserve banks, appropriate changes in the price of gold, and, as a last resort, breaking away from the gold standard. An ad hoc Commission on Stabilization would repeat or reverse the operations until the desired price level had been reached, counteracting both deflation and inflation.[8] Irving Fisher's proposals were extensively criticized by other economists. James H. Rogers of Yale pointed out that open-market operations were leading only to accumulation of idle funds (excess reserves), the commercial banks having become risk-averse after their losses.[9] Walter E. Spahr, Benjamin M. Anderson, and Charles O. Hardy discussed the idea that prices of commodities went up or down with the price of gold and that price manipulations of the latter could assure control of the former.[10] Other analysts rejected the Fisher theory of managed currency and its assumption of the business cycle as "just a dance of the dollar." Some of them asserted that the manner in which money in circulation was distributed among investors and consumers was as important, if not more so, as total quantity of money in circulation.[11]

In opposition to the *monetarist* thesis, other well-known economists stressed for a variety of reasons the importance of *fiscal* measures to combat the depression. Professor Jacob Viner drew attention to the interrelations between prices and costs and to the critical role of the government with respect to the latter. According to him, the depression could end if prices were stabilized or increased while costs declined. An important factor in this decline could be played by the reduction of taxes, "which press directly upon production," and by the lowering of utility charges and of rail freight rates influenced by the government. To cope with the ensuing lower yield of tax revenue, a sound policy would let deficits accumulate in a depression, "deficits to be liquidated during the prosperity years from the higher productivity of the tax system and from increases in the tax rates when they would do no harm." This "balanced deflation," according to Viner, was preferable to "aggressive" spending and inflation via the issue of legal tender greenbacks or borrowing from the banks: it would indeed take "extraordinary amounts of government spending" to offset the unavoidable countermeasures of a deflationary character by banks or individuals.[12] Viner's colleague at Chicago, Henry C. Simons, also argued in favor of increased government expenditures but for other reasons: according to him the collapse of confidence had set off demand for liquidity and the attempts to meet it had led to liquidations, with a resulting decline in the quantity of money.[13] Other economists, Sumner H. Slichter of Harvard, for instance, thought that government expenditures that do not depend on profit should dovetail with those that do, and thus alleviate unemployment. Slichter pointed out that business expenditures were unstable because the outlook for profits was unsettled. This was due to the fact that "discoveries of new methods, new products, and new natural resources do not occur at an even rate."[14]

It is interesting to note that in his *Treatise on Money*, John Maynard Keynes suggested in the early 1930s the need for government spending because the slump was due "primarily to the deterrent effects on investment of the long period of dear money which preceded the stock market collapse and only secondarily to the collapse itself."[15] In 1933, in an open letter to President Franklin D. Roosevelt, he affirmed that the depression could be overcome through "expanding loan expenditures plus, in second place, cheap credit, in particular reduction of long-term interest rates."[16] Finally in 1936, in his capital work, *The General Theory of Employment Interest and Money*, which was to gain a decisive and widespread influence only later, Keynes asserted that the developed Western economies tended toward "a chronic condition of subnormal activity for a considerable period." Failing appropriate (fiscal) measures expressly designed to correct the situation, the system will tend to oscillate "round an intermediate position appreciably below full employment and appreciably above the minimum employment."[17]

Though, as we shall see further on, Keynes believed also that the opportunity for investment was rapidly decreasing in the West, his theory of the system's chronic tendency toward "subnormal activity" was related to, but not identical with, the classical economists' idea of a *stationary state*—a state that a mature, developed economy was supposed to reach inevitably at some point in time. This concept of a stationary state, namely, of stagnation, which had been stressed notably by Adam Smith and later by John Stuart Mill, was vigorously reasserted in the late 1930s, particularly by Alvin H. Hansen of Harvard. Hansen affirmed that the Great Depression had taken place in an economy that had changed profoundly from the inducements-to-invest viewpoint. The nineteenth century, he explained, had witnessed *extensive* growth, with occupation of new territory and growth of population, as well as *intensive* widening and deepening of capital. Now the end of the frontier and of massive population growth and the exhaustion of growth possibilities in capital-widening industries (which accounted for the "buoyancy" of the 1922–29 period) had depressed inducements to invest. The United States had reached industrial maturity, an era of "sick recoveries which die in their infancy and depressions which feed on themselves and leave a hard and seemingly immovable core of unemployment." To cope with economic stagnation, income distribution had to be changed and public investments had to be expanded.[18]

c. **Which institutional changes should the government make?** While, as we saw, for some economists the depression was a purely *monetary* phenomenon and for others it was the result of *demand* deficiencies, for still others the trouble lay on the *supply* side of the economy, on technological changes that generated "excessive" efficiency. This latter view gained increasing acceptance among producers' associations and brought forth all kinds of planning proposals for controlling production.

Already in the early 1920s, a socioeconomic critic of capitalism, Thorstein Veblen, then of the New School for Social Research, asserted that the trouble with advanced capitalism was overproduction. If, affirmed Veblen, the volume of output is not regulated in the age of "inordinate productivity of mechanical technology," then "there will be overproduction, business depression and consequent hard times all around." Prosperity itself posited the need for a "conscientious withdrawal of efficiency" by those who controlled the country's output.[19] These ideas found powerful echoes in the 1920s, and even more so in the 1930s. Wheat farmers, cotton growers, and manufacturers agitated increasingly against "overproduction," the "inequities" of the price system, and the "dangers of competition." They stressed the need to reduce output, hold prices, and introduce measures dealing directly with the operation of business. Already during the 1920s farm leaders started to press hard for price-raising measures and obtained tariffs, regulation of marketing agencies, credit facilities, and federal recognition of cooperatives. As the depression began, these leaders revived an idea of 1926–27: measures to directly control agricultural output under government authority and with government support. This time farm leaders were able to put forward a full-fledged plan elaborated in 1929 by John D. Black of Harvard and made known throughout the country by a Montana economist, M. L. Wilson.[20] This so-called Domestic Allotment Plan—withdrawal of farmland from crop production to balance supply and demand at an "acceptable" level—was now presented as the only means for surmounting farm problems, stabilizing farm prices and farm income at a favorable level, narrowing discrepancies between farm prices and those of all other commodities, giving the farmer a "fair share in the national income," and turning him again into a good customer of industry's products.

Proposals for debt moratoriums, tax exemptions, subsidies, and other price-raising activities had been put forward by "sick industries" before the depression, notably the raw material-producing industries, which had pressed for relief measures under the slogan of "resources conservation." Differential transport rates, railroad car allotments, and licensing under a special federal commission were granted to the soft coal industry; and regulation of production by major producing states was enacted for the oil industry. What the depression then raised was the question of reorganization of industry for output planning, market sharing, and price fixing. In a detailed report presented to a hearing on Senator Robert M. La Follette's bill to establish a National Economic Council, the industrialist Henry I. Harriman, spokesman for the Committee on Continuity of Business and Employment of the U.S. Chamber of Commerce, stressed achieving for manufacturing (just as for farming) "a proper coordination of production and consumption" and "soundly steady prices." Many manufacturing producers, he explained, "would prefer to gauge their output to the consuming capacity and divide the volume of such production among the different units of industry on an equitable basis." This would require agreements among businesses and recognition that "penalties under antitrust laws which, suitable as they may have been for economic conditions of another day, are not entirely in consonance with the present day needs of industry." Planning for entire branches of industry through trade associations, Harriman continued, would assist in stabilizing their operations and employment; to pay high wages, set up reserves to tide over periods of unemployment, and provide allowances for sickness, accident, or old age, business "must be on a sound basis and production must be balanced with consumption." It is interesting to observe that Harriman also claimed that the "economists and the industrialists" of the nineteenth century had looked at the time of laissez faire "to an ever increasing population to keep a satisfactory balance between supply and demand"; now, however, the country was fast reaching a period of stabilized population with no other cure in sight for overproduction and employment instability but direct coordination and control of production under industrial trade associations.[21] Gerard Swope of General Electric also recommended that the Sherman Act be amended to permit producers "to so divide between them the demands of the given time" as to achieve a "balance" between production and consumption. The proposal clearly rested upon price fixing, restriction of output, and keeping many marginal producers in business.[22] While some industrialists did not share the hope of stabilizing any important matter of common interest through voluntary agreements,[23] it is certain that the depression strengthened propensities to share the market via agreements to allocate production or via formation of selling agencies, trade associations, and conventions to stabilize distribution.[24]

Another method of offsetting the enormous efficiency of machine industry and of slowing its advance, also suggested by Veblen, was to increase consumption and curtail saving via a more equal distribution of income. This thesis was also propounded during the early 1930s by liberal economists. Arthur B. Adams, in a discussion of the "Business Depression of 1930" held at the forty-third annual meeting of the American Economic Association in 1930, contended that the key manifestations of the depression, "overproduction and shortage in the consumers' purchasing power," were due to changes in the methods of production, which had brought disturbances in both the production of goods and the distribution of income. Adams added that other factors (the position of debtors versus creditors in the depression and high interest rates) reinforced "the lopsided distribution of the national money income to investors and to consumers." Accordingly he proposed increasing real wages, *pari passu* with increases in production and prices.[25] Hansen cogently rejected the thesis of simultaneous output restriction to bolster prices and of income redistribution to expand consumption. He pointed out that if every trade succeeded in reducing output and holding up prices "we should simply be biting off each other's nose"; control of output would stop the fall in prices and its depressing effect but would lower real income. Organized consumption on a large scale, via higher wages and unemployment insurance, would keep technical progress in check and stop "the advancing efficiency of the Machine Age." Both courses would lead to lower income. Hansen concluded that "stability, security, and a larger measure of economic equality" would be "antithetical to economic progress."[26]

Hansen's own claims that the free market makes for the utmost progress and that planning could be left to business alone were in turn sharply challenged by economists of the institutionalist school—Wesley C. Mitchell, John Maurice Clark, and Rexford G. Tugwell—all of whom advocated the need to expand social controls, namely, extensive government interventions in the economy via national planning, something far beyond the use of monetary and fiscal instruments. Mitchell declared that "the frequent recurrence of economic crises and depressions" showed that automatic functioning of the economic system was defective. No one, he added, believed any more that the business cycle was being "worked out," that even at the peak of prosperity production fell short of what it would be "if we could make full use of our facilities"; and that "business planning" could keep up not only the income of powerful corporations but also the incomes of small producers, farmers, and workers. He recommended a National Planning Board that could "draw the line between cases in which government should seek to exercise control and cases in which private initiative should prevail."[27] Clark argued that "industries, taken by themselves, do not reach all the interests that are bound up in the project of a really national plan" and that, notwithstanding the dangers, expansion of governmental bodies and authorities with respect to production "is of such vital and controlling public interest that the government cannot keep out."[28] Tugwell asserted that Frederick Taylor's methods of production had increased output to the point of "clogging all the channels of trade" and that what was needed to overcome disequilibrium, instability, and insecurity were planning boards by industrial associations, topped by a mediating and coordinating body, a United States Industrial Integration Board. The government would be represented on this body; it would engage in study and preparation of a national economic plan on the basis of which it might proceed eventually to "such a rearrangement of present industries or such a control over their actions as would meet the criteria of the plan."[29] A host of other social theorists indicated what such a plan should be and how to arrange for it.[30]

Clearly the economic profession was deeply divided and pulled in a number of directions by its contending schools. Some institutionalists focused on structural changes to determine their effect on the system's controls, while others proceeded from structural changes to map out what they believed would be the future of the system. For Veblen (who echoed the early nineteenth-century ideas of Saint-Simon), the American industrial economy had become "a system of interlocking *mechanical* processes," which required henceforth not the guidance of businessmen but that of "technical experts." The latter's revolution was near at hand.[31] For Gardiner C. Means, who was to play a role in shaping many strains of liberal economic thinking, including the theory of the "managerial revolution" and later that of the "new industrial state," three nonmarket controls interplayed with the market in the modern American economy with respect to use of resources: controls exercised by the interlocking managers of the corporate community, those exercised by organization of economic interest groupings outside of the larger corporations, and those exercised by the government. In the new setting the "old competition" had been superseded by "administrative competition" (shielding inefficiency in the great corporations), price flexibility had been replaced by price inflexibility, and the profit motive weakened or distorted beyond recognition.[32] All this, according to Mitchell, Tugwell, and many others, pointed toward the need for planning—planning that would eschew both "planless anarchy" and "totalitarianism."

POLICIES OF THE "NEW FRONTIER," 1933–37

The newly installed Roosevelt administration was all set to intervene decisively against the depression. But as we have seen, to do this it had to choose from a complicated menu of proposals. Should it follow the advice of the *monetarists*, of the *fiscalists*, or of the partisans of *institutional change*? Which possible combinations among the proposed solutions should it advocate and attempt to enact? What should be the main thrust of the federal government's interventions?

Looking back at the first hundred days of FDR's presidency, during which were enacted some of the most important measures of the new administration, Arthur M. Schlesinger, Jr., a youthful contemporary of these events, has asserted that the period was characterized by "improvisation and experiment."[33] Along the same lines, another historian, Albert U. Romasco, stated later that the New Deal combined "a wide and contradictory variety of ideological programs," and "had nothing to do with logic or consistency."[34] These generalizations are sweeping and not quite accurate.

Examination of the measures taken by FDR during the first New Deal (1933–37) and of their explanation and justifications, viewed against the discussion sketched above, reveals a coherent policy in some fundamental respects. From the emergency banking relief to agricultural "adjustment," to federal refinancing, to the breakaway from the gold standard, to federal emergency relief, to certain provisos concerning "national industrial recovery," to Social Security, and to attempts at indicative planning, emerges a policy aiming first of all to increase demand—in the language of the time, the "purchasing power" of farmers, workers, the needy, the old, the debtors. It is this thrust toward *income redistribution* that became the hallmark of the Democratic president and eventually of the entire Democratic party. As critics were keen to point out, however, FDR also assumed that "overproduction" (the piling up of unsold goods) and mandated increases in wages could be taken care of by concerted reduction in output and by increases in prices, that is by measures that canceled to an unknown and undeterminable degree the effectiveness of the measures aiming to raise the level of "purchasing power." Much of this was undoubtedly influenced both by the conflicting domestic proposals which we have reviewed as well as by various European ideologies and reforms.[35] What this two-pronged strategy did yield, however, thanks to its specific emphasis on income redistribution, was a renewed confidence in our own economic system, even though FDR was also expanding in the process, and in a highly unusual manner, the regulatory frontiers of government.

When the new Democratic administration took office on March 4, 1933, it faced what one of its spokesmen, Alexander Sachs, asserted to be "a threefold crisis arising from and represented by the price slump, bearing down on agriculture and the general overload of debt; the contraction of business activity and mounting unemployment; and the deflation of capital values and the inability of the former chief creditor and liquidator, the banking system, to meet the liabilities of its own deposits."[36] Much seemed to hinge then on what Professor Fisher had forcefully described as "the main secret of the great depressions": the "needless" dollar bulging, or its obverse, falling prices. The day after the president's inauguration, March 5, the first measure of the administration closed the banks, the beginning of its "counter-deflationary" (namely, *inflationary*) offensive. In connection with this "bank holiday" the president started a process of reform destined in his words to endow the government with a "more effective control of the monetary system" and, within the framework of the time, "of the metallic reserves of gold and silver used as its base." Step by step, from March 10 onward—with suspension of the gold standard, prohibition of the export of gold, surrender of gold and gold certificates to the Treasury, prohibition of the enforcement of "gold clause" obligations, regulation of dealing in foreign exchange, and raising of the dollar price for gold—the administration sought the Fisherian way to devalue the dollar, namely, to inflate the currency and contribute to the nominal rise in commodity prices that the president felt was "essential to restore the purchasing power and the debt payment ability of the American people."[37]

In conjunction with reestablishing the people's purchasing power and ability to repay debts, the administration and Congress strove to create a more stable environment for private investment, a more regulated and less volatile environment than at the onset of the depression. The Federal Securities Act of March 29 and the Glass-Steagall Banking Act of May 17 sought to reduce the movement of stock prices, reducing risk premiums and increasing capital values by curbing "speculative investment." The decrease in debt through the possibility of recapitalization (namely, issuance of equity security in place of bonds) was also a way to expand income by generating employment. The Glass-Steagall Act aimed to reduce risk by forcing commercial banks out of the investment banking business. It prohibited financial institutions from both accepting deposits and underwriting corporate securities; although not a Roosevelt initiative, the president supported it.

Other sector-specific measures, notably toward agriculture and manufacturing, pursued the same objectives of income enhancement in an economically safer environment. To increase the farmer's capacity to purchase manufactured goods, to relieve farm debt, to augment farm loans extended by banks, and to give the farmer "a more equal share of the national income," the president submitted to Congress on March 16 the Agricultural Adjustment Bill. The idea was to withdraw farmland from crop production in order to balance output with market demand at prices equivalent to the high prices received by farmers in a so-called base period (1909–14 for staples, 1919–29 for tobacco). Benefit payments were to be made on voluntary contracts between the government and each cooperating producer. The secretary of agriculture was empowered to enter into agreements with farmers to reduce crop acreage and to regulate prices and marketing methods. Other emergency measures provided policy directions to federally sponsored farm credit agencies for refinancing farm mortgages at lower interest rates with longer terms of repayment. This policy sought to ensure that "a farmer selling a certain volume of products in 1933 should be able, with the price he received for them, to buy the same volume of manufactured goods that he was able to buy with the same volume of farm products in the period 1909–1914" and, moreover, "to return to him his normal fair share of the national income," while reducing output surpluses that had dragged prices down.[38] Passed by Congress on May 12, 1933, but declared unconstitutional by the Supreme Court on January 6, 1936, the AAA was replaced, on February 19, 1936, by the Soil Conservation and Domestic Allotment Act. This represented voluntary soil conservation by farmers in exchange for compensation for soil-building practices. On February 16, 1938, Congress passed an Agricultural Adjustment Act that went much further than the two preceding laws. This most comprehensive act of the 1930s concerning the farmer set the terms of price supports for decades to come; try as they did, the administrations that followed—even of different persuasions—were unable to abolish it.[39]

In line with his policy of reflation, FDR submitted to Congress on May 17, 1933, a "program for national industrial recovery." As in the case of farming, this bill was predicated *mutatis mutandis* on production controls, along with wage and price fixing, with the object of increasing income. Production and price fixing was to be achieved via the cartelization of industry under government supervision, suppression of antitrust measures and of "unfair competition," and allotment by industrial "guilds" of carefully adjusted output quotas to each member. As a *quid pro quo* for cartelization and the right to reduce output, wages were to increase according to government standards for minimum pay and work; all this was to be supported by new rights extended to labor to organize and bargain collectively. Congress adopted, and the president signed on June 16, 1933, the National Industrial Recovery Act (NIRA), which included Title II, a mandate for the president to create a Federal Emergency Administration of Public Works. The president hoped that the act would "stabilize for all time the many factors which make for the prosperity of the Nation," since it would help the workers obtain "living wages and sustained employment" while providing the employers with an expanded domestic market.[40] It was greatly in the employers' interest to pay good wages and provide employment, the president stated, "because decent living spread over 125,000,000 people eventually means the opening up to industry of the richest market the world has ever known. It is the only way to utilize the so-called excess capacity of our industrial plants."[41] In fact the Act, which aimed to increase wages in a period of high unemployment, proved to be an unstable combination of the administration's ideas about expanded consumption and extensive regulation, business's aspirations for self-control without government supervision on both inputs and outputs, and labor's new taste for both collective bargaining and government-set-and-enforced standards of work and pay.[42] Long before the Supreme Court declared the Act unconstitutional on May 27, 1935, the NIRA, which had acted as a brake on output and as a stimulus to costs, had lost much of its appeal. Shortly after the Supreme Court's decision, a "skeletonized" National Recovery Administration was created, June 14, 1935, to last only until April of the next year. At that moment, as one facetious commentator put it, all that industry was permitted to do was to "agree to protect labor and to uphold antitrust and other laws."[43] The entire experience had been, according to Clair Wilcox, "like a vaccination, giving the United States a mild case of the cartel disease and immunizing it against the disease itself." What persisted from the experiment was the improvement of work standards, union recognition, and collective bargaining, which indeed continued with the National Labor Relations Act.[44]

The crowning piece of legislation aiming to expand demand was undoubtedly the Social Security Act of August 1935. Earlier the Hoover administration had reluctantly accepted the idea of federal responsibility for the financial burden of caring for the unemployed. But it took pressures by state and local authorities for adoption of the Emergency Relief and Construction Act of July 1932, which provided for unemployment relief via federal loans to the states. In March 1933 the Roosevelt administration affirmed its desire to attack unemployment via three sorts of legislation: the immediate enrollment of workers by the federal government, provision of grants (not loans) to the states for relief work, and enactment of a "broad public works labor-creating program." On May 12, 1933, the president signed the Unemployment Relief Act, which recognized that relief was a social problem for which the federal government had responsibility. Eventually the new administration enacted a comprehensive Social Security Act, creating a nationally administered compulsory system of old-age insurance, a system of unemployment compensation operated by the states under federal standards, and a system of public relief, based on federal grants to states, for various kinds of needy people. Transfer payments, "designed to provide the average worker with some assurance that when cycles of unemployment come or when his working days are over, he will have enough money to

live decently," were not only to "alleviate" needs but also to prevent or
mitigate future depressions by flattening out "the peaks and valleys of
deflation and inflation."[45]

The question of how to preserve the economy from slippages and
massive wastage of human and material resources remained a preoccupation throughout those years. While avoiding the idea of planning on
the scale of the economy as a whole, the federal government introduced
extensive regulatory and supervisory measures in industry and agriculture. Moreover, the administration established (in 1933 and later)
planning boards or committees. The National Resources Committee
(NRC) and its sections took stock of the nation's resources, production
capacity, and consumption. Beginning in 1935, the NRC became the
center for the preparation of studies concerning use of the land, water,
minerals, economic and demographic characteristics of the country, and
improvement of engineering techniques in the use of resources. The
NRC's most important study, *The Structure of the American Economy*, prepared under the direction of Gardiner C. Means, attempted both to
analyze in detail "the interrelation of the economic forces which determine the use of our national resources" and to suggest ways of coordinating them through appropriate "planning"; but its effect remained
limited as far as overall policies.[46] The administration did engage in
support of synchronized development programs concerning much-
needed soil conservation, irrigation, reclamation, reforestation, and
water use, as well as in regional developments (such as the complex
Tennessee Valley Authority) and in interregional and interurban coordination and planning. Much of this was erroneously seen by critics as
steps in the direction of a "planned economy." While recognizing that
"nothing in the direction of planning has been attempted," Edward S.
Mason noted that the *official language* used in the explanation and defense of such measures as the NIRA, for instance, was "the language of
planning." Spokesmen of the administration, from the president on
down, liked to proclaim that production had to be "adjusted" to demand,
that investment had to be "adapted" to the needs of industry, that
purchasing power had to be "allocated," and "balanced" economic process had to be secured.[47]

CONTROVERSY AND COURSE CORRECTION, 1938–41

The strategy of reflation and of increased "purchasing power," as
embodied particularly in monetary depreciation, banking restructuring,
relief for borrowers, subsidized curtailment of crop acreage, cartelization of industry with restricted output but with rising payroll, Social
Security, and verbal (more than actual) support of planning—was ques-

tioned both inside and outside the administration. Opposition grew as the president moved toward dollar devaluation and substituted a domestic-oriented policy for international action. By the end of August 1933 a group of administration experts led by Secretary of the Treasury William H. Woodin rejected the idea that monetary action could bring national recovery. A Committee on Monetary Policy opposed "currency experimentation" and asked for a return to a fixed gold standard that would guarantee reasonable expectations for profit and "an increased volume of business, which increases wages and the whole national income." The Advisory Council of the Federal Reserve Board and the United States Chamber of Commerce added their voices to the clamor for "sound money" (namely, the gold standard). They pointed out that a *general* rise in prices did not reduce the discrepancy between farm and nonfarm prices, that such a rise reduced the standard of living unless accompanied by corresponding increase in incomes, and that the government could not "order" real wage increases. Only increased profits coming out of a larger volume of business could lead to real wage increases.[48]

The rationale as well as the allegedly favorable economic consequences of the AAA and NIRA was also questioned. With regard to the AAA, Bernard Baruch pointed out that the program that aimed at reducing production by curtailing acreage did not in fact subsidize nonproduction; paying a bounty on a percentage of all products marketed would lead to increased production per acre. "Since the bounty is paid on a percentage of each man's marketing, and since price plus bounty is nearly double price alone and bounty is paid regardless of grade, the result will be to bring in all seed and feed and farm-consumed products and also waste grades even if farm requirements are at once purchased. . . . No matter what may be the price on grades full of sand, dirt, chaff, stalks, and defects, the bounty is the same."[49]

Such proadministration experts as Clair Wilcox, Herbert H. Fraser, and Patrick Murphy Malin contended that "debt reduction plus sound money, plus public works, plus tariff reduction, *without the N.I.R.A.*, would have offered us a shorter road to recovery than the one which the Administration has chosen to take." According to these economists, the consumer was made to pay both the agricultural price increase required for the cash subsidy and the price increase caused by curtailment of output. As far as NIRA was concerned, consequences were even more damaging. NIRA's attempts to restore prosperity by raising wages, reducing hours, curtailing output, and fixing prices, had boosted costs, increased prices, caused inefficient use of men and machines, and checked rather than promoted industrial activity.[50] To John M. Clark, the NIRA appeared "not as a means to stimulate recovery but as a measure to substitute work-sharing for relief." He added that increased prices due to monetary manipulations could have only fleeting effect, transfers of purchasing power from one group to another might stimulate activity but only under some conditions, and finally, increases in wages at the expense of business earnings were "not revival measures at all, but the opposite."[51]

The entire strategy of reflation and diffusion of purchasing power, "on the assumption that the causes of our ills were domestic, internal, and that the remedies had to be internal too," appeared to many critics as a pretext for diverting income from saving to consumption and for increasing wages (before increasing sales) via government borrowing and lending.[52] Critics added that wage increments do not go entirely into consumption but rather into debt paying and, further, that the push toward higher costs as rapidly as output increases, reduces profits.[53] The administration retorted that in the absence of foreign markets the "new frontier" would be domestic demand. To take advantage of this market, it had to cope with widespread unemployment and with the need to bring about the revival of the capital goods industries. The administration thought that matching purchasing power to industrial activity was a circular problem, and what really mattered was "to find the points that will start the wheel revolving."[54]

By 1937 the balance sheet was mixed; income had increased, but investment and total employment were lagging. Then, as government's expenditures contracted and the Fed doubled the reserve requirements, a sharp recession set in shaking the administration's confidence in its own measures. The outlook became dark after the early summer of 1937, when the economy took a sharp turn for the worse. As we noted, industrial production fell drastically, and with it came rapid decline in employment and in farm prices, raw materials, and wholesale commodity prices. The increase from the preceding year's GNP in current dollars was on the order of 17 percent in 1934, 11 percent in 1935, 14 percent in 1936, and 9 percent in 1937. In 1938 the GNP decreased by 6 percent. Unemployment became alarming, rising again from some 7 million people in 1937 to over 10 million in 1938.[55]

Confronted with the new downturn, the president sent to Congress on April 14, 1938, his much-discussed "Recommendations Designed to Stimulate Further Recovery." In his words, "the citizens' income of today is not sufficient to *drive the economic system at a higher speed.* Responsibility of government requires us at this time to supplement the normal processes and in so supplementing them to make sure that the addition is adequate."[56] He proposed a three-pronged attack on the recession: additional appropriations of $1.55 billion for fiscal 1938–39 ($1.25 billion to the Works Progress Administration); additional bank resources for credit by releasing approximately $1.4 billion of Treasury gold; "definite additions to the purchasing power of the Nation by providing new work," by federal expenditures and new loans of $1.46 billion (of which $1.16 billion was for public works).[57]

Were these a break with the conceptual policy framework of the past? Were they the expression of a change in use of government instruments? Did they inaugurate new views about interrelations between government and the economy? According to Arthur Smithies of the University of Michigan, this document was "the first outright recommendation by the president destined to achieve recovery through *fiscal* policy."[58] Many other economists, however, saw the president's action in a different light. Commenting on Smithies's suggestion, Gardiner C. Means, who was better attuned to the concepts of the 1930s than anyone else, retorted that it gave "undue" weight to the "fiscal" rather than to the "monetary" explanation of the president's recommendations.[59] The latter followed indeed a period of reduction in government spending. As noted, policy makers had remained concerned throughout the 1920s with the stock of money rather than with flows of incomes and expenditures. Alvin H. Hansen stressed that neither before nor after 1937 did the administration pursue a "really positive expansionist program": what it aimed at was "a salvaging program."[60] Echoing Hansen, Herbert Stein more recently noted, "it was not, in 1938 or 1939, national policy to use fiscal means—deficit spending—to whatever degree it might be necessary or thought to be necessary to achieve prosperity and full employment. Fiscal policy did not have the unlimited, residual role of doing whatever all other means in combination failed to do."[61] Driving "the economic system at higher speed" was to be achieved, according to the president, through expansion of "today's purchasing power—the citizen's income of today"—consumer buying power that had lagged behind production, just as in 1933. The president remained faithful to his ideas about the link between "mass purchasing power" and growth.[62]

LEGACIES

Deep dislocations caused by the Great Depression—generalized misery and unemployment, advancing paralysis of production and distribution, danger for institutions—brought profound changes in the country's thinking about the economy and about the role and responsibilities of government. President Hoover had wound up his election campaign of 1932 by extolling the country's economic successes during the first decades of the century and blaming the "temporary" dislocation of its "normal functioning" on the "abnormal shocks" it had received from the *outside* during the preceding three years. He warned that "new dealers" would endanger the American system through expansion of government expenditures, depreciation of the dollar, intrusion in banking and in the electric power business, and through a futile search for "employment of all surplus labor at all times."[63] The country was not in a mood to listen; it had given up belief in "automatic adjustments" and was hoping for an activist government and for a change in the public purpose.

This activism translated into measures concerning the government's involvement in income redistribution and its expansion of regulatory powers. Nevertheless, this activism rebuilt confidence in the system and steered the country away from more radical solutions. As we have seen, the measures taken affected money and banking, the environment for private investment, agriculture and industry's organization, output, pricing, and employment, conditions of work, wages, and labor-management bargaining, and, finally, social security. Some of these changes proved irreversible. In other cases the principles and assumptions on which reforms were based—concerning agriculture, social security, and in part industry—came under scrutiny. When underlying economic factors shifted with regard to interindustry and intersectoral relations, patterns of employment and technological transformation, and the scope of growth and change, reforms of the 1930s were bound to appear in a new and not always favorable light. No matter how one looks at these reforms, one cannot forget, however, that one of their motives was the necessity to cope with the waste of human and material resources generated by the depression. In fact, since then the fear of mass unemployment has never been completely exorcized from the nation's collective mind.

Some of the economic theories brought to the fore by the depression have been less fortunate than reforms of the time. Some economists may still continue to reason in regard to the business cycles either in terms of the purely *monetarist* explanation (Irving Fisher or R. G. Hawtrey), or in terms of disturbances in the *sphere of production* involving inventions, innovations, markets, and changes in desired demand (Joseph A. Schumpeter and Sumner H. Slichter), or, less likely, in terms of maladjustments in *income distribution*. Possibly they may also think in terms of all these explanations and of their multiple combinations. Perhaps fewer than in the 1930s tend to think now exclusively in terms of relative prices and of stocks of money and not *also* in terms of flows of income and expenditure.

The 1930s provided an abundance of theories concerning interplay in "industrial society" of the "centers of corporate power," government, and the rest of the population, a possible convergence of economic systems, and the nature and uses of economic planning. Some of these theories—particularly those of Veblen and Means—have had a deep effect on such influential books as James Burnham's *The Managerial Revolution* (1941) and John Kenneth Galbraith's *The New Industrial State*

(1967). Veblen beheld the future of the "incoming industrial order" as belonging to the "engineers"; "as a matter of course, the powers and duties of the incoming directorate will be of a technical nature, in the main if not altogether."[64] Burnham asserted that capitalism and socialism, the United States and the Soviet Union, as well as Nazi Germany, were all "converging", namely, "moving though by different paths toward the same or a similar form," a "form" that he called the "managerial society." This supertechnical industrial society, Burnham said, needed directors, coordinators, organizers of the processes of production, and administrators. Veblen saw clearly the coordinating need of this integrated whole, but he confused "this directing and coordinating function with the scientific and engineering work." Actually, Burnham said the engineers were merely "highly skilled workers," while real power already belonged to the *managers* in all these kinds of societies.[65]

In analyzing the American economy, Means drew attention not to the interplay of prices but to that of "controls," which according to him coordinated all the country's economic activities. He listed four "coordinating mechanisms": the *market*; *administration*; *canalizing factors* (laws and rules); and *accepted goals* (via contracts). Great segments of the economy had shifted during the past century from the market to administrative controls, whose foci he assumed to be the steadily expanding and interlocking large corporations (in industry, transportation, communications, trade, and finance) and the government.[66] Galbraith made these large corporations the nucleus of the modern economy and the locus of decision making for the economy as a whole. As we shall see in more detail later on, the "guiding intelligence" of the corporation, according to Galbraith, became not management, but (back to Veblen) the firm's technicians—engineers, product planners, market researchers, sales executives—that is, the corporation's "technostructure." It was the corporation's *planning*, its control of demand, supply, and provision of capital that changed the government's own policies and instruments from taxing to spending (civilian or military). Finally, as for Burnham, *convergence* between the industrial systems, capitalist and socialist, had begun, and its locus was within the "modern large-scale production."[67]

The contributions of the 1930s to planning fall into two categories. A large number of planning proposals had an effect, if not on policy at least on the language of the public and policy makers; it was fashionable to talk about "convergence," planning, and centralized coordination. Since then, whenever the specter of unemployment stalked, proposals for planning have reappeared. But other contributions of the 1930s to the "economics of control"—such theoretical works as those of Abba Lerner and Oscar Lange—had a lasting effect on economic theory.[68]

Since the 1930s the New Deal has been described as socialistic and the NIRA as the height of collectivism. Actually the New Deal was not even *dirigiste* in the sense of the French notion of complex state interventions through the state budget and "planning" through a vast nationalized sector. The New Deal operated through *institutional reforms*. As for socialism and its implicit Marxian connotation, Leo Rogin of the University of California has pointed out that an administration bent on collectivism would have hardly "thawed out, cleaned out and resuscitated" the banks, "bailed out" large corporations, enacted collective bargaining, showed concern for farmers, and envisaged state action in the interest of recovery and economic stabilization. Had Marx been able to envisage a large program of public works in a setting of entrepreneurial "rugged individualism," he might well have remarked that these entrepreneurs would sabotage the priming of the pump and then take the pump away.[69]

CHAPTER
2

COUNTER-CYCLICAL
POLICIES

THE ECONOMIC SCENE, 1945–60

As the powerful forces unleashed by World War II were transforming
and remodeling the economy's sectors and branches and their interrelations, concern about the future transition of the economy from war to
peace became insistent both inside and outside the government. What
forms will this transition take? What kind of shifts will occur in the
composition of output and employment and in the economy's structure?
What will happen to income distribution, consumer demand, investment
opportunities, prices? Will the private economy generate sufficient investments both to cope with the war-created shortages of capital for
nonmilitary production and to push the economy forward? Will the
government consider it its responsibility to secure full employment and
prosperity? Will it maintain the "welfare state" foundations built in the
prewar years?

   Innumerable postwar economic plans were spawned during the war
years. As early as November 12, 1940, President Roosevelt instructed the
National Resources Planning Board—the planning arm of the executive
office of the president—to "collect, analyze, and collate constructive
plans for significant public and private actions in the postwar period."[1]
By mid-1943 comprehensive planning programs were undertaken in the
Departments of State, Treasury, Commerce, and Agriculture, the Bureau of the Budget, the War Production Board, and in numerous governmental agencies. An annotated bibliography of the Legislative
Library of Congress listing the major books and articles written between
1943 and 1945 on full employment covered no less than fifty-six tightly
packed pages.[2] Besides the paramount concern with full employment,
described as "the central feature of the society that had to be constructed
in the U.S.,"[3] important wartime economic publications focused on: the

24

evolving structure of the American economy (the *Report* of the "Temporary National Economic Committee" [1941] and the studies that followed it), fiscal policies and their impact on business cycles (for example, Alvin H. Hansen's *Fiscal Policy and Business Cycles* [1941], J. H. G. Pierson's *Deficit Spending and National Income* [1941], and Abba P. Lerner's studies on "functional finance" and on the optimal allocation of resources [1941, 1943]), economic planning and its alternatives (including such antiplanning books as Ludwig von Mises's *Omnipotent Government* [1944] and Friedrich von Hayek's *The Road to Serfdom* [1944]), and postwar market prospects (Sumner H. Slichter's *Markets after the War* [1943], John M. Clark's *Postwar Economic Problems* [1943], and P. T. Homan and Fritz Machlup's *The Economics of Peace* [1945]).[4]

The widespread preoccupation with postwar prosperity and full employment, stemming from both the memories of the Great Depression and the fears of the impact of the war's achievements on postwar developments, deepened as war expansion reached higher and higher levels. Warning that "record production with large scale unemployment may reappear in an aggravated form in the postwar years,"[5] various economic publications forecasted unemployment levels of from 10 to 30 million people for 1946.[6] Asserting that a "high level of employment is not a gift of the gods nor the product of automatic market forces," certain economists such as Everett E. Hagen urged the maintenance of high levels of employment, "extremely wise social engineering, aimed at raising materially either the propensity to consume or the incentive to invest or both."[7]

At the war's end the apprehension that we might drift into a depression worse than that of the 1930s mingled with the deep desire and the determination to make full employment a fundamental feature of the postwar economy. The Employment Act of 1946, which was to acquire eventually the force of an "economic constitution," gave expression to this deep-seated wish for "a conscious and positive attack upon the ever-recurring problems of mass unemployment and ruinous depression."[8] Whatever the differences of opinion on the specific measures (fiscal or monetary) needed for economic stabilization, both the Truman and the Eisenhower administrations accepted as a key function of the federal government's policy the *moderation* of cyclical swings. The policy was to consent to partial *compensation* in the downswing and partial *restriction* in the upswing: the long track of the economy around which cyclical fluctuations will occur was supposed to take care of itself. This "cyclical mentality," as James Tobin was to call it, was superseded only after 1960, when the government's policy changed its focus and started to aim at preventing cyclical fluctuations and at keeping the economy close to a path of steady growth at a constant target-rate of unemployment.[9] It is for this reason that this chapter takes 1960 as a horizon.

Let me briefly recall that immediately after the war, the economy went through a *reconversion* phase that lasted until 1947. The sharp fall in the government's purchases of goods and services, from some $83 billion in 1945 to some $28 billion in 1946, was fortunately offset in part by large increases in consumption expenditures, gross private domestic investment, and net foreign investment. Furthermore, the government helped the reconversion adjustment via transfer payments to victims, rapid liquidation of "surplus" war property, and repeal of the excess profit tax. Employment and production declined under the impact of demobilization but from such abnormal levels that "a portion of war production could be forgone without the need to replace it in order to maintain full voluntary employment."[10] The postreconversion years up to 1960—the end of the Eisenhower administration and the cutoff point of this discussion—while registering a significant overall growth in GNP, were marred by not less than four recessions. The economy settled into its first postwar recession for almost the whole of 1949. By the turn of 1950 business renewed its forward thrust in no small measure because of the war in Korea. The expansion lasted until June 1953, when a second recession, longer than the first (thirteen months) plagued the economy until August 1954. After a new forward thrust, a third contraction took place between September 1957 and June 1958 (nine months). The upswing that began in July lasted until June 1960, when a fourth recession, spilling into 1961, closed the period under review.

Did the actual measures of the Democratic and Republican administrations converge or diverge in response to these fluctuations? Under the Truman administration, government expenditure tended to *rise* (as did its federal component), from some 18 percent of the 1947 GNP to 27 percent of that of 1952.[11] The Eisenhower administration tended to put a cap on this rise and whenever possible (1954–56) to lower it. It surpassed it once, however, in 1958, when it reached some 28 percent of GNP. In federal expenditures, the Eisenhower administration rapidly decreased the share of defense at the end of the war in Korea and maintained the welfare allocation levels at roughly 3–5 percent of GNP. The federal surplus fluctuated around 1–2 percent of GNP in either direction, while the federal debt fell continuously as a percent of GNP through both administrations, namely from 101 percent in 1947 to about 47 percent in 1960. Money supply increased at an average annual rate of 3 percent under the Truman administration and at less than 2 percent per annum during the Eisenhower years. Credit expansion was vigorous both at the end of the 1940s as well as throughout the 1950s, while interest rates pushed upward from 2.5 to 3.5 percent from 1947 to 1952, to from 3.5 to 5.5 percent by the end of the 1950s.

Real gross national product (at 1972 prices) increased at the compound rate of 4 percent per annum during the Truman administration (after the postwar reconversion years) and at less than 3 percent under the Eisenhower administration. Total employment rose from close to 59 million in 1947 to some 64 million in 1952 and to over 68 million in 1960. Unemployment tended to fall under Truman from close to 4 percent of the civilian labor force in 1947 to 3 percent in 1952, with peaks of 6 and 5 percent in the recession years. Under Eisenhower, unemployment followed an upward drift with peaks of over 5 percent (1954, 1959, and 1960), and close to 7 percent (1958). Conversely, inflation tended to rise during the Democratic administration and to fall during the Republican one: the consumer price index (CPI), which had increased by over 18 percent between 1947 and 1952, increased by some 11 percent between 1953 and 1960. The Republican administration did indeed leave an economy singularly free of inflation. (See figure 2.)

During the Truman administration, the Republicans incessantly drew the public's attention to "excessive" government spending, wage increases, and inflationary pressures. The Democrats retorted by stressing the low levels of unemployment and the appreciable rates of increase in real GNP. During the Eisenhower years, the Democrats denounced the use by the Republicans of the "inflationary scare" in order to "keep government expenditures down" and pointed to the rising rate of unemployment, the upward drift of interest rates, and the falling rate of growth of the GNP. The Republicans responded by underlining the country's prosperity and the decreasing inflation rate, without "undue" government "meddling."

Notwithstanding these significant differences, certain long-run and deep seated tendencies of the economy were not seriously affected by the change of administrations. The share of farming in the nominal GNP continued to fall, from close to 9 percent in 1947, to 6.5 percent in 1952, and to 4 percent in 1960. The share of manufacturing remained about the same throughout all these years, around 28–29 percent. The output of farming and of industry (manufacturing plus mining plus utilities) increased remarkably—the latter faster though than the former—given unequal productivities in the two sectors.

It became quite customary in the 1960s to refer to the Eisenhower years as a "troublesome period of retarded growth from the mid-1950s to the early 1960s." The claims were based on certain controversial definitions of potential output that held sway in the 1960s and that we shall consider later on. Let us note now that derivations of potential income at 4 percent unemployment, computed by Edward F. Denison, yield for the Truman years a real excess of income (at 1972 prices) over the potential of $11.5 billion and for the Eisenhower years a shortfall in relation to the potential of $112 billion.

KEYNESIAN VS. NON-KEYNESIAN
APPROACHES TO POLICY

The post–World War II years brought into the public eye, as never before, some of the deepest theoretical cleavages that rent the economics profession since the 1936 publication of John Maynard Keynes's famous book, *The General Theory of Employment Interest and Money*. These cleavages, never fully breached, concerned not only policy issues but also deeper underlying questions on the nature and *modus operandi* of the contemporary capitalist system and on the role of the government with respect to the workings of the price system, the organization of production, and the allocation of the country's resources.

The contending concepts can be presented schematically as follows. The "classical" school believed in a self-adjusting system. It affirmed that under competition, frictional disproportions between prices and costs may arise and bring about depressions that, in turn, eventually eliminate these disproportions and produce again full employment and efficient allocation of resources. The "classical" monetarists thought on their part that the rate of money supply (variously defined) was the only systematic determinant of the price level, and if the supply of money were stabilized, the free market would take care of the residual business cycle instability. In contradistinction to the classical economists' contentions, Keynes asserted that the contemporary Western economic system was a system in which resources were underutilized, markets were in chronic disequilibrium, adjustments were not always achieved via price movements alone, and agents did not react to price signals only. Our system, he pointed out, was a *mixed* economic system in which interactions of government policies and markets determine the organization of production and the total demand for the goods produced. Effective use of fiscal and monetary policies (with emphasis on the former) can combat unemployment and chronic depressions, act upon the intensity, duration, and frequency of business cycles, and largely influence the movement of GNP. Keynes set *income* analysis in a place as important as *price* analysis. His chain of reasoning ran as follows: output and employment are determined by the demand for output. This demand consists of consumption plus investment (plus government spending). Consumption is largely determined by the level of income. In turn, the latter is determined by the interplay of two sets of independent decisions concerning investment and saving. Investment varies, depending on the crucial interrelation between the returns on capital (its "marginal efficiency") and the rate of interest—combined with the impacts exercised by such factors as expectations, technological change, economic growth, and investment incentives. Prices of commodities are determined by the demands and supplies of commodities. The rate of interest itself is

Figure 2. Selected Indicators, 1948–1960

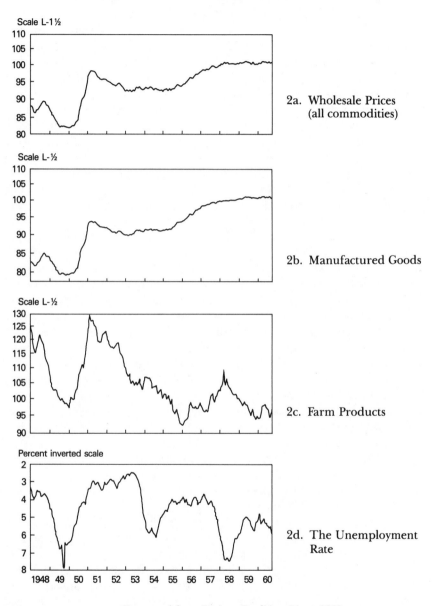

2a. Wholesale Prices
(all commodities)

2b. Manufactured Goods

2c. Farm Products

2d. The Unemployment
Rate

SOURCE: Excerpted from *Business Conditions Digest,* 1969

separately determined by the supply of money (decided by the monetary authority) and the demand for it (the active component of which is the public's "liquidity preference"): "This is how the quantity of money enters the economic scheme." Fiscal policies change income flows and induce reliable responses via a multiplier mechanism. Following this analysis, Keynes felt confident to say that "a decreased readiness to spend [by the government] will be looked on in quite a different light if, instead of being regarded as a factor which will, *cet. par.*, increase investment, it is seen as a factor which will, *cet. par.*, diminish employment."[12] Put differently, government spending alone can, in certain conditions, bring effective demand to a level at which the balance achieved between it and production will be sufficient for maintaining full employment.

As David McCord Wright pointed out, we cannot follow Keynes's line of thought and say "that the capitalist system, left to itself, will automatically bring forth sufficient effective demand." Contrary to J. B. Say's classical "law" that production creates its own demand, Keynes, as we already noted, asserted that the outstanding characteristic of our system was its capacity of "remaining in a chronic condition of sub-normal activity for a considerable period without any marked tendency either towards recovery or towards complete collapse"—a condition that could persist "failing measures expressly designed to correct it."[13] Thus Keynes derived "the most vividly known arguments for intervention even though such intervention may be quite capitalist in nature,"[14] namely, based on the market framework, not on its suppression. In the broader philosophical tradition, we may assert with Walter A. Morton—more or less facetiously—that the ideas of the three contending economic schools—classical, classical-monetarist, and Keynesian—were, *mutatis mutandis*, akin to those of eighteenth century deists, theists, and humanists. The first of these philosophies contended that the universe was so ordered from the beginning as to make divine intervention unnecessary. The second affirmed that divine intervention was occasionally beneficial. The third suggested that, to serve human needs, interventions to alter the order of nature were necessary.[15]

In the late 1940s and in the 1950s the economists' policy-oriented debates clustered around three groups of questions: (a) the policies and instruments for moderating business fluctuations; (b) the goal of "full employment" and its "costs" in terms of inflation (given statistically observed interrelations between the rates of unemployment and the rates of inflation—the so-called Phillips curve); and (c) the possibilities and the limits of government interventions for promoting "maximum" production and the general welfare. While the connective theoretical issues of the indicated debates escaped the public at large, rarely did professional discussions enjoy such widespread attention. Let us consider now in turn the indicated "clusters" of issues.

a. **On the moderation of business cycles**. The "stagnationists" of the 1930s believed that "mature" capitalism, plagued by depressed inducements to invest, was faced by an era of sick recoveries that would die in their infancy and depressions that fed on themselves. While accepting the thesis that in an advanced capitalist economy underinvestment and oversaving tend to become typical, the Keynesian theory opened up a different view of the future, not only for the more developed but also for the less developed countries of the world. Its repudiation of the classical conception of the self-adjusting system, along with its sanctioning of modifications to the workings of the price mechanism, opened up a new vista on a potentially secure future for any mixed economy with an economics-conscious government. Under Keynes's influence, an increasing part of the economics profession started to harbor the hope—others say the illusion—that "because we know the causes of depressions and stagnation, we shall therefore prevent them from recurring" and that "from now on we shall do what has never been done before."[16] From the 1940s on, technological progress began to be celebrated as the generator of investment opportunities. In the early 1950s, investment was wanted in the United States because it generated income and created employment. Rather little was said then about the concomitant expansion of productive capacity. This was, however, stressed by R. F. Harrod and by Evsey D. Domar, as we shall see later on. Keynes took the view that, if full employment were maintained long enough, the increase in productive capacity would be so rapid that the marginal efficiency of capital would decline to near zero in a few generations. (This is somewhat similar to Joseph A. Schumpeter's earlier model of zero interest rate and stationary state. It corresponds also to Frank Ramsey's "bliss" state in an undiscounted optimal growth model.)

Conversely, in some Western European countries, the socialist or semi-socialist countries, and in the less developed countries (LDCs) investment was wanted precisely because it expanded the capacity to produce. In particular, the leaders of the LDCs assumed optimistically that if they raised the rate of savings and investment and engaged in a crash program of industrialization, the disparities between their countries and the most advanced countries of the world would rapidly diminish and eventually vanish.[17] As we shall see further below, our decision makers and their advisers also "discovered" from the mid-1950s on the importance of enlarging the country's productive capacity. However, the subject of *accelerated* growth, that is the rapid expansion of the capacity itself, became central to policy decisions only in the 1960s.

As in the LDCs, optimism was also the hallmark of American economic writings in the early 1950s, but for other reasons. As the most enduring college textbook, *Economics*, had it, this was so first of all because of the new perspective of a "useful or wise employment of resources," namely, of "a better, larger, and more stable level of production and consumption, and equitable distribution of that output between individuals."[18] And second, because of Keynes's contribution of an aggregative income determination model—simple, manipulable, and relevant to policy problems—along with the use of other "exciting" tools such as input-output and linear programming, opened up broad possibilities for future policy model building. These circumstances made a future Nobel laureate in economics proclaim: "Every day, in every way, we are getting better and better."[19] All this should not, however, be construed to mean that the entire economic profession had gone over to all of Keynes's views. The most influential economists of the day proclaimed themselves partisans of the "neoclassical synthesis," namely, the integration of two different theoretical structures, the Keynesian theory and the analyses of Léon Walras, Vilfredo Pareto, and Knut Wicksell—an integration made possible by John Hicks's *Value and Capital*, subsequently developed by Oscar Lange, Don Patinkin, and others. The partisans of this synthesis did not assume instantaneous market clearing of all markets, particularly the labor markets, but they also rejected the idea of a permanent nonclearing in the absence of government intervention. Economists like Paul A. Samuelson stressed that the equilibrium position toward which the market tends is described by the classical reference to preferences, resource endowments, and motivations of economic agents, so that economic policy may well be neutral in the long run. These policies, however, are fully capable of modifying the path along which the economy adjusts to disturbances or shocks so as to reduce the cost of adjustment. In practical day-to-day policy for economies in disequilibrium, the neoclassical analysts would essentially follow Keynesian lines; however, they would not neglect to stress that *in the long run* private actions will offset government action so that the classical outcome would prevail.[20]

Even among those who called themselves Keynesians, agreement was not unanimous on the critical idea that "the right remedy for the trade cycle is not to be found in abolishing booms and thus keeping us permanently in a semi-slump; but in abolishing slumps and thus keeping us permanently in a quasi-boom"—as Keynes had it.[21] Some inclined rather toward a policy of controlling the boom so as to reduce the extent of the expected slump that would follow. The discussions among economists continued to focus, then, on the appropriate moment to call into play discretionary measures—and which one, public expenditure or tax changes—to supplement the automatic play of built-in stabilizers; on the actual or assumed incompatibility of Keynesianism with the traditional rules of "sound finance"; and on the Keynesian lack of confidence in pure monetary instruments.

In two theoretical articles that set the stage for the passionate debates that followed around these problems, Abba P. Lerner contended (in 1941 and 1943) that the central idea of counter-cyclical Keynesianism was to focus exclusively on the *results* yielded by the application of any fiscal measure in relation to its chosen goal. Rejecting the tenets of "sound finance," Lerner's "functional finance" approach, namely, "the principle of judging fiscal measures by the way they work or function in the economy," advanced the following "rules." In order to tame the cycle, the government should use government spending when total spending is too low, and taxation when total spending is too high. Further, to achieve a desired investment level, the government should appropriately adjust public holdings of money and government bonds via borrowing or debt repayment. Finally, in order to carry out this program, the government should simply "print, hoard, or destruct money as needed."[22]

There were many plans for using *fiscal policy* in the years immediately following World War II. Most of these plans asserted, however, that the flexibility of fiscal policy was more limited than was usually assumed, that fiscal policy needed to be supplemented with monetary policy, that the built-in stabilizers should be allowed to do their work, that economic forecasting was unreliable and therefore the timing of this or that measure was likely to be in doubt, and that there were other objectives in addition to economic stabilization that must be taken into account. In short, all wanted in varying degrees to limit discretionary fiscal actions to deal with fluctuations.

In a highly influential statement on "Federal Expenditure and Revenue Policy for Economic Stability" issued in 1949, sixteen economists of widely different persuasions (including the prominent representative of neoclassical economics, Paul A. Samuelson) rejected the idea of exclusive reliance on fiscal action and recommended instead a policy system centered on "automatic flexibility" and "formula flexibility." The first, exemplified by the unemployment compensation system, farm benefits, and the like, also referred to a tax system with a set of rates that would yield falling or increasing revenues in a depression or in an inflation, respectively. The second referred to tax cuts or to upward tax revisions, which would be triggered by output decreases or price increases around some prespecified levels. The sixteen also rejected the idea that the basic tenets of "sound finance" could or should be tampered with. They pointed out that the impact of spending and taxing will be different according to the *type* of spending and tax involved, that procedure lags and distortions could further affect these impacts, and that any attempt to divorce expenditures from the need for a corresponding taxation would weaken the resistance to spending without regard to its costs in terms of taxes.[23]

Other economists, like Paul J. Strayer of Princeton, for instance, wondered whether the government could vary its level of expenditures over the cycle without an ever-expanding, permanent increase of the proportion of the country's economy under government control; whether increased government spending would not discourage private investment and thus perpetuate the evil that it was trying to correct; and whether the practical application of counter-cyclical Keynesianism would not lead *simultaneously* to unemployment and inflation given the inflationary bias arising out of monopolistic trade unions and large industrial concentrations.[24] But Strayer was, so to speak, laughed out of court.

Yet soon enough, in the 1950s, the perspective of even a severe stagnation *cum* inflation appeared as very possible to other economists, long before Samuelson and Robert M. Solow identified this theoretically puzzling phenomenon in the recession of 1957–58.[25] Strayer, for instance, sketched with insight the eventual counter-productive results of fiscal measures at high levels of expenditure, debt, and rates of taxation. In his "Appraisal of Current Fiscal Theory" he noted that fiscal measures may lead to unexpected results, because the taxpayer may react with hostility to some rate schedule changes, the wage earner may resort to indirect methods in order to escape a reduction of his disposable income, and corporate taxes may lose their effectiveness. It may thus become "impossible to make any further tax increases effective in the sense that they reduce total demand."[26]

"Orthodox" Keynesians had stressed the idea that in fiscal policy we were dealing with definitive and *direct* action to increase or decrease income flows, while in monetary policy and debt management we were dealing only with *indirect* methods, via impacts on liquidity and asset structure. Anti-Keynesians countered that these views were a poor guide to the proper use of monetary instruments and to the handling of the dominant problem of that time, inflation. According to Harry Johnson, for instance, the Keynesian antimonetarist "bias" was attributable to a "crude effective demand model of income determination," erroneously combined with either the demand pull of inflation or with the cost-push theory, one approach leading "towards the prescription of fiscal policy to remedy inflation, the other towards the prescription of some form of wage and price control." Now, in practice, the first solution was very difficult to graft onto large budgets dominated by military and welfare expenditures, while the second was inconsistent with a free market economy. The underlying rationale of both approaches was the dismissal of the possibility of controlling inflation by monetary means, a wrong idea due to an obsession with the *mechanism*, rather than with the *cause* of inflation.[27] Other economists, like William Fellner, while conceding that when saving exceeds planned investment at a stable price level it may not always be possible to restore the balance by conventional easy-money policy, contended that in the opposite case it would not always be possible to restore the balance by restrictive credit policies. Fellner added that in some countries compensatory activity by central banks had a century-long history and that long before Keynes many Swedish and English economists were convinced that in business cycle analysis it was useful to attribute a crucial role to saving-investment discrepancies.[28]

b. **On full employment and inflation**. The debates on full employment bore not only on the practical meaning of the term but also on the possible trade-off between unemployment and inflation and on the failure of wages to rise or fall with the ups and downs of business. The basic Keynesian assumption of a clear-cut alternative between full employment and a situation in which all kinds of unused resources are available was branded by Friedrich von Hayek as Keynes's "most dangerous legacy." Hayek contended that unemployment is rarely general: it is usually confined to certain industries, occupations, and localities. (And, as Fellner put it elsewhere, the crux of the conceptual difficulty of unemployment is that it includes "individuals who might obtain employment if supply conditions were different on the labor market, that is, if they sought a job on different terms."[29]) Continued inflation, added Hayek, would not suppress the underlying discrepancies between the distributions of labor and of demand. To aim to secure jobs and wages at their former levels in declining industries is to perpetuate maldistributions of labor, lower productivity, and to prevent a redistribution that would eventually lead to higher employment without artificial stimuli.[30] Further, noted Hayek, the blissful illusion that prosperity could be maintained "by keeping final demand always increasing a jump ahead of costs," glosses over the fact that the latter are in the long run not independent of but rather determined by what the final demand would be. To secure "aggregate demand" over "aggregate costs" may prove impossible in the long run, since an excessive demand may act as a deterrent rather than as a stimulus to investment.[31] Henry C. Wallich, then chief of the Foreign Research Division of the Federal Reserve Bank of New York, noted perceptively that submission to the imperative of full employment was, in a sense, the obverse of submission to the gold standard. The former implied emphasis on complete *internal* stability and the latter on complete *external* stability. And he added that if we did "formally subject ourselves to the dictates of the fully employed instead of the golden calf, we might merely find ourselves repeating our past experience of attempting increasingly to by-pass or offset these dictates."[32] Referring to the Employment Act of 1946, another economist, Edwin G. Nourse, noted that ultimately Congress sought to place the act on a practical basis by devolving to professional economic advisers the obligation to provide "interpretations of the full employment goal." Eventually, a rule of thumb emerged as to what full employment actually means, with various suggestions as to the approximate measure of *un-*

avoidable unemployment (frictional, seasonal, and hard-core)—3, 4, 5 percent of the labor force—as a measure of good performance or as a trigger to government action.[33]

Until the simultaneous emergence of inflation *and* unemployment in the late 1950s, the Keynesian analysis of the equilibrium output and of an equilibrium interest rate relied on the so-called "IS-LM model" developed by Professor Sir John Hicks. This model—somewhat reluctantly endorsed by Keynes, since it modified up to a point certain Keynesian postulates—illustrated how the total demand behind the GNP (that is, changes in interest rates affecting investment spending and therefore possible income levels) interacted with the demand and the supply of money at every different income level. This model ignored, however, what would concurrently happen on the supply side of the economy, that is, to the labor market, wages, costs, and prices, as the indicated interactions take place. A statistical study made in the 1950s by A. W. Phillips showed that an inverse relationship appeared to exist between inflation and unemployment—that is, a higher (lower) inflation was co-related with a lower (higher) unemployment rate. If one assumed that these relations were *stable*, it was possible to sustain the argument that the government could, via its fiscal or monetary measures, effectively move the economy along the Phillips curve and maintain any combination of wage-rise (inflation) and unemployment it chose. The new Phillips relationship could thus be safely integrated into the Hicksian-Keynesian framework.

All this, however, raised some serious problems concerning, for instance, the persistence of excess demand for labor along with unemployment. Samuelson and Solow, treating the trade-off between inflation and unemployment as stable, affirmed that in the United States' economy of the time, in order to keep wages from rising we would have to hit an unemployment rate of 8 percent; with wage increases of 2.5 percent per annum, we would have an unemployment rate of 5–6 percent; and, with a rise in the price index by as much as 4–5 percent, we could have an unemployment rate of "no more than 3 percent." They added that if the politicians engineered a low-pressure economy in order to decrease the impact of the demand pull, it was equally possible: (1) that prices might continue to rise even though unemployment remained considerable (that is, *stagflation*); (2) that in the *long run*, say a decade, the economy could achieve higher employment and stability; and (3) that the economy could build up within itself *structural* unemployment, so that more and more unemployment would be needed to keep prices stable.[34]

The attribution of increasing structural labor maladjustments to a low-pressure economy was contrary to Hayek's contention, who, as we saw, attributed the perpetuation of maldistributions of labor to a high-pressure economy. Other anti-Keynesians of the 1950s asserted that the truly novel feature of the contemporary economy was the interaction between *wage push* and *demand pull* (full employment) and that, without preventing the "relentless push of wages in excess of the general rise in overall productivity," inflation, depression, and regimentation were unavoidable.[35] There was no "stable" trade-off between inflation and unemployment. The question of whether wages could be reduced and how, and what the actual consequences of wage cuts were with respect to demand, output, and employment, was in fact at the heart of Keynes's difference with the classical theory. Keynes contended that wage flexibility was insufficient to guarantee full employment. He denied that reductions in money wages would stimulate demand by diminishing costs and prices and therefore increase output, employment, and investment. He suggested instead the maintenance of a stable general level of money wages, since such a policy would not upset the stability of prices and would not cause fluctuations in employment in the short run. He also pointed out that necessary adjustments of the wage level could be achieved by reducing the value of money instead of reducing the wage bill.[36] Friedrich von Hayek—along with a galaxy of other economists—attacked vigorously both the contention that it was *impossible* to reduce the money wages of a substantial group of workers without causing extensive unemployment and the idea that it was *possible* to adjust the real wage level by reducing the value of money without making the employment problem worse. He affirmed that the crux of the matter was that Keynes and his followers were arguing in terms of a *general* wage level while the true problem concerned the *relative* wages of different groups of workers, industrial or regional. In the process of development, he added, relative wages are bound to change: if the money wage of no important group is to fall, then the adjustment of relative positions must be achieved by increasing all other money wages, namely, by inflationary procedures. Further, the employment problem is a *wage* problem: the subterfuge of reducing wages when they are "too high for full employment," via the deceptive method of reducing the value of money, will work for a time but in the long run will make the problem of wages an even greater obstacle than it has been to a stable monetary system.[37] Other economists, following the important works in monetary theory of Don Patinkin (and subsequently of John G. Gurley and Edward S. Shaw), pointed out that a fall in money wages and in prices could bring about a rise in effective demand to a level consistent with full utilization, since it would raise the real value of already existing money and thus stimulate the purchase of goods.[38]

c. **On the thrust of government interventions**. From the early 1940s the debate on the forms and limits of government interventions for achieving "a sustained balance" between income shares on the one hand and the growth of each sector on the other centered around various presidential policy documents. Preoccupation with high production, consumption, and the general welfare emerged from apprehensions about a possible repetition of the economic difficulties caused after World War I by the collapse of agricultural exports and income and, later, from memories of the Great Depression. Likewise the legacies of the New Deal on the relation of production to purchasing power and income distribution were a concern. The shift in emphasis from the indicated "economic balance" toward *growth* in the fundamental sense of simultaneous increases in *supply* (that is, in productive capacity even when unused capacities exist in certain industries and sectors) and in *demand* began to receive top billing in the professional economic journals toward the end of the 1950s. Extensive discussions on economic growth had occurred for the first time at the sixty-eighth meeting of the American Economic Association in 1955.[39] From then on a whole new literature on *economic growth* started to develop around the issues: What are the determinants of economic growth? How can growth be measured and composed temporarily and spatially among periods and among countries? What is the historical record of the U.S. economy in this regard? Why do growth rates differ, and what makes for accelerated or decelerated growth rates at certain periods and in certain countries? What is the relevance of growth theories and of growth models to policy decisions? What may be the effect on growth of collective goals and priorities? What is the role of centralized planning in formulating and in implementing a consistent economic policy?

Keynes's analysis of income determination and of the relation between effective demand and aggregate employment, as well as his "Short Notes" on the "trade cycle," mercantilism, and the "social philosophy" toward which his book was aiming, illuminated many of the interrelations arising in the process of economic growth. But Keynes never developed in the *General Theory* a long-run economic model. The policy implications of his theory centered on the higher or lower utilizations of an *existing* production capacity. His best alternative to depressions, stagnation, and unemployment was to keep the economy "in a permanent quasi-boom." By the mid-1950s, however, the attention of a large body of economists was focusing on the maximal growth attainable through government interventions via the removal of various constraints on both the supply and the demand sides. The Keynesian income-expenditure analysis and the newly refined national income and product accounts were put to use for "post-Keynesian" (in fact *non*-Keynesian) long-term projections of the national product and of its components; they served as points of departure for the study of faster growth. While the post-Keynesian literature increasingly focused on growth and on the idea that with proper fiscal and monetary policies we could have both full employment *and* whatever rate of capital formation the decision makers would choose, its non-Keynesian adversaries opposed the idea that the economy was a "technocratic machine." They felt that the rates of its growth could not (and should not) be determined by policy makers but rather should be left to emerge from private decisions. Further, said the non-Keynesians, the economy cannot be strained to its limits, the financial and market functions cannot be taken for granted, and a process of accelerated growth cannot but lead to inflation and to unsettling imbalances and bottlenecks. These and related issues would be brought to the forefront of economic policy discussions in the 1960s, and we shall examine them extensively at the appropriate time.

COUNTER-CYCLICAL CONCEPTS AND MEASURES

It was Arthur F. Burns, former chairman of President Eisenhower's Council of Economic Advisers, who noted in the early 1960s that with the passage of time, the Employment Act of 1946 had acquired "the force of an economic constitution."[40] Successive presidents and successive Congresses recognized indeed the continuing responsibility of the federal government to strive "with the assistance and cooperation of industry, agriculture, labor" to promote, as the act demanded, "conditions under which there will be afforded useful employment opportunities" and "maximum employment, production and purchasing power." Both the Truman and the Eisenhower administrations often stressed their commitment to the tenets of the act. But their policies and the instruments for carrying them out diverged in many respects, since they interpreted the objectives and the terms of the act in the light of very different economic ideologies, as we shall see below.

For President Truman's administrations, just as for those of Roosevelt, a fully employed, fully productive economy was one that could rely on a continuing rise in real consumption spending. Behind each decline in "real purchasing power of great numbers of consumers" loomed the danger of a depression. While the president was certainly not inclined to listen either to professional economists or to intellectuals in general, the basic ideas of his Councils of Economic Advisers, inasmuch as they were formulated within the conceptual framework of the New Deal, did correspond to his own views. The pivotal ideas of the first *Economic Report of the President* of January 8, 1947, were indeed borrowed from the New Deal, namely that "when people stop buying, business stops producing" and that the government must "remove the fear that demand will periodically be inadequate to absorb maximum production." In order to avoid shortfalls in consumer demand, the federal government was supposed to focus its attention on price-wage interrelations, on the dangers of labor-management strife, on investment activities, on income transfers, on the most effective uses of the soil and marketing of agricultural products, and on foreign aid in relation to its possible impacts on consumer demand. If prices increased, the government should establish price controls while leaning toward an upward wage adjustment, since otherwise "consumer buying will falter"; if strikes and work stoppages occurred, the government should step in because production and employment would be affected by shortages and uncertainties concerning demand and supply; if investment weakened and construction slackened, the government should call into play various incentives, since otherwise the volume of production and of purchasing power will contract; if Social Security programs were not expanded, "a desirable support for mass purchasing power" would not be provided; if agriculture were not encouraged to produce, the American diet and standard of living would be imperiled; if our methods of financing foreign trade were not adjusted, we would endanger the demand for our goods, "one of the factors accounting for a high level of employment, production and purchasing power."[41]

Subsequent *Economic Reports* disclosed a systematic tendency toward extensive interventions in the economy. As the danger of inflation became apparent at the beginning of 1948, the second annual *Economic Report* of the president proposed—possibly under the influence of the vice-chairman of the Council of Economic Advisers, Leon Keyserling—the tightening of business and consumer credit, authority to allocate "scarce commodities and services . . . to their most efficient and necessary uses," and the imposition of "rationing and price control on a highly selective basis." As for the budget, while scheduled receipts were to exceed payments, a shift from personal to corporate taxes was recommended in order to "help the income of those lagging behind the cost of living increases." For the president, any type of possible impact of the tax revisions on inflation was "outweighed" by its merit on equity grounds. Finally, the *Report* warned that "unless we achieve the *necessary* purchasing power adjustments in the price-wage-profit structure," the "continuance of maximum employment and production will be impossible."[42] (Incidentally, it is interesting to recall that the *Third Annual Report to the President* by the Council of Economic Advisers, issued at the end of that same year, 1948, remarked that abstract theory could not produce any criterion or rule of a "stabilizing relationship among wages, prices, and profits, or between any two of them" and that the best one could do was to rely on "empirical observation, reinforced by economic analysis," in order to ascertain which of their "respective movements" would contribute toward improved stability.)[43]

To increase employment opportunities, the administration felt that, as in the 1930s, the consumers' "purchasing power" had to be expanded and that adjustments in prices and incomes had to be made. Peering into the future, the administration set as an objective that GNP should increase at the rate of 3 percent per annum, with the share of consumption rising from around 70 percent to 75 percent, an objective actually never reached.[44] Indeed, 1949 brought with it a recession that lasted the entire year. The president's *Midyear Economic Report* of July 1948 extolled as the economy's bulwark against the recession the recently enacted housing program, unemployment insurance, the old age retirement system, and the farm price-support program. The *Report* then added the following revealing comments about the administration's views on cyclical fluctuations. Our position, said the *Report*, "would be even stronger if we had taken adequate steps to control inflation between 1945 and 1949." Indeed, continued the *Report*, what developed "underneath the surface of the inflationary boom" were serious price and wage distortions and losses in the purchasing power of millions. If these latent factors in the inflation had been checked in time, the break in employment and production would have been less severe.[45] In the view of the administration, inflation could be curbed only via the three-pronged measures of price controls, profit taxes, and increased transfers (including farm price supports).

As the recession ended, the *Economic Report of the President* of January 1950 stressed again, on the threshold of a new decade, that the country's main shield against periodic downturns was the expansion of demand and the promotion of certain "balances." As defined by President Truman's Council of Economic Advisers, "economic balance" was a *sui generis* "dynamic equilibrium." In this equilibrium the proportions among income shares and among the economy's sectors were adjusted so that business's income and investment matched the need to absorb the available technology, while consumers' income and spending were sufficient to clear the markets of goods. Further, expenditures were sufficiently large to provide those services "which our resources permit," while exports were sufficiently abundant to promote a prosperous and peaceful world. Only through this kind of "economic balance" between production and incomes could the various economic groups of the country prosper together instead of struggling to obtain for each one "a larger share of a static national output."[46]

As we noted, that the economy moved out of the recession is due in part to the pressures of the Korean outbreak. In the new conditions of defense emergency and rising inflation, the administration felt it necessary, early in 1951, to curtail nondefense spending, freeze prices, tighten credits, allocate scarce raw materials, extend special aid along with government commitments to purchase from certain industries, and grant additional power to defense agencies to build defense plants. But the slowing down of the inflationary pressure was accompanied by a softening of some markets and by a decline in the growth rate of industrial output.[47] To overcome those weaknesses, the president requested at the end of 1951 the renewal for two more years of the Defense Production Act (including its provisions concerning the strengthening of control on prices and credits, along with a series of his familiar measures to expand consumer purchasing power and to increase transfer payments).[48]

The last two *Reports* of President Truman, in mid-1952 and at the beginning of 1953, set out clearly the administration's economic philosophy and its concern for what it perceived to be the critical nexus between employment, production, government spending, and consumer purchasing power. The *Midyear Report* stated notably, "whether the government runs a surplus or a deficit is important, but is not of such decisive importance for the economy as to outweigh all other considerations. There have been times when a Federal surplus did not protect the economy against inflation, and other times when a Federal deficit did not produce inflation."[49] And the valedictory *Report* of January 14, 1953, added that full employment and expansion could not continue unless "based on a sound and fair distribution of the increasing product. Our economy is built upon mass markets. Unless each important sector receives a workable share of the expanding output, the expansion will come to an end because the market demand will be lacking."[50]

This concept of the economy and of the "balance" among its sectors (including agriculture), of the "fair distribution" of the expanding product and the critical importance of consumption, was rejected by the incoming Eisenhower administration. Yet, as we already noted, this Republican administration accepted also as its task the moderation of cyclical fluctuations. Defining the basic framework of its federal policies, the new administration affirmed its commitment to keeping the economy on the "narrow path" between the danger zones of inflation and contraction. This, however, did not imply either "constant steering and meddling" or attempts to cope always and fully with the unpredictability of the shifts in human behavior and with the economy's responses to the policy makers' own actions. The watchwords of the new administration were the avoidance of a *doctrinaire position* and the resort to *flexibility* when the old policies proved inadequate. Further, the new government did not view itself as a job provider: jobs must be created by private entrepreneurs, who should be rewarded for assuming "the risks of enterprise and innovation." Finally, the government pledged itself to remove interferences from the operation of markets and to divest itself of functions that belong to private enterprise. It stressed its desire to encourage the latter by liberalizing depreciation allowances, research and development expenses, the accumulation of earnings needed for expansion, and the taxes on incomes from foreign investments.[51]

The second *Economic Report* of President Eisenhower, issued shortly after the end of the second postwar recession, elaborated further the ideological approaches defined in his first *Report*. It affirmed that the administration was not interested in imparting "an immediate upward thrust to the economy" but rather in fostering a stable *long-term* expansion. This, in its view, was to be brought about not only by moderating the business cycle but also by reducing federal expenditures and eventually also taxes, by maintaining easy entry into trade and industry, by supporting research and development, and by reducing international trade barriers. Further, and most interestingly, the administration took a cautious position with respect to the dangers of recession: it rejected not only the views of those who "urge new public undertakings and unbalanced budgets as devices for augmenting private demand" but also the attitudes of those "critical of any governmental action that is designed to prevent or to minimize the rigors of depressed incomes and unemployment." It showed itself responsive to the perils of recession and attentive to the discussions then in vogue about the problems of economic change and development. It accepted responsibility not only to strengthen certain automatic stabilizers ("the floor of personal and family security") but also to modernize and expand the country's infrastructure (interstate highways, harbors, hospitals, educational facilities) and to support various programs meant to improve the nation's "human capital," which it considered an indispensable foundation for the expansion of private enterprise.[52]

The ways in which the administration "leaned against the wind," both in an inflationary and recession period, were readily observable in the period 1954–59 when such changes alternated rapidly. In the expansion period the economy experienced from the end of 1954 onward, the administration underlined with satisfaction its emphasis on *monetary* policies against a "degree of exuberance" in the economy that allegedly could lead to speculation and "eventual economic recession."[53] By the end of 1956, it rejoiced in its budgetary surplus which it considered the major contribution of its "persistent efforts since 1953."[54] As the expansion turned into a decline toward the middle of 1957, the administration proclaimed again its unshakable faith in monetary policies for "lowering the cost of credit to help business investment" along with a quite cautious resort to certain federal construction programs prompted by military needs. With hopes for an eventual economic upturn, it extolled the virtues of a "sustainable and balanced growth"—a balance it defined as consisting in an expansion capable of simultaneously assuring our defenses, satisfying our growing wants, and enabling us to assist the healthy expansion and improvement of other economies.[55] As the recession of 1957–58 passed into history, the *Economic Report* of the president stressed anew in its balance sheet the virtues of the monetary and credit policies which "can produce prompt and significantly helpful results," as well as the use of the built-in stabilizers which soften the impact of economic declines on the flow of incomes to individuals and thus on the volume of consumption spending. Though the *Report* acknowledged the possibly useful contribution of public works in a recession, it added that "little reliance could be placed on large undertakings which come on stream only after an extended interval of time."[56] Throughout these years the Eisenhower administration showed its preference for what it called "flexible" *monetary and debt management* policies, as against the "less flexible" *fiscal* instruments—sticking faithfully to the distinction made in its first *Report*.[57]

The last *Economic Report* of President Eisenhower, reviewing the country's experience under the Employment Act of 1946, recognized that the act gave "explicit expression" to the federal government's continuing interest in aspects of economic life that "had previously received deliberate Federal attention only in such emergency conditions as depression and war." But this did not mean that the act had sought "to centralize economic decision-making in the Federal government" or even to confer on it the predominant responsibility for economic growth and improvement. The decision process should be a "shared private and public responsibility" with the federal government promoting only the *conditions* under which private initiative can thrive. The priorities of economic policy, including a stable currency and protection of the "value of the dollar," were not rigidly ranked: emphasis on one—on fixed quantitative targets for employment, for instance—to the neglect of other goals "would rapidly prove self-defeating."[58]

Thus, two clear-cut economic philosophies underlined the policies and the choice of instruments during the period 1946–60. While both bore the influence of the experiences of the Great Depression and claimed conformity with the tenets of the Employment Act, they diverged considerably in many respects. For the Democratic administrations of the mid-1940s and early 1950s, the American economy was a *mixed* economy in which government's policies interplayed complexly, continuously, and importantly, with the market included in the organization of production and in the determination of the demand for the goods produced. In the Roosevelt tradition, Truman's policy was focused both on full employment and on its nexus with maximum production and the consumer's buying power. Further, if investment faltered, appropriate government spending must take up the slack. Income transfers and built-in stabilizers—Social Security payments "to help the incomes of those lagging behind," farm support programs, government-sponsored housing, rural electrification, and so on—involved both socio-ethical considerations and economic imperatives. The goal of "economic balance" implied in this context the pursuit, as far as possible and under changing circumstances, of various adjustments between *sectors'* incomes and *factors'* rewards. In short, it assumed that each important sector, and labor as well as management, must receive a "workable share" of the expanding output.[59] Put differently, the overall concept of the "welfare state" involved "government outlays large enough to permit *fiscal* policy to play a controlling role in the adjustment of aggregate demand to the [economy's] productive potential."[60] For the Republican administrations of the 1950s, the federal government was supposed to be a "firm" government as far as both receipts and expenditures were concerned and a "pragmatic" and cautious one in regard to its relations with the economy's activities outside the field of national defense. The federal government was supposed to restrict itself to *residual* functions: its roles were to stimulate the private economy, and to defer to state and local government in furthering social utilities. For President Eisenhower, there was no such thing as "a mixed economy": the private enterprise economy constituted, as it were, the entire economy. Within that sphere were to be taken all the critical decisions concerning employment, investment, output, and income. On the other hand, given the postdepression experience, the government did recognize that it had counter-cyclical responsibilities, but these were to be shared with private business and to involve other means than compensatory finance. The moderation of cyclical fluctuations was sought essentially through monetary, debt management, and credit policies and the prudent administration of the budget; a role for some built-in stabilizers (not necessarily just those concerning the farm sector) was acknowledged, and the resort to public works was recommended if it helped expand the foundations on which business rests (namely, the highway system, research, schooling, skills development). The goal of "economic balance" was viewed in a totally different context than the one propounded by the Democratic administrations. This new balance involved equilibria between the potential growth of the population, of the labor force, and of the productive capacity, as well as balances between the potential needs of national defense, the growing wants of the population, and the extent of our commitments to other nations. All these equilibria were to be achieved without losing sight of the rules of sound finance and of the need to maintain a stable, sound dollar.[61]

THE POLICY DEBATES

Under the Truman administration, the American economy was a high-pressure economy responding to a continuously expanding demand for goods and services with stepped-up utilization of its resources, manpower, and productive capacity. Under the strain of pent-up postwar demands, of the Korean conflict, and then of the cold war, the economy responded (under the prodding of the government) with the expansion of both investment in capital goods and the output of consumer goods. *Pari passu*, inflationary pressures mounted. The administration asserted that the big corporations were responsible for inflation, since they controlled the market: it was they who allegedly pushed prices upward, while the Republican party willfully labored to keep "low prices

for farmers, cheap wages for labor and high profits for big corporations."[62] To curb the inflation, President Truman requested extensive
controls and higher profit taxes. In the same vein, Adlai E. Stevenson,
the Democratic candidate for the presidency, proclaimed in 1952 that
"taxes are better than inflation" and that the best way of avoiding depression was to maintain "the buying power of the people." Through "price
supports for the farmers, minimum-wage and collective bargaining laws
for the workers, social security measures for the unemployed and the
elderly," foundations were built under the national economy.[63]

The economic critics of the Truman administration—Paul J. Strayer
for one—contended that in fact the Democratic administration had no
"positive program to check inflation." They said that the president and
his Council of Economic Advisers were giving "disproportionate weight
to the various social, welfare and other economic programs" that drew
away their attention from "the prevention of, or great reduction in the
severity of business fluctuations." Finally, stabilization could hardly be
achieved without fundamental changes in the "system of concentrated
economic control of industry, and more recently [of] labor."[64] With
respect to this last point, Gottfried Haberler stressed indefatigably
throughout the 1950s that "the novel feature of the contemporaneous
type of creeping inflation is the interaction of incessant wage push and
continuous full employment pull" and that the control of demand alone
could not yield a completely satisfactory solution of the problem.[65] As
for the farm price-support policy, the most pointed critique came from
the Democrats themselves. Repeatedly President Truman proclaimed
that "those who are willfully trying to discredit the price support program don't want farmers to be prosperous"; and Adlai Stevenson added
that "we believe, as Democrats have always believed, that our society rests
on an agricultural base," a base that must be kept solid and healthy by
farm programs to maintain farm income.[66] Yet a liberal Democrat such
as John Kenneth Galbraith pointed out that there was a "remarkable
divergence between the weight of scholarly recommendation and the
course of practical action" with respect to farm policies. He noted indeed
that the "scholarly recommendation" was heavily set against the policy of
price supports: "Inefficiency, economic isolation, monopolistic exploitation, inflation, depression, and the economic serfdom and political de-
basement of farmers are all abetted by the policy." A strong case could be
made, Galbraith added, that the technique of supporting prices by loan
and purchase was inferior "to measures which would allow prices to find
their own levels in the market and provide direct payments to sustain
income at the guaranteed levels."[67]

The distinctly different approaches of the "Eisenhower conservatives"
with regard to the pace of the economy, employment and inflation, labor
and unions, and farm policy were accompanied by all kinds of direct and

indirect attacks against the Democratic positions. They drew in their turn critical counterattacks from the economists of Democratic persuasion. Let us recall that the main thrust of the Republican attack was that the Democrats were "the party of high spending and high taxes" and that the Republicans' first order of the day was to reduce both sides of the budget and to achieve stabilization of the dollar. In opposition to the concept of a high-pressure economy—an economy requiring "full employment with both growth and stability" (a task Alvin H. Hansen equated to squaring the circle)[68]—the Republicans countered with the idea of a low-pressure economy, an economy running at a moderate pace and avoiding both inflation and depression. In the words of Gabriel Hauge, President Eisenhower's special assistant for economic affairs, the Eisenhower conservative rejected the doctrine that our economy must always "run a temperature to stay healthy."[69] Against the specter of unemployment in a low pressure economy, the Republicans pointed to the specter of inflation in a high pressure economy. And Henry C. Wallich pointed out that "unemployment hurts a number of people severely, but for the most part temporarily. Inflation hurts large numbers, usually less severely, but the damage done to savings and relative income position tends to be permanent."[70] To the Democrats' contention that wages must catch up with the prices pushed upward by corporations' control of markets, the Republicans answered that in fact the price of labor had been rising during both boom and recessions, thus exercising more or less steadily an upward push on prices.[71] To the Democrats' appeal for more taxes to support a vast reconstruction and development program, the Republicans responded that it was better to let the people have more of their earnings to spend for themselves. Finally, to the Democrats' claim that farm programs were "a must for maintaining farm income," the Republicans answered that the price supports of twelve out of 250 farm commodities had only helped to create our farm surplus problem: these supports had not led to the opening of new markets but rather to the building up of unsalable stocks in our warehouses.[72]

The core of the Democrat-Republican dispute over "inflationary pressures" may well have involved, according to some Democratic economists, "differing definitions of maximum employment and over-full employment."[73] Allegedly, Eisenhower's conception of the federal role with respect to the economy was that of a "Communal Calvinistic conscience—demonstrating and imposing self discipline, applying restraint, exercising prudence, checking excesses." Supposedly, for the Republicans, "debt is immoral if it is federal: debt is moral if it is private"; but debt was evidently a necessary complement of growth of output.[74] With regard to labor, Eisenhower was accused of having changed the National Labor Relations Board so that it had become "much more favorable to the position of the employer than that of the employee" and, further, of strengthening the "anti-labor" tilt of the Taft-Hartley Act. Specifically, Eisenhower was said to have transferred power "from government and labor to the business community," following "the trickle-down theory," according to which "if the businessman is given the opportunity to make a killing, the resulting gains will trickle down to the workers."[75] Although the Republicans had not destroyed the inherited social legislation, they were alleged to "economize unduly" on expenditures on welfare programs. The counterparts of their antitax philosophy were such obvious failings as our "slums, ugly cities, delinquency, mental illness, and overcrowded schools."[76] Finally, with respect to the farm problem, the Republicans were accused of riding "two horses at the same time": the free market and controls plus subsidies. The only solution was to limit production: "as long as there are price controls, there must be production controls."[77]

One of the most portentous phenomena of the time, clearly perceived by Republicans and Democrats alike, was the appearance of *stagflation*, that is rising prices in a recession. Booms with inflation and recessions without inflation did not necessarily follow each other: inflation and recessions could coincide. In the recession years 1949, 1954, and, even more so, in 1958, the price of labor—compensation per man hour in nonfarm industries—continued to rise, even more than the consumer price index.[78] Arthur F. Burns suggested in this connection that wages "would undoubtedly become flexible if a recession deepened into a protracted depression"—an alternative excluded in principle since "it is now the established policy of our government to use all practicable means to moderate business declines."[79] A staff report of the Joint Economic Committee of the Congress also pointed out at that time that the downward rigidity of prices may indeed be "more a reflection of the absence of any prolonged declines in business activity rather than a manifestation of strong unionism."[80]

LEGACIES

As we have seen, a large part of the theoretical discussions of the 1940s and 1950s was concerned with the problems raised by haunting memories of the Great Depression: employment and unemployment, causes of stagnation and of "unhealthy" booms, the role of the federal government and the impact of its fiscal and monetary instruments. Preoccupations with economic fluctuations were common to both the Truman and the Eisenhower administrations. Truman himself was convinced, as we pointed out, that the higher the postwar economic exhilaration, "the greater the danger that it will end up in unemployment, business distress, and recession or depression."[81] But the Democratic Keynesians focused their attention on the state of the economy rather than on the dynamics of the cycle. Contrariwise, Eisenhower's main economists centered their attention on the cycle: they were leaders or disciples of the National Bureau's business cycle research, searching to discover in the Mitchell-Burns tradition the cycle's empirical regularities.[82] The Democrat-Republican "consensus" on the Employment Act of 1946 was real with respect to the recognition of government responsibility for the maintenance of high levels of employment, but open to debate on everything else.

Much of this debate took place, willy nilly, within the analytical framework established by Keynes in the *General Theory*. Although one of the notable features of the *General Theory* is the absence in it (except in a "Short Note" at the end) of the traditional focus on the business cycle as the substratum of the phenomenon of unemployment, Keynes pointed out that it was logical to assume that amounts of private investment, which are highly variable over time, are not automatically equilibrated to full employment savings by an efficacious endogenous economic process. The "consensus" on the Employment Act in essence expressed recognition of this potential disequilibrium. For the Democrats this implied that large government outlays must be made to overcome the disequilibrium, namely, that *fiscal* policy must be the major instrument for discharging the government's responsibility for output and employment levels. For the Republicans this implied first of all an appropriate *monetary* policy. As Haberler put it: "Monetary policy would be sufficient, in most cases at least, if the monetary authorities were prepared to extend the scope of their operations, as Keynes proposed [?] to purchases and sales of long dated securities or possibly equities. If final policy is required, it need not imply increased government expenditures and extended government activities. It could be of the milder, less interventionist form of varying revenues."[83]

Above all, the consensus on the Employment Act did not imply a Democrat-Republican coming together at the heart of hearts of Keynes's theory—"on the sum and substance of his heresy," as Professor Samuelson once put it—namely, on the absence of "an Invisible Hand channeling the self-centered action of each individual to the social optimum." What the Democrats maintained was that, left to themselves, people will *save* in a depression and thus lower society's capital formation and *spend* in an inflation, thus pushing higher the price spiral. For the Democrats this implied the need to counteract individuals' actions in a recession via government spending, income transfers, and the expansion of consumption. Keynes had suggested that, up to the point where full employment prevails, "measures for income redistribution that are likely to raise the propensity to consume may prove positively favorable to the growth of capital."[84] The Republicans accepted reluctantly the idea of income transfers and welfare payments but never ceased to question their validity and legitimacy from the point of view of the economy as a whole.

Further, while the Democrats advocated a tax system falling more heavily on the portion of income saved, and thus counteracting a fall in the propensity to consume, the Republicans saw economic salvation in tax cutting and business incentives.

These and similar divergences nurtured many economic discussions of the 1940s and 1950s and led to exhaustive examination of Keynes's heritage and to the opening of new directions in the development of its theoretical implications. The presentation and reformulation of Keynes's model—in literary, graphic, or mathematical representation—engaged first of all J. R. Hicks (1937), J. E. Meade (1936–37), L. Tarshis (1948), I. O. Scott (1951), E. Lindahl (1956), and W. L. Smith (1956). Important facets of the theory were exhaustively probed—for example, the consumption function, by Hansen (1946), J. H. Williams (1948), and J. S. Duesenberry (1949); the role of the rate of interest, by O. Lange (1938) and R. F. Harrod (1946); the level of effective demand and its fluctuations, by Samuelson (1946); changes in employment and unemployment, by Haberler (1946) and A. P. Lerner (1956); the supply functions, by F. J. deJong (1954, 1955) and D. H. Robertson (1955); and the "rigidity" of wages, by H. W. Arendt (1949) and I. O. Scott (1951). The debates on what does or does not survive of the *General Theory* and various strands of Keynesianism become an unavoidable anniversary exercise, for example, for J. R. Schlesinger (1956), W. Fellner (1957), and H. G. Johnson (1961).[85]

Recall that Keynes, who was influenced by the stagnationist idea that opportunity for investment was rapidly decreasing in the West, asserted in the *General Theory* that it would be very possible that "the prolongation of approximately full employment over a period of years would be associated in countries so wealthy as Great Britain and the United States with a volume of new investment, assuming the existing propensity to consume, so great that it would eventually lead to a state of full investment" in the sense that no further investment in excess of replacement would be desired "soon, say within 25 years or less."[86] Now, as we shall see, when Keynesianism triumphed in the United States as a guide for both presidential and congressional economic policies, it triumphed under the particular form of *Keynes cum growth*. This was to be a policy of systematic expansion of investment and of productive capacity along with adjustments in the aggregate demand to the needs of an ever-expanding potential of the economy. Thus, after a quarter of a century of "approximate full employment," what came to be stressed by the Keynesians and by the partisans of the neoclassical synthesis was not the prospect of a "state of full investment" but rather the opposite: a state of underinvestment requiring more than ever government's activism and government investment. All this in the name, of course, of true "Keynesianism." We turn to these issues in the next chapter.

CHAPTER

3

GROWTH-ORIENTED POLICIES

THE ECONOMIC SCENE, 1961–74

Preoccupation with the "lagging" U.S. rate of economic growth with respect to those of the other industrialized countries, the Soviet Union, and China became widespread at the beginning of the 1960s. The Democrats were emphasizing the crucial connection between growth (henceforth understood as expanding the capacity to produce) and a high and stable level of employment. The Republicans were stressing the importance of the relation between growth and economic freedom, efficiency, and stability. But Democrats and Republicans alike viewed growth as the critical factor in the "deadly competition . . . not only with the men in the Kremlin, but the men in Peking," to use the expression of the 1960 Republican candidate for the presidency, Richard M. Nixon.[1] Eventually the Kennedy and Johnson administrations and, up to a point, also the Nixon administration made the acceleration of economic growth a key goal of their economic policies. Throughout the years of these administrations, from 1961 to about 1974, certain basic problems of growth never left the center of the government's and public's attention. Some of the main questions raised included the following: Would the U.S. be able to achieve and maintain over the long haul high rates of growth? Could the economy be kept at high levels of employment without severely harming its economic stability? Were high growth rates the result of war-fed booms, or were sustained high increases achievable in a peacetime economy? And, what uses should be made of the growing outputs and incomes?

Under the Democratic administrations, the country meandered first through a peaceful stretch of increasing growth rates with reasonable price stability and slowly falling unemployment rates (1961–65). It then went through an unsettling period, burdened by a deeply frustrating

51

war in Vietnam, during which the economy started to display increasing inflationary pressures and low levels of unemployment (1966–68). After transition to a new Republican administration and a short phase of decreased defense spending, the economy passed through a number of years of slowing growth rates, increasing inflationary pressures, and rising unemployment rates. When the Democrats transferred power to the Republicans, they pointed to 106 months of rising GNP—a period of "unprecedented prosperity" thanks to their "vigorous and more consistent application of the tools of economic policy [which] contributed to the obsolescence of the business cycle pattern and the refutation of the stagnation myths."[2] The Republicans, who had contended all along that much of this had been a war-induced boom, wondered whether they could now match the growth record of their predecessors. They soon asserted that they had in fact to bear the brunt of the needs of redirecting the country's resources, of liquidating the consequences of the Vietnam War, of carrying out large cutbacks in civilian and military employment and in defense spending, and of coping with long-neglected and unchecked inflationary pressures. As we shall see, the Republicans were indeed confronted by hard, unpleasant, and finally ineffectual choices between inflation, stagnation, and price controls.

Notwithstanding these different situations and avowed preferences for differing instruments, under the Democrats as well as under the Republicans the share of government's total outlays increased throughout these years, from some 27 percent of GNP in 1960 to around 28–29 percent up to 1966, and then to around 30–32 percent throughout the balance of the period up to and including 1974.[3] During all these years the share of federal outlays as a percentage of GNP stayed at about 20 percent, while the share of transfer payments to individuals increased steadily from around 5.5 to 8.5 percent of GNP, and the share of defense expenditures dropped, at first slowly and then rapidly, from some 9 percent to less than 6 percent. Though each year the budget was in deficit, the federal debt as a percentage of GNP dropped continuously from roughly 48 percent of GNP in 1960 to 25 percent in 1974. The money supply increased at an accelerating rate from roughly 4 percent per year during the period 1961–68 to around 6 percent during the Nixon administration—notwithstanding (or because of) systematic efforts to freeze prices and wages. On the basis 1967 = 100, the consumer price index (CPI) increased from 91 in 1960 to 104, and then shot up rapidly, reaching 147 in 1974. Wholesale prices of all commodities increased rapidly from 1973, under the impact of the increases in both food and oil prices. (See figures 3a and 3b.) The prime rate charged by banks increased from around 5 percent in 1960 to a little over 6 percent in 1968 and then rose to almost 11 percent in 1974.

In real terms, GNP (at 1972 prices) increased at the rate of 3.6 percent

Figure 3. Selected Indicators, 1961–1974

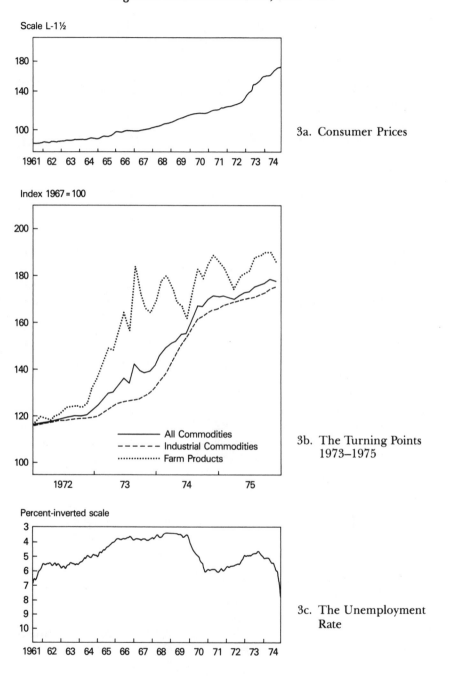

Scale L-1½

3a. Consumer Prices

Index 1967 = 100

— All Commodities
--- Industrial Commodities
········· Farm Products

3b. The Turning Points
1973–1975

Percent-inverted scale

3c. The Unemployment
Rate

SOURCES: *3a, 3c, Excerpted from* Business Conditions Digest, *April 1984*
3b, Excerpted from Economic Indicators, *Prepared for the JEC by the CEA, 1975*

per annum for the period 1961–74, or at the rate of 4.5 percent per annum during the Kennedy-Johnson years and of 2.8 percent per annum during the Nixon years. The number of persons employed rose impressively from close to sixty-nine million in 1960, to over eighty-one million in 1968 and to almost ninety million by 1974, even though unemployment fluctuated in the early 1970s between 5–6 percent of the labor force. (See figure 3.) The sectoral changes displayed tendencies already clearly observed in the preceding period. At current prices, the share of agriculture in GNP fell from 4 percent in 1960 to 3.7 percent in 1974; that of manufacturing from 28 percent to 23 percent. In real terms, however, the share of agriculture fell even more steeply (from 4 to 2.5 percent) while that of manufacturing actually increased (from 20 percent to over 21 percent).

A comparison of the actual and potential income computed by Edward F. Denison at 4 percent unemployment, yields for 1961–65 a shortfall of some $51 billion (at 1972 prices) and a surplus of some $26 billion for the period 1966–68. For the Nixon years the shortfall would be on the order of over $253 billion. Comparisons of the GNP rates of growth for the U.S. and the industrialized countries, on the one hand, and of the Soviet Union, on the other, indicate that the United States did significantly approach the average rates of its economic or political competitors during the period considered. For 1961–65, 1966–70, and 1971–75, the United States registered real GNP increases on the order of 4.7, 3.9, and 3.1 percent, respectively—as against 5.2, 4.8, and 3.1 percent for the whole of the OECD (the Organization for Economic Cooperation and Development, grouping twenty-five countries including the United States), and 5.0, 5.2, and 3.7 percent for the Soviet Union, according to Western compilations.[4] Such comparisons, much in fashion in the 1960s and early 1970s, were, however, based on controversial assumptions and on only roughly comparable data.

DEVELOPMENT, GROWTH, AND WELFARE

The literature on economic development and growth reached its peak in the late 1950s and early 1960s. Soon after World War II, a large number of economic studies began focusing on the developmental problems of the less developed countries, on various issues in capital formation and growth theory, on planning methods, and on optimal macroeconomic policy. Much of this literature came to shape the thinking and the activities of policy makers and economists here and abroad, not only in the 1960s but for years to come.

Two distinct groups of analyses must be considered in this regard: a Soviet and a "Western" one, with a number of interesting similarities but also numerous disagreements. Within these two groups, one must further distinguish the writings on economic development and those on growth. The economic development theorists attempted to fuse ambiguously quantitative growth and qualitative "structural" changes, to integrate into economics socio-historical frames of reference, and to map variously defined developmental "stages," assuming "intrinsic" qualities or shortcomings for given sectors and industries. The growth theorists confined themselves to the study of dynamic interactions among economic variables only. All these types of studies relied in certain ways on the literature of economic control, which provided models and mathematical underpinnings.

The post–World War II Soviet development theory remained rooted in Marx's conception of "historical materialism" expounded in 1859 in the preface to *A Contribution to the Critique of Political Economy.* Soviet growth theory was predicated on another part of the Marxian corpus, namely on Marx's two-sector model published in 1885 in the second volume of *Capital.* In Marx's historical materialism, development is triggered by independent technological-social changes that take place in a society's "base." The base comprises both productive forces (productive techniques and the work force) and productive relations (ownership forms and "class" relations). The base, and the changes within it, shape and modify the society's "superstructure," that is, the governmental, religious, legal, and cultural set-up, which in turn react upon the base. Successive bases and their corresponding superstructures—feudalist, capitalist, socialist—are steps on a ladder leading to the final, supreme stage of communism. The requisites for development are thus concomitant socio-technological changes.

Marx's two-sector model attempts to disclose the functional relations that must obtain in virtually *any* system in the processes of a steady state or growth. The economy is comprised of two sectors: a sector of *producer* goods (namely, of capital and raw materials, Sector I) and a sector of *consumer* goods (Sector II). In the steady state, the output of producer goods equals the replacement demand for these goods in both sectors. In growth, the demand for producer goods is larger in Sector I, and smaller in Sector II, than the former replacement needs. It is the allocation of the producer goods output between the two sectors that determines the system's pace of growth. According to Marx, only a "rising organic composition of capital" (namely, increasing depth of capital) can sustain the level of profit and with it the process of "accumulation" that guarantees growth.[5]

While the development schema formed the substance of Soviet "Political Economy," the two-sector model provided the foundation of Stalin's strategy for economic growth, namely, his choices with respect to investment allocation as well as those of his successors. This strategy, defined in

the 1920s, stressed the importance of securing a large share of accumulation in the national income and its preferential allocation to
Sector I (and within it particularly to steel, electricity, and machinery). A
growth model developed by G. A. Feldman pushed the Marxian logic to
its limit: it mapped the maximal growth rates obtainable when all investment (that is all the output of Sector I) is directed to Sector I, while
Sector II takes care of both the maintenance and renovation of its
equipment while providing the consumer goods needed by the society as
a whole.[6] The instrument for carrying out the indicated Marxian-Feld-
man strategy was, from 1928 onward, extensive centralized directive
planning. Until the 1980s, when the principles and methods of this
system came under close scrutiny in the Soviet Union itself, orders were
issued to industries, branches, and plants enforcing the policy makers'
preferences. These orders were based on certain macrofigures computed on the basis of both the two-sector model and of a pyramid of
loosely coordinated "balances" of resources and allocation, involving a
vast array of producer and consumer goods. The allegedly high rates of
growth yielded by the "Soviet model"—namely, by the Soviet-type centralized organization of the economy and by its directive planning during the 1950s—exercised a deep impact not only on the leadership of less
developed countries but also on the decision makers of the advanced
European countries.

The Western literature on development and on growth—at times
reinforcing Soviet contentions and at others differing from them—
displayed more variety and imagination and also deeper cleavages. Some
textbooks on development recognized explicitly that development and
growth had "separate meanings," though the development literature
tended to use these terms interchangeably. Charles P. Kindleberger and
Bruce Herrick, for instance, noted in their text, *Economic Development,*
that while growth means "more output," development "implies more
output and *changes in the technical and institutional arrangement by which it is
produced and distributed.*"[7] Most other texts, however, equated growth
with development. The latter was often illustrated with Marx's stages and
at times with other similar grand historical schemata (which, incidentally,
had flourished particularly in the writings of the German historical
school of the nineteenth century).[8] Many development discussions centered on the contemporary stages theory of W. W. Rostow (involving five
stages from the traditional society to the "high mass consumption" society) as well as on other modern schemata of "transitions" from agriculture to industry.[9] To this day, development literature remains
anchored in a kind of historic-socio-geographic institutional framework
of stages and phases dominated by "virtuous" or "perverse" differences
among sectors and industries. Thus, as Lloyd G. Reynolds noted, "development theory is concerned with total economies in certain regions of

the world and at an early stage of economic evolution": it "interpenetrates the sectoral specialties rather than stand alongside them."[10] According to these texts, surmounting the gaps between traditional and modern production requires governmental action, an appropriate strategy of development, and a directive economic plan—essentially, massive direct control intended to supplant the price mechanism—thus converging with the Soviet recipes. The Western literature on development has always been hostile to the market, which it has viewed as being either ineffective, unreliable, or irrelevant for the problems now encountered by developing nations. It has tended to assert that the "price mechanism must be suppressed" insofar as the determination and the compositions of investment and foreign trade were concerned.[11] Concessions to shadow pricing were made only in the theoretical discussions on planning. Much of the literature on development focused a great deal of its attention on the question of which planning *strategies* were preferable—namely, a strategy of massive investment over a group of mutually supporting industries (so-called "big-push" or "balanced growth" strategy) or a strategy of preferential development of certain sectors or industries (so-called "unbalanced growth" maintaining "tensions, disproportions and disequilibria").[12] Writings contrary to these theses—for instance, those of Harry G. Johnson, Theodore Schulz, and Peter Bauer—emphasizing the *market* as "the preferable instrument" for development received little attention in these texts. "Dissent on development" has never been fashionable.

The Western literature on economic growth, aggregative in nature and dealing with the broad tendencies of a growing economy, was shaped primarily by the works of Harrod, Domar, Solow, and Swan.[13] Its roots were in a number of seminal writings published before World War II. Already in 1939, Roy F. Harrod explored within the Keynesian framework the conditions in which an economy could achieve steady-state growth, that is, proportional increase of output and of all inputs ("balanced growth") given constant labor increments and constant capital-output ratios. Harrod showed that the equilibrium rate of growth—designated as the "warranted" rate of growth (g_w)—required that it should be equal to the rate of savings (s) divided by the capital-output ratio (k). With fixed capital coefficients and with labor inputs increasing at the natural rate of growth of the labor force (n) capital must grow at an identical exponential rate if each additional worker is to be equipped with the same amount of capital. When s/k is equal to n and when full employment is maintained through time, we are in a "golden age." If $g_w > n$ the economy falls eventually into a cumulative disequilibrium once the full employment barrier is hit. Conversely, if $g_w < n$, unemployment emerges. If investors anticipate more (less) than g_w, the actual rate of growth of demand will exceed (fall short) of g_w resulting in a dangerous imbalance, cumulative inflation, or cumulative deflation. Conclusions concerning similar knife-edge imbalances of the growth path were reached after World War II by Evsey D. Domar, who concentrated on the dual role of investment, namely, on its simultaneous generation of a growth of demand and a growth in supply (in productive capacity). The Harrod-Domar formula $(g = s/k)$ became a favorite reference of policy makers and a planning tool, particularly in the less developed countries, for the purpose of setting targets for savings (investment) to "secure" a desired rate of national income growth.

Discarding the Keynesian framework as inappropriate for long-term analysis and setting aside as unrealistic the assumption of fixed coefficients, neoclassical economists placed the growth discussion on a general equilibrium basis and resorted to an aggregate production function allowing for substitutability of labor and capital. If capital accumulates at a rate different from units of labor, the capital-labor ratios change, causing factor prices to change. It was Robert M. Solow who opened up a new perspective on growth with a celebrated paper "A Contribution to the Theory of Economic Growth" (1956). Replacing the Harrod-Domar constant capital-output ratio with a flexible capital-labor ratio, Solow showed that not one but a *range* of balanced growth paths were possible, that the equilibrium rate of growth was *independent* of the saving rate, and that *technological* change determined the permanent growth of output per unit of labor input. Put differently, he demonstrated with a one-sector model that all full-employment constant saving rates paths would eventually approach the steady-state path (satisfying the Harrod-Domar condition, $s = kn$) and that in the long run the economy's growth will settle down to the growth rate of the labor supply plus the rate of technological progress. Noting that the growth of productive capacity (that is, a move away from the steady-state equilibrium) has two components—the underlying steady-state natural rate of growth and a "transitional" type of growth resulting from changes in the output invested—Solow pointed out that the latter type of growth would be maintained only with a steady increase in the investment quota.[14] His model stimulated a powerful development of neoclassical studies on growth. Subsequently, two-sector models were also developed by James Meade, Hirofumi Uzawa, Ken-ichi Inada and others and received sustained attention in the professional literature.

Other writers examined the theoretical aspects of optimal growth, linking their models to the pathbreaking papers of Frank Ramsey (1928) and John von Neumann (1936). Assuming, in the tradition of Ramsey, that the objective of economic growth depended uniquely on the path of *consumption* as foreseen in the future, various model builders of the 1950s and 1960s explored the implications of resource allocation with respect to the utility of the present versus future generations when decisions are taken about consumption and savings by a single decision maker representing the society. These models yielded the conditions for the existence of optimal paths and the properties of these paths (they did not, however, postulate an institutional framework in which to implement these plans). Following von Neumann's lead in demonstrating that in a multi-sector economy the maximal growth rate was achievable when there is proportional growth of all stocks, other model builders showed that a planner would also achieve a maximal growth rate and obtain a given capital stock with a specified composition at some point in the future, if he placed the economy on a path closely approximating the von Neumann path (called the turnpike path) for most of the planning period. Following both the Ramsey and the von Neumann traditions, still other economists developed models showing the turnpike property of consumption planning. These and similar explorations helped either to gain insights in the ways in which "some broad strategies for planning ought to be formulated" or to establish frames of reference for comparing the efficiency of intertemporal allocations and the desirability of the rates of growth realized in plan-directed economies. Then, thanks to shadow prices, the optimal planning models have also yielded important comparative implications for market-directed economies.[15]

As we saw above, the indicated models postulated a single decision maker operating in the name of the society as a whole. In a decentralized economy the government obviously does not make all the allocation decisions; there are also individuals and firms free to maximize their own objectives under their own constraints. As Jan Tinbergen showed in his *Theory of Economic Policy* (1952), the government, a decisive player, has at its disposal an array of instruments from which it can choose, and which it can combine, in order to achieve a given goal in an optimal way. Could not the government of a "mixed" economy use its instruments in order to control—not directly, but indirectly—not only *public* investment but also *private* consumption and investment decisions? All these decisions are complementary in the present and in the future; they compete for the same resources and *should* indeed be taken in the light of one another. The government's instruments are not only allocative (for example, government investment) but also able to influence the private allocation decisions (for example, via taxes and the creation or retirement of debt). Using a "dynamic analogue" of Tinbergen's model, Kenneth J. Arrow and Mordecai Kurz set out to show that it was indeed possible to calculate a publicly optimal policy with respect to all consumption-investment decisions in the society. They defined a given allocation policy as "controllable" by a set of instruments "if there exist values of the instruments varying over time in general, which cause the private and government sectors together to realize that policy." And they concluded that "if there is a sufficient number of these instruments and if they are powerful enough, the publicly optimal policy . . . and, indeed, virtually any feasible policy, is controllable, in general with stable instruments." If the latter are few and ineffective, then the optimal policy is not controllable and the problem is to find the second best optimal policy or to stabilize the instruments needed to achieve the controllable policy.[16]

The surge in development and growth theories, in planning models and techniques, in the analysis of optimal and "controllable" policy choices, in the study of the structuring and steering of complex technological systems (which evolved from research in military problems) engendered overoptimism with respect to the controllability of our "mixed" economy. Confidence in controllability reached its zenith in the late 1950s and early 1960s. As Paul A. Samuelson put it at the time, "whatever rate of capital formation the American people want to have, the American system can, by proper choice of fiscal and monetary program, contrive to do." And further, "I repeat, with proper fiscal and monetary policies, our economy can have full employment and whatever rate of capital formation and growth it wants."[17] The twilight of business cycles was accepted as a fact. The modeling of production activity—input-output, activity analysis—combined with the policy models, put at the disposal of the policy makers and their advisers new and enticing methods for processing and analyzing massive and complex types of data. The deeper issues of information feedback—concerning not arrays of numbers, but the eventual reactions arising in the economy from the expectation of *future* policy actions—which had been hotly debated in the discussions on planning in the 1930s, had almost vanished from sight, except for a brilliant paper by John F. Muth introducing rational expectations, whose importance would be grasped only later. These optimistic developments coincided with an increasingly broad public consensus that the country's growth rate was far too low in relation to that of the major industrialized societies and that what was now needed was accelerated growth.

Yet it should be noted that the economics profession remained divided as to whether the government should intervene primarily in order to foster the expansion of the country's productive capacity; whether it actually could do so effectively; whether the intended shift from a *corrective* economic policy (with respect to business fluctuations) to a *propulsive* policy (with respect to growth) would not in practice soft-pedal the target of full employment; and, last but not least, whether the use of certain rules rather than of discretionary government powers could not better ensure the achievement of certain objectives, including that of economic growth.

Speaking in the name of the academic pro-Kennedy "growthmen," James Tobin asserted that intervention by the government to foster growth meant intervention "to affect the composition of current output and society's provision for the future." Acting for the public, the government would decide for them collectively "to supplement (or diminish) the provisions for the future they are making individually." In practice, he added, "a strong pro-growth policy would restrict consumption by taxation or by economy in government's current expenditure" while increasing government savings "by making investments on its own account, subsidizing the investment of others, or by channeling tax money through the capital markets into private investment."[18] Such statements were not received favorably everywhere. Among Democrats, conflict arose between the academics and the trade union economists of older generations: for the latter, growth policy meant "undifferentiated government spending, plus transfer programs and wage increases to raise consumption demand by wage earners and other households of high marginal propensity to spend."[19] As for the Republicans, Herbert Stein undoubtedly correctly voiced their doubts when he addressed to Tobin the following question: "Let us assume that we have discovered that we are saving too little. . . . Why should individuals require the help of government in order to carry out impartial savings decisions if that is what individuals want to do?" And further: "There is no critical mass that the savings must reach. It is not necessary that everyone should save in some particular way, which has to be specified by a central authority."[20] Unlike Stein, Harry Johnson, also a conservative, considered that the government's actions and decisions with respect to the economy had "a legitimacy at least equal to that of private decisions," but he also refused to view the government as the "super ego of the society, concerned with looking after the best interests of the ongoing nation" and to consider its decisions as "always designed to serve the social interest."[21]

Could the government actually accelerate the growth process? On this issue the "growthmen" had to contend with the growth theorists, namely, often with themselves. Did not growth theory show—on the basis of the theorists' own assumptions—that in the long run the growth rates of the GNP (and of aggregate consumption) were exogenously determined by the growth of the labor force and of technology? Then, why restrict consumption today? Again, Tobin pointed out that the long run allowed a lot of room for maneuver in the interval. Society faces hypothetical parallel consumption paths: the higher the path, the higher the economy's capital intensity and the higher the savings ratio needed to maintain it. Eventually, capital intensity would converge to its natural value, but in the meantime—that is, for decades—the society could move from the lower to the higher paths, thus controlling its rate of growth. Further, the "growthmen" asserted that the consumers "would give a positive present value to feasible increases on future consumption," but the opponents of faster growth denied it. These critics suggested that to facilitate growth, what was needed was not necessarily a macropolicy of increased savings (reduced consumption), but rather microreforms of the fiscal system coupled with policies destined to make competition more effective. Be that as it may, it is interesting to recall in passing that while our "growthmen" emphasized the trade-off of less consumption today for more consumption in the future, the Soviet "growthmen" always emphasized less consumption today for more producer goods tomorrow—in order to "catch up with and surpass the United States."

In the pre-Keynesian days, the objective of macropolicy was price stability, and its recognized instrument was monetary policy. After the Keynesian revolution, the achievement of full employment called forth by an effective demand became the primary target of macropolicy, and fiscal policy became its instrument par excellence. With the advent in the 1960s of the so-called "New Economics," the objective and the underlying logic of macroeconomic policy were henceforth referred to, in Walter W. Heller's terms, as "Keynes *cum* growth." This formula tended to obscure rather than to clarify what was henceforth involved with respect to both policy and instruments. The key objective became not only the achievement of a high rate of utilization of manpower and of the available capacity but also continuous expansion of that capacity itself and the closing of the "gap" between actual income and the economy's expanding potential. The "shift in targetry"—as Heller put it—from a policy of full employment to a policy of expanding potential output (the supply side) and of closing the "gap" between income (the demand side) and the output produced, these changes were neither clearly understood nor readily accepted even by the "traditional" Keynesians. Further, the "new economists"—within and outside President Kennedy's Council of Economic Advisers—and the president himself eventually converted the broad qualitative goals of the Employment Act of 1946 into specific quantitative goals, namely, a high employment target of 4 percent unemployment and a growth target of 4 percent per year.

While not entirely independent of one another, these targets were arrived at by different routes and for different reasons. The hypothetical magnitude, "potential output," was defined as being the output that would obtain when the unemployment rate is 4 percent. Thus the unemployment rate was taken "as a proxy variable for all the ways in which output is affected by idle resources." The "leap" from unemployment rate to potential output was made by assuming that "whatever the influence of slack economic activity on average hours, labor force participation, and manhour productivity the magnitude of all these effects are related to the unemployment rate."[22] The idea that the condition of high employment could be defined by a single statistic, that the number in question was known within a narrow margin, and that that rate would for all practical purposes remain constant was a widespread belief. The

Council of Economic Advisers took the 4 percent as an approximation of *unavoidable* unemployment. According to Tobin, the 4 percent was actually chosen with an eye on the Phillips curve, namely, on the 4 percent *inflation* that accompanied 4 percent unemployment in the mid-1950s. Moreover, the advisers of President Kennedy felt that a more ambitious unemployment target would have been considered then by many influential critics at home and abroad as "irresponsibly inflationary."[23] As for the rate of growth, two studies on the growth potential of the U.S. economy had made a great impact at the time. A 1960 study by James W. Knowles (part of a series of studies for the Joint Economic Committee of the U.S. Congress, directed by Otto Eckstein) focused on the U.S. potential in terms of an aggregate production function, and a 1962 study by Edward F. Denison (published under the auspices of the New York Committee for Economic Development) examined this potential on the basis of each separate element affecting the "basic determinants of growth" and their possible combinations. Denison had concluded that the U.S. economy's "natural" rate of growth was on the order of 3 percent per annum and that even major changes in the investment in physical and human capital could not significantly change this rate. Knowles, however, estimated the rate as being 3.9 percent with a half percent on either side for low- or high-growth policies.[24] Finally, the National Planning Association, President Kennedy, and his Council of Economic Advisers estimated that "a moderate policy program favoring economic growth could make potential output rise at something like 4 percent a year between 1960 and 1970—perhaps even a little faster, and if the path to 1970 winds up at full employment, the actual annual growth rate could exceed 4.5 percent."[25]

To achieve this goal greater "government activism" was said to be needed. This "activism" was to be exercised on the "basic determinants of growth," since the growth of productive capacity was largely limited by the rate at which these determinants could be expanded and improved. Agreement existed all the way from applied to theoretical economists— from Simon Kuznets to Samuelson, from Denison to Solow—that these determinants were the quantity and quality of manpower, the size and structure of the existing capital stock by industries and branches, the level of technology and the degree to which it could be made effective, the conditions of access to natural resources, and the efficiency with which these resources were allocated. Difficulties arose in evaluating the relative impact on growth of each variable—for example, of education in general and of particular types of education, of the role of "embodied" versus "disembodied" technology, and so on—so that general agreement on the "basic determinants" did not necessarily imply agreement on any particular legislative package meant to affect them.

The question of instruments suggested significant differences on two distinct planes: among the Democrats (including President Kennedy's advisers) concerning the appropriate use, with respect to full employment and growth, of government spending versus tax reduction; and between the Democrats and the Republicans concerning the emphasis on fiscal versus monetary policies and the broader issue of government discretion versus government's submission to rigid rules.

As we shall see further on, a long, drawn-out discussion took place among President Kennedy's advisers (in and out of government) on the opportunity of a tax reduction for both overcoming the prevailing recession and for stimulating economic growth. Some high-ranking "new economist" advisers, like Tobin, who believed in massive support for investments, tax credits, and easy money, opposed the idea of tax reduction. He affirmed that there may be other ways to expand demand and utilization than tax reductions "while at the same time providing both more stimulus for and more economic room for capacity-building uses of resources now idle." It is worthwhile to recall all this, since after the eventual adoption of the tax reduction measure in 1964, the tax cut was hailed as the purest "Keynesian" triumph of the "New Economics."

Neither the partisans of the primacy of fiscal instruments, nor the advocates of the importance of monetary measures, ever asserted that their opponents believed that money or fiscal policy respectively did not matter. What both groups were convinced of was that their opponents had not grasped fully either their respective differences concerning long-term objectives, or how much the use of their own instruments mattered in order to reach these objectives. In the name of the "fiscalists"—an expression we use here as a shorthand term without any pejorative connotations—Walter W. Heller, the chief architect of the "New Economics," stressed that only heavy reliance on the budget could guarantee the maintenance of steady growth. He derided, moreover, the "monetarists'"contention that the control of money supply was the key to reach their own objective, namely that of economic stability, and summoned them to indicate which specific variable—M_1 (currency and bank deposits), M_2 (M_1 plus time deposits), or some other measure of the money stock—should be used as the guiding indicator. In the name of the "monetarists" Milton Friedman asserted first of all that the quantity of money mattered for certain *nominal* magnitudes. Changes in money supply affect the *fluctuations* in nominal (and real) income in the short run, and in nominal incomes and prices in the long run. Certainly, he added, changes in the relation of taxes and spending affect the division of income between what is to be spent by the public and what by the government. But fiscal policy by itself had "no significant effect on the course of nominal income, on inflation, on deflation, or on cyclical fluctuations": it had effects only in conjunction with monetary changes. In order to provide a stable background for the economy—to "keep the machine well oiled"—and avoid counterproductive, perturbing wide swings and lags in monetary policy responses, Friedman proposed the adoption of a kind of surrogate for the gold standard, a "publicly stated policy of a steady rate of monetary growth" (something like 3 to 5 percent per year). Heller retorted that "a fixed-throttle money-supply rule" would be destabilizing and would place the policy makers in a "hopeless" standby position while the economy would go through "long periods of economic slack or inflation."[26] It is important to note though that both the "fiscalists" and the "monetarists" believed that economic controllability was indeed achievable but by their own means and in the pursuit of their own different objectives (that is, growth, on the one hand, and the dampening of economic fluctuations, on the other).

Expectations of an ever-increasing GNP and reliance on the government's ability to control the economy and to direct its changes, to maintain full employment, to increase productive capacity, to guarantee reasonable price stability, to eliminate poverty and to raise the standard of living, these were the hallmarks of the first half of the 1960s. But, eventually, a rising tide of inflation, the disappointments created by the Vietnam tragedy—an apparently futile yet costly war in human and material resources—the deep frustrations generated by social inequalities in employment and income, the increasing urban decay and its tensions and fears, the generally deteriorating environment—all concurred in deglamorizing growth. Paradoxically, the very setting of quantitative national goals for employment, output, and stability institutionalized "the creation of discontent." Indeed, these goals became standards by which to judge not the future but the present. And as the present tended to diverge from the successful pursuit of both full employment and stability, recession and inflation seemed even harder to bear. Furthermore, congestion, urban overpopulation, pollution, natural resource depletion, along with the attacks on "growthmania" toward the end of the 1960s and the beginning of the 1970s, became subjects not only of journalistic pronouncements but also of a new economic literature on environmental protection and management, on externalities, on the valuation of public goods, on cost-benefit analysis, and on the repercussions on the environment of economic policies. The new literature pointed out that ecological stability required at the extremes either the changing of the structure of society—by implementing zero-growth and zero population growth—or, conversely, the adoption and enforcement of a policy of systematic redirection and/or reduction of certain outputs to allow man to continue to use the ecosystem for high productivity. The literature on "ecological stability" was roundly criticized as lacking understanding of the market mechanism. On the other hand, the policy of growth redirection was to be elaborated and variously implemented from the early 1970s as an increasingly significant adjunct to the perennial policy issues of employment, growth and stability.

On the threshold of the 1970s, President Nixon predicted that the gross national product would grow over the next ten years by 50 percent, that is, by more "than the entire growth of the Americn economy from 1790 to 1950." Did that mean, he added, that we will be "50 percent better off, 50 percent happier?" Or is the truth on the side of those who see a "fundamental contradiction between economic growth and the quality of life?" The president rightly answered that neither of these two assertions was entirely correct. He then affirmed his belief that "continuous vigorous growth provides us with the means to enrich life" and stated that the question ahead was not whether to "abandon growth," but rather how to direct it.

GROWTH TO STAGFLATION

The issue of economic growth had played a central role in the presidential campaign of 1960. Both candidates stressed again and again the need to accelerate the country's growth. Pointing to the fact that the United States had, in 1959, the "lowest rate of economic growth of any major industrialized society in the world," John F. Kennedy asserted that with a "really healthy rate of growth" we could have full employment, pay for all the defense the Republicans said "we can't afford," have the best schools for our children, and the best-trained teachers. And if we are going to grow, he added, "we must adopt fiscal policies that will stimulate growth and not discourage it." "I don't believe in big government"—he affirmed during his first debate with the Republican candidate, Vice President Nixon—"but I believe in effective governmental action . . . I think it's time America started moving again." While denying that the country was "standing still" and emphasizing the importance of private initiative, Nixon also asserted throughout the campaign that "growth at a maximum rate" was the order of the day: "I would say that my goal, and I think the only proper goal . . . is a maximum growth rate." The disagreement concerned the means, not the objective.[27]

As President Kennedy's sentence, "It's time America started moving again," became, as it were, the watchword of his administration, he asserted in his first "State of the Union" message of January 30, 1961, that the time had come to "show the world what a free economy can do— to reduce unemployment, to put unused capacity to work, to spur new productivity and to foster economic growth."[28] However, the actual course the new administration followed in that year was a cautious one. Looking back on that first Kennedy year, Paul A. Samuelson, who had been an adviser to the president, noted that what had astonished him most was how the lawyers in the new administration "believed their own rhetoric—that the country was going to get moving by speaking about getting it moving; and it was a great surprise and required some education for them to realize that you had really to *do* things to achieve vigorous growth and prosperity."[29] Actually, the president's cautious course was due in part to his own uncertainty as to what precise steps to take immediately, in part to his lack of strength in Congress, and in part to the suggestions of his own economic advisers. Indeed, the president's "task force" on economics, chaired by Samuelson and including "exclusively Keynesian economists" such as Walter Heller, James Tobin, and Seymour E. Harris, had suggested caution in the report they delivered to the president on January 6, 1961. This report—subsequently credited exclusively to Samuelson and included in his collection of *Scientific Papers*—was indeed not strongly Keynesian. It diagnosed a "recession imposed on top of a disappointingly slack economy," proclaimed the need to shift in the period just ahead "toward a more vigorous fiscal policy" but warned against "erring in the direction of activism" and of trying to undo in a year "the inadequacies of several years." It specifically advised the president to go slow on public expenditures, to consider a tax cut only if the economy improved little in 1961, and it precluded a cheap money policy given the precarious state of the balance of payments.[30] The president's "Program for Economic Recovery and Growth," announced on February 2, 1961, and applied during the year, involved only accelerations of federal purchases and procurement, extension of unemployment benefits, liberalization of social security benefits, and other similar measures. With respect to monetary policy, the president's Council of Economic Advisers emphasized the need for a "twist,"—a boost for declining long-term interest rates in order to keep the flow of credit into the capital markets and a halt in the decline of short-term interest rates that directly affected the balance of payment. This cautious course drew severe criticisms from the liberals who accused him of following "Eisenhower's economic ideology" rather than modern fiscal theories.[31]

The president's approaches to economic policy started to change rapidly during 1962. In his first *Economic Report* of January 1962, after noting that recovery had "carried the economy only part of the way to the goal of maximum production, employment and purchasing power," he established the quantitative targets of 4.5 percent output growth, 4 percent unemployment, and 2 percent for inflation to prevent the economy from straying "too far above or below the path of steady high employment." To prevent further recessions he then recommended the enactment of standby presidential powers for temporary income tax reductions and for public capital improvements, as well as the strengthening of the unemployment insurance system. Further, he stressed the need for both the labor leaders and the managers of our major industries "to hold the line on the price level in 1962"—labor, by accepting the productivity benchmark as guide to wage objectives; managers, by practicing equivalent restraint in their price decisions. By June 7 of the same year, he announced that in order to avoid recovery being "cut short by a new recession," he had decided to offer for action by the next Congress as of January 1, 1963, "an across-the-board reduction in personal and corporate income tax rates"—namely, a net tax reduction.[32] Finally, on December 14, 1962, he gave the following indications about the proposed tax cut: "I am not talking about a quickie or a temporary tax cut . . . I am talking about the accumulated evidence of the last five years that our tax system, developed as it was, in good part, during World War II to restrain growth exerts too heavy a drag on growth in peace time."[33]

The distinctive elements that characterized both Kennedy's stamp on economic policy and the makeup of the "New Economics" were thus in full view by the end of 1962. These, as we already noted, were in terms of *goals*, their quantification and a shift from moderating cyclical swings to closing the "gap" between actual and potential outputs; in terms of *instruments*, the launching of guideposts for prices and wages to secure stability, the use of a "monetary twist" to disassociate investment effects from impacts on the balance of payments, and an across-the-board tax cut—not expanded government spending or easy money—in order to overcome the recession and to achieve the set rate of growth.

Observing rather condescendingly President Kennedy's evolution toward "modern economics," Seymour E. Harris noted that the president, who had been at first "allergic" to the new teachings, had started to move slowly in the right direction while still remaining "uncertain about the economic trends" and "fearful of Congressional intransigence"; finally, during an address at Yale in June 1962, Kennedy not only disposed in a masterful fashion of various "myths" encumbering public ideas about economics but also delivered there "the most advanced views on fiscal policy ever made by a president." Walter W. Heller, the chairman of President Kennedy's Council of Economic Advisers, indicated also somewhat patronizingly that the Yale speech stood out "as the most literate and sophisticated dissertation on economics ever delivered by a president (and he wrote much of it himself)." While Heller added that the president also "molded the diversity among his adversaries . . . into a harmonious consensus," actually the president had quite a hard time making positions on the tax cut acceptable not only to Congress and to the public, but also among his own economic family.[34] In 1963, in his *Economic Report* of January 21, the president reported that a Committee on Economic Growth, which he had appointed in the summer of 1962 (chaired by Heller), had urged "the central significance of prompt tax reduction and reform in a program for economic growth."[35] In his "Special Message to Congress on Tax Reduction and Reform" of January 24, which followed the *Report*, the president proposed enactment of such a program in 1963 to become fully effective on January 1, 1965, and specified its content: reduction in the individual income tax level, in the rate of corporate income tax, in the normal and surtax rates, and in the treatment of capital gains, along with various revisions in the tax law and in the tax structure.[36]

Was a tax cut on top of a budget deficit really warranted immediately? What exactly would be its impact on growth? Were better alternatives not available? The 1963 *Annual Report* of the Council of Economic Advisers responded that indeed the country did not then face a cyclical emergency of the type faced in 1949, 1953, or 1957, "compelling immediate action." But unemployment and excessive capacity were affecting both the current output and the prospects for long-run growth: "The need for early action lies then, not in imminent recession but in continued waste of manpower and machines and in thwarted opportunities for more rapid growth." Initially the tax cut will increase the deficit, but proper financing will ultimately add to the expansionary effects of the tax cut.[37] The president went further in defense of the tax cut. He emphasized that the budget, then in deficit, would certainly be succeeded by a balanced budget in a full employment economy: "Total output and economic growth will be stepped up by an amount several times as great as the tax cut itself," and "a *balanced federal budget in a growing full employment economy* will be most rapidly and certainly achieved by a substantial expansion in national income, carrying with it the needed tax revenues."[38] Incidentally, this crucial idea of evaluating the impact of a budget policy not on the basis of the surplus or deficit it actually yields but of the surplus or deficit it would yield at full employment—an idea already expounded in the *Annual Report* of the Council of Economic Advisers in 1962—had been around since the wartime discussions on postwar fiscal policies and had first come to be identified with the New York Committee for Economic Development (CED).[39]

All this drew fire from various quarters—with some of the critics shifting positions as the debate gained momentum. The powerful chairman of the House Ways and Means Committee, Wilbur Mills, for instance, who had first contended that the function of taxes was to raise revenues not to manipulate the economy, asserted subsequently that he would accept a tax cut if he received assurances that expenditures would be controlled better than in the past. After the president assured him that this would indeed be the case, he rallied himself to the tax cut in order to avoid "more rather than less government spending in the future."[40] Arthur Burns and Raymond Saulnier, two former chairmen of Eisenhower's Council of Economic Advisers, argued that a tax cut would only increase the budget deficit and have a minor impact on employment.[41] Leon Keyserling, the former chairman of Truman's Council of Economic Advisers, and Gerhard Colm believed that what was needed was not a tax cut but more federal spending to redirect demand where there was not enough employment expansion, plus more consumer spending via wage increases.[42] The monetarists, including a future chairman of the Council of Economic Advisers, Beryl W. Sprinkel, asserted that a tax cut was a minor element in economic policy and that what was really needed to stimulate the economy was an increase in money supply.[43] Even the president's own economic family was far from unanimous. John Kenneth Galbraith, then Ambassador to India, pleaded from New Delhi that the economy should be stimulated by rising expenditures and warned that a tax reduction would permanently lower government's ability to command resources.[44] The "liberal economists," among whom Samuelson ranged himself along with Tobin, E. C. Brown, and R. A. Musgrave, argued that growth involved increases in net capital formation at the expense of current consumption. "While it was right," wrote Samuelson, "that fiscal policy should receive much emphasis, it is in the realm of monetary policy that a mixed-enterprise like ours can do the most to slow down or step up its rate of growth." And Samuelson added, "a strong growth-inducing policy of monetary ease, if it succeeds in producing overfull employment, can be combined with an austere fiscal policy, in which tax rates are kept high enough and/ or expenditure rates low enough so as to remove inflationary pressures of the demand-pull type and to succeed in increasing the net capital formation share of our full employment income at the expense of the current consumption share."[45] In the same vein, Tobin noted in his Richard T. Ely Lecture at the annual meeting of the American Economic Association in December 1963, that even though the *major* impact of the proposed tax reduction was to stimulate consumption, it would simultaneously increase capital formation also. In that sense it may be called a "growth measure"; but, he added, "there may be ways to expand demand and utilization to the same degree while at the same time providing both *more stimulus for and more economic room for* capacity-building uses of resources now idle."[46]

Eventually, it was President Johnson who assumed the responsibility of carrying out with Congress the key elements of Kennedy's program. In his "State of the Union" Message of January 8, 1964, the new president invited Congress to make its session known as the one that "enacted the most far-reaching tax cut of our time" and that did more than any other Congress on civil rights, on an all-out "war on human poverty," on unemployment, on the health needs of the elderly, and on education— on what were to be called the "Great Society" programs. In defense of what the new administration viewed as the most "urgent" task, the tax cut, the Council of Economic Advisers stressed in its 1964 *Annual Economic Report* that the tax cut was the prime mover toward more rapid growth. Recalling ideas already expounded in the 1962 *Report*, the council pointed to the need for periodic budget adjustments in a growing economy in order to avoid the expansion-retarding impact of rising tax revenues as income grows and as tax rates remain unchanged ("fiscal drag") or, conversely, in order to take advantage of this same phenomenon perceived as an opportunity for a tax cut ("fiscal overspend"). The *Report* then asserted that the tendency of the "full-employment surplus" to build up to expansion-retarding levels pointed to the need for a tax cut and stated that such a cut would represent a "giant step" toward removing "a burdensome fiscal restraint *before* the economy levels off or goes into a recession." According to the council it would also provide "a framework for continued vigorous growth."[47] That is indeed what the tax cut was all about. When it was finally enacted in February 1964 even its adversaries regarded it as the act that more than any other came to "symbolize the fiscal revolution" and the "great achievement of the Keynesian New Economics."[48]

Recalling the performance of the economy after the tax cut, Professor James Tobin noted that "throughout 1965 the management of the domestic economy under the New Economics was a great success, and was generally perceived as such."[49] That year the GNP had grown by 6 percent, prices had risen only by slightly over 2 percent, and unemployment was down to 4.5 percent. Reviewing the 1965 balance sheet, the 1966 *Economic Report* pointed out with satisfaction that the total output of only seven other countries in the world was as large as the *increment* of the U.S. output in 1965. Yet the same *Report* also noted that Vietnam had become an increasingly serious problem with respect to the maintenance of "balanced prosperity." By then, two hundred thousand U.S. soldiers were in action in the war in Asia, as compared to twelve thousand advisers in mid-1962, and Vietnam was absorbing billions of dollars, accounting for some 1.5 percent of the GNP. While the president assured the country that "prosperity did not depend on our military effort," the rising defense needs were becoming an important factor in the economy, which was pressing relentlessly toward the full use of its resources. To insure against the rising risk of inflation, the people were asked to accept a fiscal "bits and pieces package" (as Arthur M. Okun had called it) concerning withholdings on individual taxes and acceleration of corporate income taxes. Foreseeing the inflationary danger, the *Annual Report* of the Council of Economic Advisers noted at the end of 1965 that a "simple mechanical offset of the fiscal drag" was not "a satisfactory rule for fiscal policy" and that "some fiscal drag should be allowed to operate" when aggregate demand threatens to exceed supply.[50] Arthur M. Okun, then a member of the Council of Economic Advisers, indicated subsequently that the members of the council had told the president that a general tax increase was needed to head off inflation and to offset the extra defense spending but that the president had felt that he could not get this kind of action from Congress. At a loss, Okun noted, "the principles of fiscal policy do not tell us *what to do*" if the necessary antidote prescription for inflation "cannot be filled." Adding that "the January 1966 budget marked the first defeat of the new economics by the old politics," Okun remarked that the new economists had repeatedly stated, against the "skeptics," that the fiscal stimulus could be turned off in time to stave off inflation, but, since for political reasons this could not be done, "the skeptics won the debate."[51]

The government's lack of resolution to enforce the necessary restrictive action in face of inflation may have been, however, only part of the problem. The other part, just as significant, may have been the increasing doubts of at least some of the new economists themselves about the feasibility of achieving and maintaining simultaneously the goals they had set out to reach and were so sure they would reach at the beginning of the 1960s, namely, full employment and price stability. Indeed, reflecting in 1972 on the experience of 1966, Tobin asserted that it had become "painfully clear" that "the economists do not have enough tools of foresight, analysis and policy to enable the government to avoid or offset shocks to the economy" and that "macro-economic policies, monetary and fiscal, are *incapable* of realizing society's unemployment and inflation goals *simultaneously*. This dismal fact has long stimulated a search for *third* instruments to do the job: guideposts and income policies, on the one hand, labor market and manpower policies, on the other."[52] Incidentally, the guideposts launched in 1962 were subsequently hailed by their conceptual designer, Walter W. Heller, as the means of the new economists for "testing new concepts and broad policy approaches" that eventually "educated" business and labor, achieved some wage and price moderation, and were the "least evil" for coping with the conflict between full employment and stability.[53] For Milton Friedman, however, guideposts "do harm even when only lip service is paid to them" because, when there are inflationary pressures, "the government monetary (or, some would say, fiscal) authorities are responsible." To which Robert M. Solow, a former staff member of the Heller council, answered that some education or some arm twisting can "reduce at least temporarily" the normal level of unemployment in the economy but that when widespread excess demand exists in the economy "guideposts are almost certain to be ineffective and, if they were effective, they might in fact not have entirely desirable effects."[54]

The 1965 euphoria, when as Tobin put it "too much was claimed and even more came to be expected," was followed from 1966 on by an increasing malaise. Frustrations with the socio-economic conditions and with the war, as well as with the choices that they were forcing on the country, favored the increasing affirmation of an alternative macroparadigm: monetarism. The new economists' 1967 proposal of bringing into balance unemployment and inflation via a "quick and fine tuning," involving a combination of higher taxes (a temporary surtax plus suspension of investment tax stimulus) with easier money (and lower interest rates along with more stable financial markets) were derided by the "monetarists." Our ignorance of monetary-fiscal impacts was still so large, stated Sprinkel, for instance, that attempts at "fine tuning," particularly once the economy had achieved full employment of resources, "will almost certainly lead to serious error." Restoring monetary growth at about 3 percent per year and avoiding tax increases or investment credit suspension would more likely avoid a recession and maintain economic growth. Skeptical, Tobin remarked that neither the managers of fiscal policies nor the managers of monetary policy "could dedicate this policy to any simple single indicator of what they ought to be doing." In point of fact, he added, there was no striking statistical relation between money supply and economic activity, or between the increase in money supply and the rate of increase of the GNP.[55]

The president's *Economic Report*, transmitted to Congress in February 1968, acknowledged that economic growth had slowed down in 1967 and that the cost of the Southeast Asian war had been "steadily increasing." He pleaded for fiscal restraint and stressed again that "we must demonstrate that we can use fiscal policy flexibly—that we can raise as well as lower taxes." Renewing his request for a temporary 10 percent surcharge on corporate and income taxes, he emphasized that the difficulties faced by the administration with respect to inflation were not at all transitory. After stating that "we must do what we can to minimize price increases in 1968," he added prophetically: "But we must also settle in for a long hard fight aimed toward 1969, 1970—and 1980."[56] In fact, the administration was uncertain and ambivalent about the choices it should make with respect to growth and inflation because of conflicts over the war versus the "great society."

In a kind of balance sheet for the Kennedy-Johnson years, the valedictory 1968 *Annual Report* of President Johnson's Council of Economic Advisers contrasted the achievement of eight years of unbroken expansion (from the recession trough in 1961 to the fourth quarter of 1968) with the four recessions that plagued the economy between 1948 and 1961 and with the thirty-month average duration of previous expansions. This unbroken expansion, it stated, was the result of keeping up with the growth of potential GNP and of closing the income gap by means of needed stimulative actions such as the tax cut, that is, via discretionary policies called forth as needed (jointly with or against the play of the automatic economic stabilizers). Unfortunately, there were shortcomings of economic policies that could be traced to "difficulties in achieving prompt and appropriate adjustments in fiscal policy." The break in price stability had started when the military buildup began in the second half of 1965 and the administration had been faced since then with the dilemma of how to "balance" the dreadful losses associated with unemployment, and the inequitable income effects produced by inflation.[57]

The troubled Johnson administration left the scene without "hail or farewell" in a highly distressing social atmosphere. The new Republican administration came in with great hopes not only of keeping the growth rate up but also of curbing inflation while avoiding an increase in the unemployment rate. As Herbert Stein noted subsequently, the incoming Nixon administration "shared the general view of the time that economic growth in the United States would continue at a high rate—4 percent per annum—for the next decade."[58] The new Council of Economic Advisers thought that no radical departures from existing policies were needed in order to maintain that rate. With respect to curbing inflation the new administration wanted to make one point crystal clear: it rejected the idea of wage and price controls. It dismissed as ineffective any kind of exhortations to labor and management to follow wage and price "guidelines" and accused the previous administrations of having resorted (up to 1966) to "jawboning" in order to put the blame for inflation on the leaders of the private economy instead of on its own policies. The new administration asserted that it would not resort to any forms of income policy: "We will not take the nation down the road of wage and price controls," proclaimed President Nixon.[59]

On the threshold of the 1970s, looking back at the preceding decade, the administration described the 1960s as a period of both great economic growth and "overblown rhetoric" (concerning its "wars" against poverty, misery, disease, and hunger). Noting that during the first half of the 1960s we had price stability while unemployment averaged 5.5 percent and that in the second half we had relatively full employment but with escalating prices, the president and the Council of Economic Advisers placed the onus of inflation on the *government's* policies—"often the cause of wide swings in the economy" —and on the doctrine that the economy could be managed "mechanistically." To keep inflation at bay the new administration decided to focus solely on demand management via the adoption of a "moderate posture" for both fiscal and monetary policies. The administration was convinced that it could restrain aggregate demand that had nourished the inflation and do so without generating any significant increase in the unemployment rate.[60]

Critics of the administration, such as John Kenneth Galbraith for instance, denounced the idea that the implied choice between inflation and unemployment was a "benign" one, that "reasonable price stability could be combined with a tolerable level of unemployment." Recalling that to keep inflation down the Keynesians used to place the emphasis on fiscal measures to control spending, while the monetarists were now claiming that what was needed for that purpose was to control spending from borrowed funds, Galbraith asserted that high employment and stable prices could not be achieved simultaneously without price and wage controls. This thesis was decisively rejected by the chairman of the Council of Economic Advisers, Paul W. McCracken.[61]

The demand management measures ushered in a recession in 1970. The credit crunch of 1969 and early 1970 pushed interest rates up and jolted the financial markets. The GNP declined in the fourth quarter at an annual rate of 4.8 percent, unemployment fluctuated around 6 percent, and inflation proved frustratingly persistent. The president's *Economic Report* of February 1971 warned in alarming terms that the administration was "facing the greatest test of the post-war era." This test concerned the capacity to attenuate the declines in output and employment caused by the efforts to reduce inflation and defense spending. To achieve this attenuation the administration would engage in a special type of fiscal activism, an activism tempered by a constraint set upon the president's freedom of action, namely the "principle that expenditures should not exceed revenues that the tax system would yield under conditions of full employment."[62] This somewhat puzzling "Keynesianism"—the president was quoted as saying "We are all Keynesians now"—elicited some pointed comments from the Keynesians. Abba P. Lerner, for instance, rightly noted that this Keynesianism involved only "a *partial* displacement of the pre-Keynesian principle of balancing the budget, by the Keynesian principle of 'balancing the economy'" but it did not "include a recognition that the *maintenance* of full employment could call for a deficit or a surplus." And Robert Eisner asked: "But what is the new fiscal discipline that accepts the constraint of a balanced full employment budget *regardless* of the consequences for employment and output?"[63]

After a spurt in the first months of 1971, the economy started sagging and the prospects for the rest of the year darkened. Inflation continued to hover around 6 percent. The likelihood of unemployment reduction appeared doubtful, and the pressures on the balance of payments increased. In a rapidly engineered policy reversal, the administration proclaimed on August 15, 1971, the introduction of a "New Economic Policy toward unemployment, inflation and international speculation." It took two sudden and simultaneous dramatic measures: an "emergency measure," namely wage and price controls, and "a permanent reform in the international monetary system," namely suspension of the convertibility of the dollar. The pledge of "not taking the nation down the road of wage and price controls"—controls denounced by the president on June 17, 1970, as "an easy way out but really an easy way into more trouble," and consistently repudiated by his economic advisers—was glossed over and soon forgotten. The introduction of controls seemed to yield some of the hoped-for results. Real output increased in 1972. The ratio of unemployment fell, and the GNP price deflator decreased. This first full year of wage and price controls since the Korean War was, as the president's *Economic Report* put it, "a very good year." To create further conditions for a growing economy "far less defense oriented and much less inflationary," the controls were modified (with special attention to the problem areas of food, construction, and medical care costs). The Congress was asked to extend the controls to April 1974, and the federal government put at the "top of the list of economic policies for 1973" the restraining of federal expenditures.

The second full year of controls, however, did not turn out as well as the first one. Real output continued to grow, and unemployment fell slightly, but inflation rose rapidly with food prices and energy in the lead: farm prices rose at their fastest rate since 1917, accounting for 51 percent of the rise in the consumer price index (CPI); another 11 percent of the rise in the index was accounted for by the higher prices of energy purchased directly by the consumer, resulting from an Arab oil embargo. Thus the inflation rate outstripped the earlier period of controls as well as the earlier period without controls. To cope with the rise in food prices, to encourage the expansion of production, and to assure the stability of supplies, the administration announced that it was freeing "the American farmer to produce as much as he can" and that the American food price level and the consumer will be "directly influenced by the forces of demand and supply." (A decade later the farmer would bitterly regret his heavy indebtedness for the massive investment effort that this expansion called for and the rise in land prices that ensued.) To cope with the sudden Arab oil embargo, the administration stressed the need to ward off the danger of an economic slowdown because of the energy shortage and, to prevent the rise in fuel prices from pushing inflation higher. Further, the administration committed itself to a so-called Project Independence, aiming "to develop the capacity for self-sufficiency in energy supplies at reasonable costs."[64]

While nominal controls continued until April and while the Nixon administration was in the throes of a deep political crisis, the economic situation deteriorated further. By July 23, 1974, a Senate resolution calling for the convocation of a "domestic summit" of the nation's leaders to formulate "a unified plan of action to restore stability and prosperity" noted that "the American economy has in recent months reached an alarming state of instability and uncertainty combining reduced economic growth, corrosive inflation, high unemployment, venture [?] capital, serious changes in energy supply and pricing, unanticipated and destabilizing commodity shortages and growing international economic and financial uncertainties."[65] Following the Senate resolution, a Conference on Inflation met in Washington in September 1974 (shortly after the passage of powers from President Nixon to Gerald Ford). Twenty-eight economists representing a fairly broad spectrum of the economic profession participated in the discussions. The proposals put forward at that most critical juncture in the country's economic situation by Milton Friedman, John Kenneth Galbraith, and Walter W. Heller, for instance, were the familiar ones. Friedman indicated that the only effective cure against the raging inflation was restrained government spending and moderation of the rate of increase in the quantity of money. Professor Galbraith stressed that the only way of dealing with the price-wage spiral was "price control and wage management" to be conducted "by people who believe in it." Heller asserted that in its fight against inflation the Federal Reserve was squeezing out too much of the "productive life blood" and that it should "back off" some. Paul A. Samuelson rightly pointed out that the country's "number one problem" was not inflation alone but rather stagflation, which "has two sides to it: [i]t has a flat economy; it has an economy where unemployment is going to grow." This situation, he concluded, required "compromising among evils" and "a long-term siege which pays equal attention to the recessionary aspects and inflationary aspects." It was this statement that Senator Hubert H. Humphrey considered "the most important finding of this conference, namely, that the country had to deal with two public enemies—inflation and recession."[66]

It would be erroneous, however, to conclude that this particular statement reflected any kind of "general consensus." Reviewing the 1974 situation, the *Annual Report* of the Council of Economic Advisers, chaired by Alan Greenspan, stressed a different approach. The *Report* (written by William Fellner and Barry Chiswick) indicated that those who had focused in the past on the alleged trade-off between unemployment and inflation must have finally perceived that this trade-off lacked stability and that what mattered was a "time trade-off" concerning the inflation itself. It was a choice, first, between accepting difficulties of adjustment *before* the accelerating inflation approaches its limit or later, *after* the accelerated inflation had set in. Second, it was between facing the lag between production and price response, or moving into a "controlling" system with all the deficiencies the latter entails.[67] The only unanimity evident in all this was the underlying acceptance of the decisive role of the government's activity as a function of both the diagnosis of the state of the economy and of different ideologies.

CRITIQUE OF "KEYNES *CUM* GROWTH" POLICIES

As John Hicks rightly pointed out, the "age of Keynes" began in practice at the end of World War II and ended in the mid-1960s. In the U.S. it continued into the 1960s in the modified form of "Keynes *cum* growth." When the 1960s boom faltered, the policies that had been seen as being able to correct the cycle and provide for growth were now perceived as producing inflation and a deteriorating quality of life— deterioration affecting both the "sociosphere" and the "biosphere" as well. Let us consider some of the theoretical connotations of these controversies.

In the 1960s, the most extensive critique of the New Economics was formulated by the "monetarists." The latter term implied, in Milton Friedman's interpretation, adherence to the "quantity theory of money," namely, to the postulate that monetary changes exert a dominant influence on general business conditions. The controversy between the two "camps" became the central issue in macroeconomics. Distinguished economists took part on either side of the debate, though the main arguments of the dispute were exchanged in the public dialogues of Heller and Friedman. These discussions involved not only critical evaluations of their respective ideas about policies and instruments but also examination of the underlying conceptions of the economic system and of its *modus operandi*, of the causes and consequences of the key issues of unemployment and inflation, and of specific measures needed to cope with them.

Recall that Keynes had posited that "the outstanding characteristic" of the modern capitalist system was that "whilst it is subject to *severe fluctuations* in respect to output and employment, it is not violently unstable. Indeed it seems capable of remaining in a chronic condition of subnormal activity for a considerable period without any marked tendency either towards recovery or towards complete collapse." The system's cyclical fluctuations were due mainly to fluctuations in the marginal efficiency of capital "aggravated by other significant short period variables of the economic system." In conclusion, Keynes asserted that "the duty of ordering the current volume of investment" in order to reach full employment could not be left in private hands.[68] The "new economists" pointed out further that changes in employment and production were affected by changes on either side of the federal budget: in the words of the 1962 *Report* of the Council of Economic Advisers (the Heller council), federal purchases of goods and services and transfer payments "add to private income and thereby stimulate consumption and investment; federal taxes, on the other hand, reduce disposable personal and business incomes and restrain spending." Counter-cyclical automatic defenses built into the federal fiscal system cannot either prevent "a large and prolonged recession" or let recovery pursue its course, since as soon as the pace of the economy quickens the rise in federal revenues slows down the recovery process.[69] Thus the need for flexible discretionary budget policies. But these policies themselves need not focus on the minimization of the fluctuations around a norm: the policy emphasis can and should be shifted toward an ever-rising potential of the economy and toward gap closing and growth. Such a policy, according to Heller, involved "a commitment to an active, positive, and continuous use of the instruments of modern economics to keep demand at levels that will make full use of the economy's potential and keep that potential growing—without inflation." Steady advances in the breadth, promptness, and accuracy of statistics, in fact-gathering and forecasting techniques had indeed made possible this shift to a more active policy: the idea of replacing discretionary policies with submission to some stale fiscal or monetary rule was dismissed as totally unwarranted.[70]

The monetarists retorted that the view of a fundamental instability of the private sector had far-reaching implications: it determined "an activist and highly interventionist policy" and cast the government in the role of "ultimate stabilizer." As Karl Brunner, for instance, noted, the alternative hypothesis reversing the Keynesian view argued that "the private sector is essentially a shock-absorbing, stabilizing and self-adjusting process. Instability is produced dominantly by the operation of the government sector."[71] Further, the monetarists argued that aggregate demand was the result of a stable demand for money because of the inherent stability of the private sector and of an unstable supply of money because of the fluctuations induced by the monetary authorities. Thus, changes in aggregate demand were explained by changes in the money supply rather than by changes in the marginal efficiency of capital. Monetary impulses counted as a major factor for variations in output, employment, and prices. While asserting that the government budget did "matter a great deal," Friedman added, however, the caveat that by itself the state of the budget had "no significant effect on the course of nominal income, on inflation, on deflation or on cyclical fluctuations." Fiscal actions, namely, changes in taxes and spending, unaccompanied by changes in money had in the short run only a transitory impact on the GNP. The effectiveness of fiscal policy was, according to Friedman, based only on "a priori reasoning." The activist strategy—described by Heller himself as "fine tuning" and later discarded also by him as an unhappy addition to "the gallery of gaffes in economic-policy semantics"—was dismissed by the monetarists as counter-productive agitation.[72] "Frequent alterations in the degree of stimulus or restraint [were] more likely to destabilize the economy than achieve avowed goals," noted Beryl Sprinkel. He then added that these alterations were usually ill-timed; they resulted in complications because of the conflicting policy views of the monetary-fiscal authorities, and were in fact based "on ignorance of detail concerning monetary-fiscal impacts." Forecasting had improved but "not sufficiently to serve the needs of an activist policymaking group." A steady rate of growth in the money supply would prevent wide fluctuations, though it would not guarantee "perfect stability."[73] The available evidence, remarked Friedman, casts grave doubts indeed on producing any fine adjustments in economic activity by fine adjustments in monetary policy (at least in the present state of knowledge). The best criterion for monetary policy remained the control of the "quantity of a monetary total," be it currency plus adjusted deposits, or this total plus commercial bank time deposits, or a still broader total.

Keynesians and monetarists diverged further in their interpretations of the nature and meaning of unemployment and of inflation and on the conditions in which inflation arose and developed. Keynes viewed all cyclical unemployment as *involuntary*, causing loss of income to the unemployed and loss of output to the society. According to the *General Theory* we may have, before full employment, a succession of "semi-critical points" at which an increase (decrease) in effective demand will tend to raise (lower) in a discontinuous fashion wages in relation to market prices. These points, where a further increase in effective demand would be liable to cause a discontinuous increase in wage rates, were designated by Keynes as "positions of semi-inflation"—in contrast to a state of "true inflation," which would arise when full employment was reached. At that latter moment, any attempt to increase investment still further would necessarily set up "a tendency in money-prices to rise without limit, irrespective of the marginal propensity to consume." Thus, before full employment "there is no previous point at which we can draw a definite line and declare that conditions of inflation have set in."[74] The New Economics strategy as formulated in the 1960s emphasized as its standard of economic performance the reaching of the economy up to its potential: then, noted Arthur M. Okun, "ideally total demand should be in balance with the nation's supply capabilities. When the balance is achieved, there is neither the waste of idle resources nor the strain of inflationary pressure."[75] A different approach, also descending from Keynes, started from the contention that the theoretical opposition between the states of unemployment/full employment was too sharp. As Hicks pointed out, if one discards the opposition, then one could assert that there was "a wide band" in which there was "a relation between the rate of wage-rise and the rate of unemployment," namely, a behavior as the one illustrated by the Phillips curve.[76] In the same spirit, but with somewhat different arguments, Tobin asserted also, but in the early 1970s—almost a decade after the heyday of the New Economics—that "the postwar experience destroyed the identification of full employment with the economy's inflation threshold," that there may be inflation without aggregate excess demand, and that there was indeed an "inflationary bias" in the economy due to the fact that "random intersectoral shocks keep individual labor markets in diverse states of disequilibrium."[77]

With respect to unemployment, the monetarists—in contrast to the Keynesians and in agreement with the classics—distinguished between current receipts and income. They viewed most cyclical unemployment as a consequence of fluctuations in current receipts. These fluctuations would alter the permanent or anticipated income streams and consumption only if they would cause "a reevaluation of the main level or variability of earnings from particular occupations and in the aggregate."[78] Attacking the widespread belief that monetary growth tended to stimulate employment while monetary contraction tended to retard it, Friedman posited that for any given labor market structure there was a natural level of unemployment at which real wages and productivity tended to be broadly consistent. The new economists' setting of an unemployment target and relating it to a firm estimate of the U.S. economy was unwarranted. Attempts to maintain unemployment below the natural level will lead to perpetual inflation at an accelerating rate. The Phillips curve was meaningful, but it was mislabeled: the supply and the demand for labor depended not on *nominal* but on *real* wages. In the long run, there was no stable trade-off between inflation and unemployment, but rather between unemployment today and unemployment at a later date.[79] The new economists eventually responded to the natural rate hypothesis—which was to play an important role in economic policy decisions under Republican administrations—that money wages do not adjust rapidly to clear all labor markets each day: excess supplies of labor take the form of unemployment, and excess demands take the form of unfulfilled vacancies. The overall balance between unemployment and vacancies cannot be controlled by overall monetary and fiscal policies.[80]

These and other conceptual divergences shaped the respective views of the Keynesian *cum* growth camp and its opponents, concerning, for instance, the wage and price guideposts to stem inflation, the impact of the "big 1964 tax cut" to stimulate the economy, or the exact impact of the policy changes meant to close the gap between actual and potential income. In defense of the guideposts of the Kennedy administration, the new economists had asserted, as we already pointed out, that major wage bargains and price decisions assumed "national importance" when they were "regarded by large segments of the economy as setting a pattern." Friedman replied, we recall, that the guideposts could have no significant effect on the rate of price rise: the new economists confused a part of the economy with the whole economy and further confused nominal magnitudes with real magnitudes, that is, dollars with what the dollars will buy. (Tobin retorted eventually that the guideposts did not deserve the scorn that they often attracted because there was indeed an arbitrary, imitative component in wage settlements, and that maybe it could be influenced by national standards.) With respect to the big 1964 tax cut, Heller contended that it was "the most overt and dramatic expression of the new approach to economic policy . . . the capstone of postwar policy for putting the U.S. economy more or less permanently into the full-employ-ment orbit."[81] In a "Friedmanesque" rejoinder, Sprinkel retorted that the 1965–66 growth had been due simply to the fact that at the time there had been around a lot of unemployed labor and capital. Heller finally responded that "some of the Friedmanites fail to recognize that if fiscal policy actions like the 1964 tax cut can do no good, then fiscal policy actions like the big budget increases and deficits associated with Vietnam can also do no harm." In short, the "Friedmanites should recognize that they can't have it both ways."[82]

Last, but not least, what was in practice the appropriate size and the actual impact of the policy measures meant to close the GNP gap? William Brainard pointed out that when policy multipliers are uncer-tain—and a number of economists have furnished widely varying esti-mates of both fiscal and monetary multipliers—a policy stimulus injected in order to close a GNP gap may lead to overshooting and to an acceleration of inflation, while, conversely, a policy restraint adopted in order to eliminate overheating could push the economy into a recession. We saw that Friedman had asserted that attempts to push unemployment below the natural rate would lead to accelerating inflation: this could only reinforce the significance of Brainard's warning against the danger of overshooting the policy target.[83] This debate is still open.

In time, this controversy was followed by a volley against the very goals of the New Economics rather than against its techniques. The attacks were carried out by a heterogeneous group that, according to Tobin, comprised "environmentalists, pacifists, anti-materialists, Galbraithians and neo-Marxists." With the help of various arguments it claimed that economic growth was an "unworthy social goal." As we have briefly indicated before, the issues brought to the fore in these attacks con-cerned particularly the "proper" size and the distribution of the U.S. population, the nature of education and the relation of science to "social purpose," the impact of input-output relations on the environment, and the interrelations between growth, "consumerism," and welfare. With respect to population, the main questions addressed were the proximate possibility (or the necessity) of zero population growth and of its impact, likewise on the dangers of accepting ever-greater concentrations of population in already crowded metropolitan regions. With regard to education, the problems aired were the quality and "relevance" of an ever-growing educational system to the possible "need" to deemphasize expansion along traditional lines, and to the lack of "social purpose" of modern science and technology. With regard to input-output and the environment, attention was drawn to the dangers caused by the deterio-ration of the "biosphere" and of the "sociosphere," to the need to assess the cost-benefits of production by taking into account its dysfunctional results, and to the adverse side effects of various technologies. Concerning the consumer, a vast popular literature developed on "consumerism," along with more serious analyses of federal interventions in matters relating to the safety of raw materials, processes, products, and places of work.

The polemic writings on "consumerism"—notably those of John Kenneth Galbraith presenting a "hapless" consumer manipulated by unscrupulous corporations that decide what new and often worthless products to dump on him, in what quantities, and at what prices—were quite fashionable at the end of the 1960s. Other economists opposed to the "growthmania," like E. J. Mishan, for instance, who was also in vogue at the time, stressed in particular that changes in the GNP were not acceptable as an index of welfare, that there was a critical need for diverting investable resources to the "replanning" of towns and cities, that resources were wasted in the drive for efficiency and in the acceleration of innovations, that it was unlikely that proper substitutes could be found for the rapid exhaustion of nonrenewable resources, and that the consumer was indeed adversely affected by product innovation and the output of "unnecessary" goods.[84]

By 1972 the National Bureau of Economic Research was moved to devote a colloquium to the questions: Why economic growth? What is its effect on welfare? What do we get out of economic growth? Do we really want growth as much as we thought we do? At that colloquium, William Nordhaus and James Tobin presented an interesting essay focused on the interrelation between GNP and economic welfare. They constructed for the purpose an experimental "measure of economic welfare" (MEW), essentially a comprehensive measure of the annual real consumption of households. To obtain it, they rearranged various items of the national statistics: they reclassified GNP expenditures as consumption, investment, and intermediate goods and services; they imputed for the services of consumer capital, leisure, and household work; and corrected for various "disamenities of urbanization." The authors' conclusion and general message was, in the words of one of the discussants, that "the economy, though subject to improvement, has been churning out, even in its present imperfect state, final consumer goods or sources of welfare, or their equivalent in leisure, at a substantial rate of growth." As might be expected, the closing remark of the colloquium was that in the final analysis growth did matter, even if one took into account all the consequences of growth.[85]

LEGACIES

Much of the development economics that flourished in the 1960s constituted, as Deepak Lal rightly put it, "a quest for new economics." It did indeed revive mercantilism *cum* "stage theories" and put forward some new "stages" or "transitions" meant to capture the grand sweep of history and the diversity of successive or coexisting economic systems. It did castigate systematically "colonialism," "neoimperialism," and the multinationals to which it attributed *inter alia* a large part of the poverty of the Third World. And it employed much effort to justify government *dirigisme*—centralized planning and direct controls—in order to supplant the alleged inefficiencies and distortions of the price mechanism.[86] An offshoot of all this was also the reflourishing of a variety of models of convergence between capitalism and socialism, namely, of the presumed evolutionary, qualitative transformations of the United States and/or of the USSR that would make these societies become increasingly alike. Some of the best known theses on convergence rejuvenated theories already in circulation in the 1930s. Among these, the most influential were those of Galbraith—to which we have referred previously—and those of Jan Tinbergen and W. W. Rostow.

Recall that in the Galbraithian vision the capitalist and socialist economies (and societies) come to resemble each other more and more because technological developments make the superseding of the market by economic planning and direction necessary in both systems. The economic nucleus of the "mature" state is formed by the complex of large corporations. Just as for Thorstein Veblen, the technicians—what Galbraith calls the "technostructure"—constitute the corporations' guiding intelligence. To implement their decisions, the corporations bind the consumer to their needs, bring the supply of capital and labor under their control, and extend their influence deeply into the state. (All this of course is just a reversal of consumer sovereignty.) Convergence between the capitalist and the socialist systems begins "with modern large-scale production, with heavy requirements of capital, sophisticated technology, and, as a prime consequence, elaborate organization."[87] In the Tinbergenian vision, the aims of economic policy are almost the same in both systems, namely, a more equal income distribution and rapid economic growth. All other purposes of economic policy are reducible to either of these goals. Since the aims are similar, one and the same optimal order is valid both "West" and "East." The West moves from the traditional factory optimization and management to the complex organization and coordination of "hundreds of thousands of simultaneous actions" for entire industries, sectors, and, finally, for the economy as a whole. The East moves away through experience from the total nationalization of the means of production, comprehensive planning, tight centralization, and direct instrumentalities.[88] Finally, in the Rostowian conception, all societies lie "in their economic dimensions" within one of five stages, ranging from the "traditional society" to the "high consumption" society. These growth and change stages unfold in an invariable sequence unless some extraordinary event distorts the normal process. In this scheme the Soviet system "is a kind of disease which can befall a traditional society if it fails . . . to get on with the job of modernization." Then, as income per capita reaches a certain level, the communist system overcomes the disease and society enters also into the phase of high mass consumption, for which it develops the "sectoral complexes"—industries and services—that it then requires.[89]

In answer to the Galbraith conception, J. E. Meade rightly pointed out that it was strange to assume that systems increasing in complexity, in which technically sophisticated productive processes and inputs produce increasingly differentiated products, would tend toward clumsy and inefficient "quantitative planning" to supplant price and market mechanisms. In fact, the Soviet Union itself has tried to use "prices"—administratively determined prices—in order to introduce "rationality" to its own centralized system of administrative-directive management. Furthermore, the Hungarian or the Yugoslav systems, onto which more or less extensive introductions of market mechanisms have been grafted by a variety of covert or overt administrative manipulations, have certainly not been examples of success to be emulated. In response to the Tinbergenian schema one may have pointed out that the concepts of income distribution and economic growth have never been the same in the two systems and that, moreover, the ideas of their leaders about the "optimal regime" differ drastically. Rostow's idea about the gravitation of the Soviet Union toward the U.S. sectoral complexes of high mass consumption assumed implicitly that the latter was precisely the universal "optimal regime." What all these theories had in common was a *deterministic* outlook. The Soviet leaders who proclaim to be determinists have rejected, however, any Western ideas of convergence in lieu of their own concept of convergence into universal communism. In the meantime, Soviet writers have proclaimed that their country had reached "mature socialism" (a counterpart of the "mature capitalism" stage of the U.S.) and that the actual problem of the two systems was not "convergence" but rather "coexistence" and "growth-competition."[90]

In the interval, growth theory and policy went largely out of fashion. Writing in the early 1970s, William D. Nordhaus and James Tobin noted melancholically, "A long decade ago economic growth was the reigning fashion of political economy. It was simultaneously the hottest subject of economic theory and research, a slogan eagerly claimed by politicians of all stripes, and a serious objective of the policies of governments. The climate of opinion has changed dramatically."[91] Another decade later, looking back at the economic growth of the 1960s, Robert M. Solow wondered: "Where have all the flowers gone?"[92]

Actually, as far as growth *theory* was concerned, it continued to be discussed and developed, but only as a subset of the far more-encompassing *capital* theory. Growth theory had been concerned with the issue of how growth in total output could be achieved by centrally planned choices and instruments affecting savings, investment, consumption, and the allocation of capital across sectors, given a natural rate of growth of labor and exogenous technology. In contrast, capital theory, which has taken off particularly since the early 1970s, began focusing on a larger set of problems. It centered its attention on various formulations and mechanisms of intertemporal resource allocation. Moreover, it returned to the Walrasian framework in the sense that it looked simultaneously at income determination and at prices and also considered alternative mechanisms—centralized or decentralized—for the realization of inter-temporal allocation. Further, it studied both aggregate and disaggregate models, the most typical of the former being the one- and two-sector growth models. (C. J. Bliss asserted that capital theory was interested only incidentally in special cases and particular growth models; according to him, the capital theorist "found nothing more boring than a catalogue of growth models.") Finally, capital theory tried to investigate the broader question of uncertainty in a totally different framework than the Keynesian one (focused on the vagaries of investment and the unpredictability of interest rates). The capital theorist assumed that the "controller" of the economy knew the parameters of the underlying stochastic process governing the economy's transition law. At the most general level the capital theorist considered the issue of efficient alloca-tion rather than that of growth. Put differently, the capital theorist did not feel precommitted to a growth path but considered steady-state or declining paths as well. He attempted to define different efficiency criteria that would lead him to comparison of centralized versus de-centralized mechanisms and to the characterization of pricing of effi-cient allocations. In short, capital theory developed as an extension of equilibrium theory and of production theory in order to take into account the role of time and had absorbed within it the more narrowly focused growth theory.[93]

With respect to the conflict between the Keynes *cum* growth theoreti-cians and the monetarists, and in regard to growth policy in general, it became increasingly obvious by the beginnings of the 1970s that demand management, which had worked for most of the postwar years, was now unable to resolve the conflict between unemployment and price stability. Inflation was developing alongside idle capacity and unemployment, with no excess demand. Looking back in the early 1980s to that period, Paul A. Samuelson asserted that 1961 through 1965 had in fact been a "too lucky period to be extrapolated." At that time the economy had been "exceptionally free of the disease of inflation," and even without the disastrous Vietnam War "we would have run into the problem of over-heating and incipient stagflation" as the 1960s unfolded. Samuelson added that stagflation negated "simple Keynesianism more cogently than the hypotheses and claims of any of the schools of monetarism." He then ranged himself among "sophisticated Keynesians [who] are as critical of versions of old-fashioned Keynesianisms as monetarists are."[94] Unfortunately, Samuelson left us in the dark as to when these schools had appeared, how they differed from one another, and who belonged to them and for what reasons. Be that as it may, with respect to growth policy, Erik Lundberg of Sweden pointed out that, on the basis of both the U.S. and the European experiences, in practice the estimation of "gaps" between actual and potential production was "a very treacherous exercise"—partly because of the interdependence between the demand and the supply factors—and that the measurement of total productive capacity independent of new price relations and demand structures was very "doubtful" given the existence of "sick industries" with overcapacity. A "sufficient" growth rate for GNP with a consequent rise in productivity continued, however, to be regarded as a necessary condition for moderation in wage bargaining and a low inflation rate.[95]

Two specific groups of policies of the period had a large effect on the budget and on the economy for years to come: the "war on poverty" programs of 1964 and the environmental program of 1969–72. President Johnson's "war on poverty" initiated some new programs and consolidated and expanded the coverage of some programs already on the books. These concerned: (i) human investment programs destined to increase earnings capacities (namely, compensatory education and skill training; extension of coverage of minimum wage laws); (ii) earning replacement programs designed to alleviate precipitous declines in income (unemployment insurance; disability compensation; Social Security); and (iii) provision of goods in kind and services including health care (direct in-kind programs for food; low-income housing; hospital insurance and medical care). In 1965, the last year before Vietnam, these social programs represented 25 percent of the federal budget and 4.5 percent of GNP; by 1980, following subsequent extensions and additions, the programs absorbed 48 percent of the budget and 11 percent of GNP. Although aimed against "poverty" (equated with a given low-income level), a large part of the programs eventually contributed a significant income transfer to both low- and middle-income people, mainly old. The analysis of these programs and of their impact led to important public debates and to a vast economic literature on inequality and poverty, on progressive taxation of income and wealth, and on the impact of such measures on incentives to work, take risks, and save. The legislation concerning the environment took shape between 1969 and 1972 under the Nixon presidency. The National Environmental Policy Act of 1969 (NEPA) led to the creation of a Council on Environmental Quality in the executive office and, by the end of 1970, to the establishment of the Environmental Protection Agency (EPA). Between 1970 and 1972 Congress passed two fundamental acts that established air and water pollution control strategies for years to come. Although earlier environmental statutes were extant, the new laws—the Clean Air Amendment of 1970 (CAA) and the Federal Water Pollution Control Amendments of 1972 (FWPCA)—established new goals and standards for air and water quality, set specific deadlines for cleanup and formulated procedures and mechanisms for regulation and enforcement that are still in force. The analysis of environmental policy led also to the development of a vast and interesting literature on the economics of the environment (on the environment and welfare economics, on methods of determining optimal amounts of pollution, on environmental policy and the distribution of costs and benefits, on resource conservation, and on the impacts on growth).

CHAPTER

4

ANTISTAGFLATION POLICIES

THE ECONOMIC SCENE, 1974–84

In the nine years from November 1973 to November 1982, the American economy experienced no less than three recessions, two of which were severe. The first one, the longest and deepest since the Great Depression—erroneously called by some as the latter's "second coming"—was soon baptized the Great Recession. As we already pointed out, first a rise in food prices and then oil price shocks, caused by the Arab oil embargo, hit the economy in the fourth quarter of 1973. The first big hikes in the price of oil rapidly accelerated the inflation and precipitated the fall in stock market prices. The recession dragged on from November 1973 to March 1975 (sixteen months). Food prices and oil played major roles in both the 1973–74 acceleration of inflation and in its deceleration in 1975. Since the economy had peaked in November 1973, one might have expected that the forecasts made in January 1974, either by the Council of Economic Advisers or by the best known private forecasting groups, would contain gloomy perspectives for the year ahead. But nobody was willing at the time to predict a great recession, and some forecasters (for example, "Roundup") predicted "zero growth but not for long" with a resurgence of the economy by mid-1974. Actually, at the time Gerald R. Ford succeeded President Nixon in mid-1974, the economic downturn gained momentum, turning sharply further down in the fourth quarter. The trough was not reached, however, before the end of the first quarter of 1975.[1] The second recession, which unfolded under the Carter administration against the background of a further increase in inflation stimulated by a new oil price hike, was actually brought about by an ill-advised imposition on consumer credit which drove down sharply and unexpectedly consumer spending. The recession lasted from January to July 1980 (six months). Finally, the third

89

recession, engineered by the new Reagan administration to bring down the inflation, was severe and prolonged. It deeply affected the economy from July 1981, shortly after the beginning of the new administration, until November 1982 (sixteen months).

These recessions combined with accelerating rates of increase in wages and prices (particularly the startling jumps in food and oil prices), upward surges in interest rates, and increasingly large budget deficits. They were also accompanied by rapidly expanding unemployment, alarming reports on faltering U.S. productivity rates, losses in the U.S. technological leadership in a number of fields, and a deterioration in the country's balance of trade. The concomitant high inflation rates (with peaks in 1973–75 and 1980–81) and the high unemployment rates (with peaks in 1974–75 and 1982) clearly show the high points of the Great Stagflation. (See figures 4a and 4c.) The sense of crisis imparted by all this was not fully overcome even when the rate of inflation was pushed down to roughly 4 percent by 1984, the rate of unemployment settled to a so-called natural rate of around 7 percent per annum, and the rate of growth reached 6.5 percent.

The Great Stagflation, which could be considered as ended by 1984 — appropriately, we take that year as the cutoff date of our discussion—like any great economic debate raised challenging problems for both economic theory and policy. As Gottfried Haberler had noted earlier, "the policymaker who had just mastered the principles of modern Keynesian macroeconomics was now confronted by a distressing dilemma: if he applied expansionary measures to reduce unemployment, he would accelerate inflation; if he adopted restrictive measures to curb inflation, he would exacerbate unemployment."[2]

Why did prices and wages continue to rise from the Great Recession on, notwithstanding excess supply of labor and capacity? Why did stagflation reach so suddenly, in 1974–75, intractably acute levels? What kind of proposals were the economic advisers offering the policymaker concerning the policy instruments to be used? What impact did these peculiar circumstances have on economic thinking and on its fundamental paradigms?

Consider briefly the main characteristics of the Great Stagflation in relation to those of the periods previously examined. Recall that in the 1930s, the vision of the "stagnationists" was that of a "mature" economy plagued by a dearth of opportunities for private investment, devoid of room for extensive growth, confined to mere replacement of existing capital upon retirements, accumulating savings idly—all of which set in motion a downward spiral of consumption, prices, incomes, and production. Such an economy could experience only "sick recoveries" that would die in their infancy and depressions that would feed on themselves and leave "a seemingly immovable core of unemployment."[3] As

Figure 4. Selected Indicators, 1960–1985

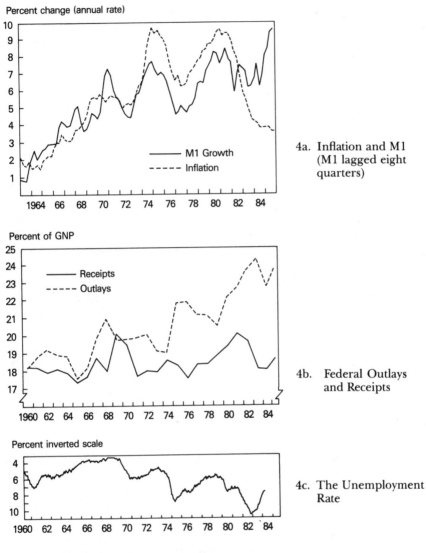

Percent change (annual rate)

M1 Growth
Inflation

4a. Inflation and M1
(M1 lagged eight
quarters)

Percent of GNP

Receipts
Outlays

4b. Federal Outlays
and Receipts

Percent inverted scale

4c. The Unemployment
Rate

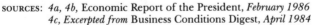

SOURCES: *4a, 4b,* Economic Report of the President, *February 1986*
4c, Excerpted from Business Conditions Digest, *April 1984*

used in the 1970s, the term stagnation in stagflation referred to a slowly growing inflation-ridden economy. Recall that during the Great Depression the 1929 real GNP was not reached before 1937, when a recession set in, and that the pre–Great Depression level was not surpassed, even slightly, before 1939. For that entire period, the yearly rate of growth had been only 0.3 percent. During the postwar years 1947–60, real GNP grew at the compound yearly rate of 3.5 percent and during the growth-oriented period 1961–73 at the compound rate of 4.1 percent. In the ensuing eleven years 1974–84, real GNP grew at less than 2.4 percent per annum.[4]

Deflation prevailed in the Great Depression, when the precipitous fall in prices and wages along with the spreading unemployment were viewed as the key issues. Throughout the 1930s the consumer price index (CPI) continued to remain far below its 1929 levels even by 1940. Contrariwise, in the Great Stagflation, it was inflation that was viewed as the critical problem, and the acceleration in the rate of increase in prices and wages was watched with apprehension. After the liquidation of the post–World War II inflation bulge, prices had risen at an average rate of 0.5 to 1 percent per year between 1949 and 1960, except for temporary surges in 1951–52 and in 1957, when the change in the CPI was on the order of some 3 percent. After a phase of creeping CPI increments during 1961–65, with annual rates of increase of 1 to 2 percent, the rate of increase accelerated to 5.5 percent per year from 1967 to 1970, falling and then surging again by 1973 to 8 percent and by 1974 to over 12 percent, following the extraordinary increases in food and oil prices. After falling again and fluctuating between 5 to 9 percent per year, the yearly rate of change of the CPI increased to as much as 13 percent by 1979 under renewed pressures from oil prices. The index was brought down to 9 percent in 1981 and then kept to around 4 percent per annum in the ensuing years up to 1984. (On the rate of inflation measured by change in the implicit price deflator for GNP, see figure 4a.) In June 1974, as inflation was accelerating, Paul A. Samuelson asserted that the phenomenon was in fact "rooted deep in the nature of the mixed economy," an economy in which "the electorate of all political persuasions" was not willing to accept high rates of unemployment and in which the government's attitudes had "shifted the odds against stable prices (and of course against falling prices)." Moreover, added Samuelson, inflation had gathered strength from the "synchronous reappearance" of the business cycle, a cycle that had been tamed in the "Age after Keynes" but that was "by no means yet dead" (though Samuelson himself had proclaimed it so a few years earlier).[5]

It was certainly true that in the "Age after Keynes," the share of government expenditure in nominal GNP had risen continuously, from some 27–28 percent (of which 18–19 percent was federal) in 1960–66, to some 30–31 percent (20–21 percent federal) in 1967–73, and 31–33 percent (21 to 23 percent federal) in 1974–80. This upward thrust did not stop, however, with the advent of the Reagan administration and with its change in policy emphasis. The indicated percentage indeed rose further, to 33–35 percent (21–25 percent federal) in the early 1980s. Great efforts had been made from 1979 on to tighten the growth of the money supply (except in 1980–81) and to restrain inflation, while the rates of unemployment drifted upward. But the combination under the new administration of increased government spending on defense and on interest on the debt, along with a policy of tax cuts in 1981–83, expanded enormously the discrepancy between outlays and receipts leading to increasing deficits. (See figure 4b.)

Interestingly, the Great Stagflation and its concomitant business cycles did not, however, alter significantly some of the basic tendencies of the post–World War II economy. Consider private domestic investment, for instance. It tended as before to grow, though only at a moderate pace— from some 15 percent of the GNP in the 1950s and early 1960s, to 15 to 16 percent in the mid-1960s and early 1970s, and then to 16 to 18 percent from the mid-1970s to the early 1980s, with half of these totals going to plant and equipment. While, as we have pointed out, in the Great Depression much of the stagnation fears had been generated by an anticipated inadequacy of investment opportunities, in the Great Stagflation some analysts pointed to the drop in productivity growth and to an alleged dearth of capital for meeting the available and prospective investment opportunities. As before, however, the tendency of the sectoral changes continued in their by then familiar directions. The share of agriculture, forestry, and fishery contracted, falling from about 3.5 percent of the nominal GNP of 1974 to 2.5 percent of the GNP of 1984. The share of manufacturing fell also from 23 to 21 percent—though in real terms it stayed about the same (around 22 percent of real GNP). As we noted above, stagflation did not imply a no-growth economy: between the benchmark years 1974 and 1984, real agricultural output increased by 22 percent, manufacturing output by 28 percent, goods output by 30 percent, and services by over 28 percent. Exports increased also by 38 percent, but imports increased even faster, by close to 70 percent, enlarging the deficit on current accounts. Finally, notwithstanding the high unemployment rates, total civilian employment increased from close to 87 million gainfully employed in 1974 to 105 million in 1984.

As was the case with the Great Depression, the Great Stagflation also set off searches for different ways of doing things. "Keynesianism" became the first target, both as a way of thinking about the economy and as a way of managing it. The search for solutions beyond Keynesianism involved, on the theoretical plane, discussions about the validity of the Keynesian analytical core, about the logic and effectiveness of its aggregate demand orientation, and about the relevance of the econometric models built on the theory's premises. On the pragmatic plane, the search for new solutions expressed and reassessed the traditional concerns about business-government relations. The conflict between the tendency pushing toward further expansion in the scope and degree of government intervention in the economy and the tendency of limiting the role of federal government in the society and of reassessing its priorities grew continuously from the middle of the 1970s on, reaching a climax at the beginning of the 1980s. Skepticism about the ability of the government to manage the economy so as to rapidly restore full employment with stable prices and steady growth, spread incessantly and helped finally to usher in a new administration which reshaped the national agenda and changed the priorities of the federal budget.

ECONOMISTS' RESPONSES TO STAGFLATION

Modern monetarism, modern classical economics of the rational expectations persuasion, and the more eclectic "supply-side economics," etched out their characteristics and put forward their conclusions directly in opposition to: (a) the organizational principles of Keynes's theory; (b) its policy implications; and (c) its uses in the building of econometric models. Let us consider these issues in turn.

a. **The organizational principles**. As we have already pointed out, Keynes built his theory on his perception that our economic system tended toward a condition of subnormal activity; full employment was a rare or short-lived occurrence, and, typically, oscillations "round an intermediate position avoiding the gravest extreme fluctuations in employment and prices in both directions" were usual. He then showed how the volume of output was determined by aggregate demand at current prices and pointed out that fluctuations in investment "were most often at the bottom of the phenomenon of fluctuations in employment." He finally asserted that the level of prices was separately determined by cost trends (primarily the level of money wage rates). Hicks let money and finance enter this system, so to speak, marginally via the IS-LM framework. Whatever the subsequent additions, refinements, and syntheses—some of which were extremely useful for both economic analysis and policy—Keynes's "apparatus of thought" and his ways "of looking at how the entire gross national product is determined and how wages and prices are determined by it" have not been modified in most of the main macroeconomics textbooks still in use.[6]

In the New Economics or in the Keynes *cum* growth phase, an important distinction was added to all this between actual and potential output—the first determined by effective demand, the second, separately and distinctly, by the growth of factor inputs. The change seemed theoretically innocuous: potential output was described as a target to be reached by an activist policy influencing both demand and supply. In relation to Keynes's *General Theory,* however, the change was theoretically significant. What Keynes had set out to do was to show what determined the *actual* amount of income or, which is the same thing, of employment. What he pointed out—and what he said was the "substance" of his *General Theory*—was that what called forth an increase in employment (in any given situation of technology, resources, and factor costs) was whether the effective demand exceeded the aggregate supply price of output. In the New Economics potential output became exogenously dependent, as in Robert M. Solow's model, on various "growth" determinants. Keynes's paradigm thus became combined with certain analytical results arrived at within a different, non-Keynesian framework. The frontal criticism against Keynes's paradigm, and against Keynes *cum* growth as well, gained momentum in the mid-1960s but reached a climax only after the onset of the Great Stagflation. Let us consider briefly the salient points of these critiques that first took exclusively the form of modern monetarism, then of so-called rational expectations, and then of "supply-side economics."

The monetarists stressed indefatigably that Keynesianism in whatever form had little to say about inflation. It did not recognize that the growth of money supply was the major determinant of the nominal magnitudes of the GNP in the short run and of prices in the long run and that erratic changes in money supply engendered macroeconomic fluctuations. The monetarists (and other critics) noted, moreover, that the Keynesian system "faltered in dealing with supply-shocks" (namely, the oil price shock) because of its neglect of the supply-side elements.[7] The leaders of the rational expectations school—increasingly known as "new classicals"—attacked Keynesianism from the vantage point of the classical world, in which private choices determine what, how, and for whom to produce and in which these choices are made on the basis of rapidly adjusting prices and wages. The modern rational expectations school affirmed that individuals optimize on the basis of the information available to them and that *all* markets, including the labor markets, clear at all times. Hence they dismissed as unwarranted Keynes's crucial contention that unemployment was to a large extent involuntary, and asserted that labor markets cleared rapidly after shocks, while wages moved to balance supply and demand. Other critics, like Friedrich von Hayek, for instance, rejected altogether Keynes's analysis in terms of aggregates—namely, macroeconomics as such—since such an analysis "wholly concealed" the constant reallocation of resources taking place in the economy.[8] Finally, the "supply-siders" (about whom more below) affirmed that the Keynesian emphasis on aggregate demand was misplaced and that supply was the real determining factor of all economic activity.

b. **Implications for Policy**. Keynes's key policy target was to pull the economy up to full employment level. The fulcrum of the policy was the posited stability of the relations among the economy's aggregate flows. By making deliberate choices for the flows it controlled—namely, the budget—the government, the policy asserted, could impact the overall level (not the composition) of all other flows.

Monetarist critics argued that government's interventions disturbed the orderly stability engendered by the operations of the private economy. Recall that Keynes viewed the private economy as tending to stabilize in an under full employment equilibrium. The monetarists also posited stability of the private economy but took a different view as to which equilibrium was stable. Further, while Keynes viewed use of the government's instruments as having beneficial outcomes, the monetarists' position was that their use was destabilizing and therefore nefarious. The government should avoid interfering with the market, should shun price-wage programs, and should comply with a fixed rule concerning the money supply—if it wanted to insure normal growth.

For a short while various new theoretical models were advanced with respect to employment disequilibrium (for example, by Robert Barro and Herschel Grossman). But development in this direction was overshadowed by the advent of the rational expectations school. The rational expectationists pointed out that if, by definition, all markets clear—and the labor markets clear like all the others—only misconceptions about real wages and/or relative wages could create the illusory appearance of a short-run Phillips curve (and of trade-offs between unemployment and inflation rates). Changes in policy alter both the time path of the decision variables and the behavioral parameters governing the rest of the system: for policy measures to really affect the short-run behavior of real aggregates—as the Keynesian policy attempted—the disturbances would have to be both "imperfectly anticipated and imperfectly perceived" by the private agents. (Or, "the effectiveness of government measures rests on the inability of private agents to recognize systematic patterns in fiscal and monetary policy"—an inability difficult to accept, since people do bet in their own interest and would not make the same mistakes in the same direction year in, year out.) Keynes had formulated the "sub-discipline called macroeconomics" in order to explain the business cycle [?!] which he could not fit within the classical framework: but fluctuations can and do arise in such a world when individuals react to unanticipated changes in variables that impinge on their interests—and as the government's ability to offset these initiating changes turns out to be very limited.[9]

c. **Econometric Model Building**. While rejecting the Keynesian theory, Robert E. Lucas and Thomas J. Sargent, the theoreticians of rational expectations, claimed that the "Keynesian Revolution" had succeeded in the United States because Keynesianism "lent itself so readily to the formulation of explicit econometric models." This, they added, accounted "for the dominant scientific position it attained by the 1960s." It was the transformation of "macroeconomics into a quantitative, *scientific* discipline, the development of explicit statistical descriptions of economic behavior, . . . the introduction of the use of mathematical control theory to manage the economy" that made Keynesianism significant.[10] The monetarists had rejected the Keynesian models, their implications, and their forecasts as both imperfect and unreliable (though actually one could build somewhat similar all-purpose models, just as imperfect, in the monetarist tradition, with different policy implications and different forecasts neither more accurate nor more reliable).[11] The adherents of rational expectations, while praising the Keynesian "revolution in method," also rejected the Keynesian macroeconometric models as lacking "a sound theoretical or econometric basis." They tried to build instead, not a single "all purpose model" but a variety of small equilibrium models of their own, "used to interpret various economic phenomena and to experiment with hypothetical government policies"— models in which agents were rational and the impulses that trigger business cycles are mainly unanticipated shocks.[12] Yet this building of highly simplified policy-interpretative models raised also an insuperable dilemma. In the words of Thomas J. Sargent and Neil Wallace, "In order for a model to have normative implications, it must contain some parameters whose values can be chosen by the policymaker. But if these can be chosen, rational agents will not view them as fixed and will make use of schemes for predicting their values. If the economist models the economy taking these schemes into account, then those parameters become endogenous variables and no longer appear in the reduced-form equations for the other endogenous variables. If he models the economy without taking the schemes into account, he is not imposing rationality." This was described as the "conundrum" facing the rational expectations economists: they are necessarily confined to *interpretative* models and cannot construct what they naturally desire, namely a model with normative implications.[13] Even in a dynamic policy coordination game—in which the government responds to the public reaction, and the public responds to the government correction—the conundrum is not broken.

Different both in scope and sophistication from either monetarism or rational expectations, the so-called "supply-side economics," which had its vogue in the early 1980s, did not advance any complicated set of arguments against the Keynesian analytical core, its policy implications, and its econometric model building. All supply-siders did not necessarily emphasize the same policies.[14] Some supply-siders, like Martin S. Feldstein, believed that the unemployment observed in the United States in the 1970s did not reflect inadequate demand but was rather due "to the government policies like unemployment insurance, welfare restrictions and the minimum wage that reduced the effective supply of labor." They emphasized accordingly the need to reduce the "entitlements" created by welfare policies, to eliminate waste, and to end the Social Security subsidizing of the "middle classes." Other supply-siders emphasized the need to broaden the tax base, cutting the marginal tax rates and deregulating industry, because they believed that taxation and overregulation had affected adversely the incentives to work, save, invest, and take risks. Tax cuts and deregulation would give business the necessary stimulus for expansion. In the early 1960s the Keynesians had seen an opportunity for a tax cut in the fact that, on account of economic growth, tax revenues had been rising faster than the intended government expenditures and were thus hindering the attainment of full employment. The Keynesians ended up by achieving a reduction in tax collection by a combination of narrowing the tax base and rate reduction (for example, investment tax credits and accelerated depreciation). The supply-siders, who recommended a tax cut during the Great Stagflation, did it because they thought that would limit government spending and above all would reduce marginal tax rates that adversely affected incentives, investment, and the expansion of the supply of goods and services. "This different perspective is the essence of the supply-side revolution in economic policy," declared one of its leading advocates, Paul Craig Roberts. Finally, certain supply-siders, particularly followers of Arthur B. Laffer, put forward extravagant claims for the tax cut policy. They projected a rapid rise in output following a tax cut, swift increases in revenue toward the level previous to the tax rate cut, sharp rises in savings, and a painless reduction in inflation. Thus, they predicted, the deficit will be reduced or the deficit would perhaps increase, but at a slower pace than the increase in national savings. These exorbitant claims led to certain quantitative misallocations and gave a bad name to supply-side policies, as we shall see later on.

The adherents of yesteryear's New Economics decided in the early 1980s to rename their brand of economics "mainstream economics" and did not remain insensitive to all these critiques. While, as Samuelson put it, stagflation itself had "negated simple Keynesianism more cogently than the claims of any school of monetarism,"[15] actually the mainstream economists showed a great degree of flexibility and adaptability to all criticisms. They synthesized monetarism and rational expectations. They started to indicate that money did indeed enter into output determination, not solely, of course, but along with other policy variables like government and technology. They added further that expectations had to be taken into account as a way of explaining financial markets (including interest rates, stock prices, and foreign exchange rates), if not also as an explanation of the slower adjustment of the labor markets. They conceded that "people do learn fast" and that solutions to yesterday's macroeconomics may not work today, since the people may have adapted their behavior in light of yesterday's solutions. Eclecticism thus became the hallmark of "mainstream" economists, who condescendingly looked down on the "early neanderthal Keynesian models" (Samuelson's expression) that they themselves had made popular previously.

According to William D. Nordhaus—co-author with Paul A. Samuelson of a new edition of the latter's basic textbook, *Economics*—the "neo-Keynesian synthesis" of the 1980s became an even further extended (namely, modified) version of the New Economics of the 1960s.[16] Its main element—the crux of everything—was the distinction between *actual* and *potential* output. The former is thought of as "demand," the latter as "supply"; potential output is viewed as determined by the growth of factor inputs with the rate of technological change exogenously given; actual output is to be considered as basically determined by aggregate spending "as in the Hicksian IS-LM curves." It was pointed out that fiscal policy "appears to have substantial impact on actual output at least in the short-run," while monetary policy has substantial effects on output, but "the uncertainty is much greater for the former than for the latter." Finally, while "some early Keynesian thinking held prices and wages to be approximately constant up to the point where the economy hit full employment," the new view is different: "Inflation is taken to be the sum of inertial, cyclical and volatile or random forces." In these conditions, the neo-Keynesians asserted confidently that they could look upon monetarism as "a special case of the neo-Keynesian synthesis." Indeed, as further noted by Nordhaus, "the monetarists accept the distinction between actual and potential output, as well as the view of the determination of the potential output of the Neo-Keynesian synthesis. The major difference lies in the view of output determination and the inflation process." The "new-classical macroeconomics" (that is, the rational expectations school) may also be viewed as accepting "the long-run but not the short-run half of the neo-Keynesian synthesis," that is, that it views the economy "as in neoclassical equilibrium, though subject to random shocks." Only the supply-siders were excluded from all this, since they failed *inter alia* to "grasp analytically" the distinction between actual and potential output.

It should be noted that synchronously with all these theoretical debates, the search for policy strategies "beyond Keynesianism" were also very active throughout the decade considered (mid-1970s to 1984). In turning now to these specific issues, we group the main problems as follows: (i) the analysis of the economy's "deficiencies"; (ii) the proposals concerning strategies and policy coordinations; and (iii) the interrelations between deregulation and "competitiveness."

As a point of departure for the entire discussion, we take, as most appropriate, the legislative efforts made primarily by Senator Hubert H. Humphrey in the mid-1970s to amend the Employment Act of 1946 and to promote national economic planning—an idea first advanced by a private group, the Initiative Committee for National Economic Planning, co-chaired by Wassily Leontief and the trade union leader, Leonard Woodcock. The bill, S1795, introduced in the U.S. Senate on May 21, 1975, aimed to amend, in fact to expand, the framework of the Employment Act in order to provide for the development and adoption of a "balanced economic growth plan." The proposal, appropriately titled the Balanced Growth and Economic Planning Act of 1975, was viewed by some as "the last product of the New Deal thought" part of which might "almost have been written by [Rexford G.] Tugwell and [John R.] Commons," as Craufurd D. Goodwin put it.[17] It focused on the "structural deficiencies" of the economy and on its "imbalances" and urged the establishment of an Economic Planning Board in the executive office of the president with the task of preparing the plan. This bill was followed by a revised version, S50, introduced in the U.S. Senate on March 16, 1976, under the title the Full Employment and Balanced Growth Act of 1976, which set as goals the achievement of full employment and the preparation of a yearly plan for employment and growth. Congress "extracted the legislation's teeth" before approving it as the Full Employment and Balanced Growth Act of 1978 and created "an 'unworkable monster' by loading the bill with an agglomeration of conflicting policy statements."[18] While this legislation did not produce much substance, its preparation and the discussion it elicited further fueled an already abundant literature on both the economy's "deficiencies" and the planning and coordination of governmental decision-making processes. We turn to these issues now:

(i) **The Economy's Changing Structure and "Shortcomings."** The discussions on the economy's "deficiencies" and "imbalances" drew impetus from the decline and the retrenchment of our basic industries—steel and autos—the allegedly continuous expansion of the service sector relative to goods producing, the faltering of productivity growth rates, "shortfalls" in the rates of capital investment, the loss of leadership in certain technological exports, the greater cyclical instability in industries sensitive to interest rates and to international trade, the energy problem, and, last but not least, the increasingly hurtful competition of Japan and its overt policies to promote industrial growth. The shutdown of plants and the massive loss of jobs in the old-line industries were attributed by some to a general process of "de-industrializing."[19] Yet, as Charles L. Schultze pointed out, the United States had been one of only three major industrial countries—Italy and Canada being the others—with any increase in manufacturing employment during the 1970s. U.S. manufacturing, the largest and most conspicuous of our economy's major sectors, made some important and desirable structural adjustments at the time— shifting toward high technology sectors and those making capital goods and synthetic materials—while simultaneously doubling its total exports.[20] It was true that throughout the post–World War II years, our primary activities—agriculture, fishing, forestry, mining—had continued to shrink and to grow in efficiency at a time when the *principal* service sectors increased their share of national income. These increases, however, varied as between finance, insurance and real estate, legal, health and education, transportation, wholesale and retail trade, and the public service.[21] These shifts did not represent, as it was fashionable to contend at the time, a "qualitative" scientific and technological upheaval, a revolutionary transition from an "industrial" to a "post-industrial" society, that is, from a society producing goods to one importing them.[22] They represented in fact inevitable changes in an economy continuously adjusting to the impulses of both domestic and international markets (for example, the so-called "merger mania").

What about the "decline" in the growth of productivity? The index of output per hour of all persons in the total economy, and the related multifactor productivity index, according to a variety of estimates, showed declining rates of growth from 1965 to 1973 and an even steeper decline during the following decade, 1973–82. Various productivity studies attributed this decline in rates to changes and/or shortcomings relating to capital, labor, and to government's policies. With respect to capital, particular emphasis was placed on an alleged decline in capital formation on lower savings constrained by rising costs of capital services, on the deleterious impact of inflation on capital returns, on rising energy costs and on antipollution requirements leading to massive premature discarding of equipment. With respect to labor, attention was drawn to intersectoral shifts of labor from higher to lower productivity occupations, to declining rigor and relevance of education and training, to increased numbers of the unskilled, the young, and women in the workforce, and, last but not least, to outdated management skills and practices emphasizing quantity rather than quality. With respect to government, the onus was placed on wide swings in its fiscal and monetary policies, on rising federal spending and deficits that supplanted more productive private spending and investment, on regulations and tax-based penalties that hampered innovations and lowered capital returns.[23]

Examining this "crisis" in the context of long-run productivity growth of comparable countries, William J. Baumol of Princeton suggested a different interpretation. He pointed out that the available long period data on productivity and related variables showed a reasonable convergence of output per labor hour among industrialized countries. Almost all the leading free enterprise economies moved in this respect closer to the leader over the past century or so (1870–1980), and the post–World War II data suggested that this process of convergence (not of systems but of productivity rates) extended to the "intermediate" and centrally planned economies as well. The fruits of a successful productivity-enhancing policy (for example, through an extraordinary investment effort) did not benefit exclusively those who made the extra effort: these fruits were ultimately shared by others so that a nation's innovation record depended heavily "on how rapidly and well it can learn from the advances of other countries." Last but not least, Baumol pointed out that U.S. productivity growth had in fact been surprisingly *steady* over the indicated century—a conclusion corroborated by the results of other studies.[24]

In connection with the discussions on the fall in productivity growth rates, attention was often drawn to an alleged loss of U.S. technological leadership to the rise of Japan's competitive technological capabilities and to the displacement of certain U.S. exports by newly industrialized countries. The "loss of leadership" was alleged to be due *inter alia* to a declining rate of growth in research and development expenditures (by industry, government, universities, and others), a slowdown in the U.S. growth rate of its engineering labor force, a decrease in the development and in the export of new and improved products, and a fall in the rate at which innovations were produced and diffused in the U.S. economy.[25] It may be pointed out that an in-depth evaluation of the technological changes that took place at the time may have required some additional telling indicators: productivity growth and technological change impact on the production processes. Not only do they reduce the labor force and possibly also capital, but they affect simultaneously the bundle of intermediate goods these processes require. These structural impacts could be ascertained through detailed analyses of input-output tabulations and through appropriate calculations showing how the input requirements for the final bill of goods of, say, 1980 would have been different if it had been produced with the technologies of 1939, 1947, 1958, and 1972. Such an exercise was done by Anne P. Carter in 1970, but only for 1961. It showed not only how the requirements of labor and capital changed and how intermediate goods tended to substitute for both labor and capital but also how certain production establishments were growing specialized, "buying goods and services from outside suppliers rather than making them in-house," and which particular intermediate inputs were those with the more rapidly growing or shrinking requirements, possibly affecting domestic and foreign suppliers as well.[26] With respect to international trade, it was certainly true that the U.S. share in the world trade of manufactured goods, measured in value terms, had declined from the mid-1960s to the 1980s, reflecting adjustments in both our own manufacturing production and in the growth of foreign countries' exports benefiting from the openness and increasing interdependence of the world economy. But the U.S. also shared in this expanding market: foreign trade as a percentage of GNP increased dramatically from 7 percent in 1960 to double that percentage in 1980. Exports of manufactured goods increased from some 9 percent of the U.S. production of manufactures in 1960 to about 19 percent in 1980— with imports increasing somewhat faster, from 5 to 23 percent of domestic production.[27] Anyway, one must not overlook the fact that these issues were not independent of fluctuating exchange rates whose adjustment could make up for "a multitude of sins" both of ours and of our competitors.

Consider now the related question of capital formation and the size of investments. In the early 1970s it was claimed that there was a "capital shortage" of between $1–3 billion in order to ensure a 1980 capital stock sufficient to meet the needs of a full employment economy, of pollution abatement requirements, and of decreasing dependence on oil. This contention drew some sharp and cogent rebuttals that *mutatis mutandis* apply as well to the "shortage" of capital needs to keep up with the rates of investment of other industrialized countries or with "adequate" productivity levels. Robert Eisner of Northwestern University answered that "any argument that there is a capital shortage either implies a literal failure of market clearing or some standard external to the economic system": in fact, these discussions relate rather "to imagined disparities between the amount of capital or the rate of investment which some individual or group asserts we *should* have and what appears to be forthcoming." Eisner then added that "we are told that for some reasons of state or religion, we must accumulate capital more rapidly in order to grow faster. . . . But this would be at the expense of current availability of private and public goods and services. Is it necessarily desirable that we have more in the future than in the present?"[28] Martin S. Feldstein of Harvard pointed out that the "capital gap" idea implied that the demand for capital would continually exceed supply as if interest rates and the cost of equity would not move to equalize them. He also added that the idea of capital shortage in relation to, say, full employment confused "the occasional desirability of a *temporary increase* in the capital stock with the desirability of a *permanently higher* saving rate and correspondingly large capital stock." Yet Feldstein as a good supply-sider did assert that "we saved too little" because high marginal rates of taxation had distorted the choice between consumption and saving in favor of the former. He found that "both savings and economic welfare would increase if taxes on capital income were reduced and replaced by a tax on consumption with equal yield and progressivity." His favorite target was Social Security, which allegedly reduced private savings and therefore national savings.[29]

(ii) **Policy Strategies and Coordinations**. "Planning" used as a broad term for various types of coordination of policies and actions is often loosely applied to very different concepts. For instance, it may refer to an *integral* system of coordination of (a) all public policies with the view to achieving consistency among all governmental actions; (b) all plans and forecasts of both the public and the private sector, with a view to establishing a kind of "firmed up" expectations framework serving as an indicative guide toward the future for the economy as a whole; and (c) all the operations of the economy with a view to centrally controlling and directing them according to planners' preferences. Planning may also refer to a *partial* system of coordination of certain government policies or of certain economic sectors, aiming at modifying specific aspects of production, consumption, and distribution. Planning may finally concern a *method* of improved decision making, predicated on the analyses of quantitative relations between goals and instruments and aiming at the most appropriate choice among the latter with the view to obtaining an optimal result.[30] The movement for national economic planning of the mid-1970s, promoted in the United States with the goal of achieving full employment and growth, had been initiated, as we said, by the Initiative Committee of leading businessmen supported by a number of well-known economists and by various congressmen and their staffs.[31] It aimed explicitly at enacting measures going beyond Keynesianism. As Senator Jacob K. Javits, the cosponsor of S1795, put it, the proposed Economic Planning Board must consider "the implications of a lower economic growth in employment opportunities and the educational system. The manipulation of aggregate demand is inadequate to deal with such a problem. . . . Planning offers the American people a road map to national objectives."[32] While it was not entirely clear from the wording of the bill what kind of planning its promoters had in mind, one may surmise that they aimed at some form of indicative planning—like the ones in high fashion in Europe in the 1950s and 1960s—but with priority for the mandated federal spending programs and federally designed public jobs created explicitly to cover employment shortfalls. Hardly had the 1975–76 movement for national economic planning died out, than a new "planning" drive took its place: a drive for establishing ad hoc governmental institutions capable of centrally controlling, stimulating, and pruning industrial activities; a drive for putting the government in the position of requiring industry to engage in certain types of production in exchange for special aid; a drive for formulating an "industrial strategy" with a view to systematizing the aggregate impact of government's activities and interventions with respect to industry. Aiming to "revitalize" manufacturing, institutionalize "wheeling and dealing" on behalf of society, channel investment in order to hasten the growth of high-tech industries and cushion the fall of "mature" industries, the proponents of institutional change and of "strategies" of industrialization had one central preoccupation in mind: to better counteract—while at the same time to imitate—Japan's Ministry of International Trade and Industry (MITI). The latter, supposedly, was smoothing the way for the industries it expected to be that country's "cutting edge" in future world markets.

The movement to increase government's role in orchestrating a great forward push for manufactures reached its peak in the early 1980s. Among its main advocates were Lester Thurow, of the Sloan School of Management at Massachusetts Institute of Technology, Amitai Etzioni (a sociologist and employee in the Carter administration), and Robert B. Reich of the School of Government at Harvard University. Stating that we were "England in 1900 . . . already slipping rapidly relative to the other advanced industrial countries," Thurow asserted that we had to learn from the Japanese *where* to go and from the French *what* instruments to use. He suggested that we needed "an elite group in bureaucracy that says: Hey, this is vital, even though the public is not concerned by it or the problem isn't visible yet"; a government capable of "practic[ing] triage and kill[ing] off" weak companies unable "to develop the new products needed to fight off Komatsu"; the "national equivalent of a corporate investment committee," a kind of updated version of the Reconstruction Finance Corporation—in short, centralized institutions "with the kind of clout that can be used in the American economy."[33] Etzioni claimed that overconsumption and underinvestment during the 1950–80 decades had created a "maintenance gap" that could be bridged only if resources were released to the private economy but channeled to the capital goods sectors and to the expansion of infrastructure.[34] Reich —whose 1983 book, *The Next American Frontier*, was viewed by the Democratic leadership as a part of the party's 1984 presidential platform— affirmed that the U.S. needed to regain "an institutional capacity to view industries as a whole and to fashion policies that complement and support one another" in lieu of its industrial policies "formulated in countless bargaining arenas administered haphazardly." It needed to remove its "ideological blinders" concerning the notion that "the government should refrain from interfering in the market," put an end to the irrelevant debates about the "artificial categories . . . free market or centralized national planning," and realize that the true choice it faced was between protection or "coordinated industrial policies" helping both the emerging new industries and the declining old ones to adjust to new conditions. In sum, Reich suggested the need for a kind of return to a *sui generis* mercantilist centralized institutional control, with an appropriate high-tech strategy: "We have contrived for 200 years and more to decentralize economic power in order to avoid just the kind of authority that we are probably going to need to make this [government] agency capable of negotiating quid-pro-quos with various industries. . . . We have forgotten that government can indeed act strategically in a very positive way to strengthen a nation's industrial competitiveness."[35]

A number of prominent economists rebutted the proposals advanced by the advocates of industrial policies. They rejected as dangerous the creation of an "elite bureaucracy" and of "super-boards" empowered to pick winners and bail out losers, and they noted that the surest way to multiply subsidies and protectionist measures was to legitimize them under the heading of "industrial policy." Robert M. Solow, for instance, pointed out that the hallmark of industrial policy was selectiveness and that "how selection is to be made is what differentiates one version of industrial policy from another." In the proposed schemes, a super-agency—say, an updated Reconstruction Finance Corporation—would receive requests from companies and decide on subsidies by negotiations case-by-case: thus, "to a very large extent, successes would be created by the agency, not discovered by it."[36] Enormous pressures would be brought to bear on such agencies. Answering a specific industrial policy proposal emanating from a group headed by investment banker Felix Rohatyn, Irving Shapiro, former chairman of Du Pont, and Lane Kirkland, head of the AFL-CIO, which called for a development bank with federal and private funding primarily to help revive old industries, the *New York Times* remarked in an appropriately entitled editorial "Industrial Policy—Industrial Politics": "Conventional political pressures could all too easily bring damaging remedies that favor one industry or region over another, or invoke protectionist measures, at enormous costs to consumers and competition."[37] With reference to this kind of process, the former chairman of the Council of Economic Advisers, Charles L. Schultze, noted that its true results would be "resources . . . misallocated, incentives for industrial efficiency reduced, and competitive forces blunted." Actually, "we know precious little about identifying before the fact a 'winning' industrial structure. . . . The winners emerge from a very individualistic search process, only loosely governed by broad national advantages in relative labor, capital, or natural resource costs. . . . The likely outcome of an industrial policy that encompassed some elements of both 'protecting the losers' and 'picking the winners' is that the losers would back subsidies for the winners in return for the latter's support on issues of trade protection," cogently concluded Schultze.[38]

"Industrial policy," as defined by Thurow and Reich, was warmly espoused by the Democratic candidate in the presidential election of 1984, Walter F. Mondale. But it went down to defeat with him and, because of that, was proclaimed "dead"—but, as it turned out, prematurely. It reappeared indeed soon under a new brand name, "national competitiveness."

(iii) **Deregulation and "Competitiveness."** From the early 1970s a *regulatory reform* movement gained increasing influence both in the government and in the business community. Paradoxically, this movement, first directed exclusively against so-called "old style regulations," began to gain ground precisely as a wave of "new style" or "social regulations"— concerning environmental controls, workers' health and safety, and consumer product safety—started to extend rapidly to entire industrial sectors. Eventually, the "new style" regulations also came to be challenged, as we shall see later on. Four successive presidents, Nixon, Ford, Carter, and Reagan, were to take an active role in promoting regulatory reform and were to send numerous bills on this topic to Congress. In time, stockbrokers' fees, railroads, trucks, buses, airlines, petroleum, telecommunications, cable television, radio stations, air cargo service, savings and loans institutions, banks, securities issuers, and other industries were to be deregulated in varying degrees.[39] The demand for deregulation, or for reductions in the scope of regulation, was justified on the grounds that regulations were extremely costly, obsolete, contradictory, and were resulting in misallocation of resources, slower technological advances, and higher prices.[40] Moreover, regulatory reform provided an appropriate way of reducing inflationary pressures, removing restraints on competitive markets, and reacting to the popular objective, smaller government. Phasing out policies and regulations that restrained competition, restricted production, and raised prices would make the economy freer, more flexible, and more competitive. Launched successfully in the 1970s, competitiveness, in addition to deregulation and the removal of various market restrictions, became a convenient label for resuscitating and remodeling "industrial policies" and for reorienting the policies affecting "the ability of U.S. industry to mobilize capital resources effectively to compete with other trading nations" (read Japan).[41]

When the 1984 presidential election seemed to have sealed the fate of the Thurow-Reich proposal for a national "industrial" policy, the idea actually migrated to the states where, as the managing editor of *Harvard Business Review*, Alan M. Webber, said, "it took root not as industrial policy but as *in state-level economic strategies.*"[42] In certain states the state governments made decisive efforts to invest in education and in workers' training, to improve infrastructure, to provide venture capital to entrepreneurs, to reduce taxes and thereby provide implicit subsidies, and to promote state products in new domestic and foreign markets. On the basis of the evident success achieved along this way by certain states, Michigan or Massachusetts, for instance, the proposal for a global "competitiveness strategy" (read industrial policy) regained strength. Thus, a president's Commission on Industrial Competitiveness, established in June 1983, recommended at the beginning of 1985 a string of proposals, some of which were highly reminiscent of the Thurow-Reich suggestions. The commission recommended notably: creation of a federal Department of Science and Technology "to promote national policies for research and technological innovation"; creation of "R&D partnerships" between the government and private companies; the restructuring of the tax system "that would lower the bias against savings and investment and against specific uses or users of capital"; improvement of education, particularly in engineering and business, and the encouragement of employee training and retraining; changes "in policies affecting trade performance, trade policymaking formation, antitrust policy, export controls and trade law remedies for foreign trade practices that adversely affect America's ability to compete."[43] This comprehensive and ambitious "strategy" was not followed, however, but the pressures for such policies have not lost strength and are quite likely to become a serious political factor in the near future.

THE SHIFT TOWARD NEW PRIORITIES

A solid link had been established during the New Deal between the government's policy and the economic objectives of full employment and growth. Deflation then affected the economy, and the main preoccupation of the government was to "reflate" the economy. In the post–World War II years successive recessions (unemployment) and inflations started to loom larger on the horizon, and the main preoccupation of successive administrations was to avoid these pitfalls while insuring stable growth. Notwithstanding changes in philosophies, emphases, and tactics from one administration to the next, the New Deal link survived. The Great Stagflation shattered the confidence of both the policy makers and the public in the government's capacity to achieve simultaneously full employment, stability, and steady growth. While under Presidents Ford and Carter the federal government's involvement in the economy continued to grow along traditional lines—namely via increased spending in a recession—it was clear by then that a substantial portion of the public perceived the government as being too large, its involvement in the economy as too extensive, its budgets as growing too fast, and its deficits as a major cause of persistent inflation. The social program of the Great Society, which had expanded the scope of welfare initiated by the New Deal and which had promised to remove poverty, upgrade education, and restore urban quality, seemed in less than a decade strangely anachronistic. It was by then "looked on as a failure or, at best, as delivering far less than originally promised."[44]

Continuous policy hesitations and alternations of promises, regrets, and then retractions seemed to become the rule of the presidency under Ford and Carter. A promise to fight resolutely against inflation was followed at short notice by tax increases and a rapid return of fire against recession; announcements of tax cuts were followed by cancellation of these same announcements; the stressing of the need for massive "deregulation" was accompanied by expanding "new style" restrictions. Policy reversals and obvious uncertainty about how to manage the economy in the puzzling surroundings of combined unemployment and inflation (when the trade-off between them had ceased to operate) finally prepared the terrain for a deep change in policy orientation and in government priorities as well. Let us recall briefly the disturbing reversals that ultimately led to this deep change.

When the presidency was transferred from Richard M. Nixon to Gerald R. Ford at the beginning of August 1974, the new president affirmed that inflation and energy were to be his paramount problems. He asserted the need for "fiscal and monetary discipline" and in October 1974 proposed a tax surcharge as an anti-inflationary measure. But by the beginning of 1975, apparently alarmed by the persistence of the Great Recession that by then was in fact drawing to an end, he shifted the emphasis of his policy from "whip inflation now" (WIN) to tax cuts prompted by the need to improve the economic outlook and to create jobs. While he continued to assert the necessity to slow down the rate of spending, and while he pointed with dismay to the rapid increases of transfer payments to individuals, he now proposed an anti-recession tax cut of $16 billion. "I recognize," said the president, that this "adds to an already large Federal deficit [and] might delay achieving price stability. But a prompt tax cut is essential."[45] In his budget proposal, which included a sizable deficit, the president noted: "I regret that my budget and tax proposal will mean bigger deficits temporarily, for I have always opposed deficits. We must recognize, however, that if the economic recovery does not begin soon, the Treasury will lose anticipated receipts and incur even larger deficits in the future."[46] Congress responded with a tax cut of $21 billion. Because of this tax cut and of an associated one-time increase in Social Security payments, real disposable income rose sharply in the middle of 1975. The president's *Economic Report* of January 1976 suggested again that the same policy of tax cuts, hopefully accompanied by budget restraints on spending, would be continued in 1976 even though the economy had bottomed out of the recession. He proposed notably a new annual tax cut (of $28 billion), various "cushions" for unemployment, and finally, the expansion of regulatory reform in order to achieve "a better combination of market competition and responsible government regulation."[47] Congress responded by increasing spending more than the president had bargained for. In his last *Economic Report* of January 1977, after complaining that Congress had decided "to increase spending far more than I wanted and to cut taxes far less than I wanted," the president attempted to resort systematically to measures that were to be baptized five years later as the "great supply-side revolution": he proposed "a series of permanent tax rate reductions" along with various tax cuts for business destined "to encourage the investment that will mean good steady jobs for our expanding labor force."[48] The *Annual Report* of the Council of Economic Advisers attached to this *Report* contained also some interesting corrections concerning two well-established concepts in the literature of the council: the first concerned the "full employment" budget; the second, the estimate of "potential output." As we already know, President Nixon had vowed in July 1970 that he would "never violate" one basic rule for the budget, namely that "expenditures must never be allowed to exceed the revenues that the tax system would produce at reasonably full employment" defined as implying 4 percent unemployment. This "essential discipline of an upper limit of the spending at all times," however, started to be questioned from 1974 on, when it was pointed out that the level of the full employment revenues was after all not the only relevant consideration for spending and that the 4 percent criterion itself was debatable. By 1975 there was a return, at least in words, to the old-time religion of a balanced budget. The notion of potential output, much in use in the 1960s, had been based on the assumption of full utilization of capital and land, accompanied by a 4 percent unemployment rate taken as a target to be reached by appropriate policies. The new estimates of the potential introduced in 1977 included both a benchmark for capital utilization—namely a rate of capacity utilization of 86 percent—and a rate of unemployment—pushing at the time toward 5 percent. These changes were recognized as "major improvements" by President Carter's Council of Economic Advisers, which eventually perfected further the notion of the potential by taking into account trends in productivity and in the growth rate of the labor force. The concept of potential output, as defined in the 1960s, had been tied to the notion of full employment, a goal to be reached by closing the "gap" between the actual and the potential. As modified in the 1970s, the notion of the potential acquired more economic sophistication but lost in the process its original connotation.[49]

During the 1976 presidential campaign, Jimmy Carter criticized Ford's "timid" objective of achieving only a modest noninflationary growth, at a time when unemployment was hovering around 7.5 percent. Early in his first year in office, President Carter proposed to stimulate growth by a package of tax cuts for 1977 and 1978 (for longer-term job creation). After some delays, the 1977 tax cut was cancelled; the president now felt that the country needed more than various isolated measures.[50] It needed an "economic strategy . . . to restore full prosperity." This strategy would aim simultaneously at the adoption of an effective national energy plan to reduce dependence on imports and the deficit in the balance of payments; at a reduction in federal spending and in the federal deficit; at a decrease in taxes, accompanied by tax reforms to promote capital expansion and enhance productivity; at an improvement in the programs concerning "structural unemployment among the disadvantaged"; at a reduction in inflation by a deceleration in wage and price increases and an overhauling of outmoded regulations. With such measures output could increase by 4.5 to 5 percent, unemployment could be reduced by one-half to one percentage point each year, the rate of inflation could be lowered, and, finally, the international "climate" could be improved by promoting economic recovery throughout the world.[51]

The second *Economic Report* of the president, however, had to change radically the course of economic policy: once again inflation had the top priority, given the new OPEC oil price increases which dimmed the prospects for growth. Further, the growth rate of potential output for 1973–78 had been only in the order of 3 percent annually, and the same rate could be projected for 1978–83. The downward revision of potential output reflected an actual fall in productivity growth which, during the years considered, had slowed down to 1 percent per year. The recovery from the Great Recession of 1973–75 had been completed in 1978, and a switch had to be made now "from efforts to strengthen growth in economic activity to measures to restrain inflation." This required fiscal and monetary discipline, efforts to contain the expansion of aggregate demand—the course of fiscal policy had shifted toward restraint during 1978—and the reinforcement of the voluntary wage and price program by the inclusion of "an explicit numerical ceiling for wage and fringe benefit increases as well as a price deceleration standard for individual firms." This complex stop-and-go program, which obviously added new restrictions, was accompanied by the promise that the administration would continue to dismantle regulations in other directions (for example, surface transportation) and that it would make sure that both the design of individual regulations and their cost effectiveness would be tightly controlled.[52] This second *Economic Report* contained in fact more than the explicit recognition of the dangers of inflation: it included also a short but telling epitaph for the expansionary-minded Keynesian policies pursued by the Democratic administration. This was formulated at the highest policy level by a Democratic-oriented Council of Economic Advisers, then composed of Charles L. Schultze, Lyle E. Gramley, and William D. Nordhaus. Indeed, the council's *Annual Report* stated clearly that the problem of "structural unemployment," which represented "an unacceptable waste of economic resources and a severe social problem[,] . . . cannot be dealt with by an expansive aggregate demand policy without generating further inflationary resources." Continuous efforts to avoid recessions and the growth of stagflation had indeed blunted the tools of the "fiscal revolution" of the 1960s. Wage and price increases remained "relatively inflexible in the face of slack demand. . . . Reductions in output and major increases in unemployment are no longer as effective in slowing the rate of wage and price increases. The resulting loss of output, of jobs, and of human dignity pays only modest dividends in lower inflation."[53] Unwittingly, the administration resorted to an ill-advised imposition on consumer credit that backfired in a large and unexpected way. Consumer spending fell drastically, and a sharp recession gripped the country by the beginning of 1980. The recession, which lasted six months, was followed by a spurt of growth, while the annual rate of inflation continued to rise to a new peak.[54] (See figure 4a.)

The Council of Economic Advisers' *Annual Report* for 1979, transmitted to Congress in January 1980, recalled that the 1978 Humphrey-Hawkins Full Employment and Balanced Growth Act, enacted with the support of the Carter administration, had set "interim goals" of 4 percent overall unemployment (3 percent for adults) and 3 percent for inflation for 1983. These solemn but hollow promises duly re-registered, the *Report* added that the indicated unemployment goal would be deferred for 1985 and the inflation goal to 1986. This, however, could not be achieved "by relying solely on aggregate demand policies." The goals required a continued application of restraint in monetary and fiscal policies, compliance with voluntary pay and price standards, improved productivity, reduction of impacts from outside inflationary shocks, regulatory reforms, and many other things. The task set now was "a long-term reduction in the nominal growth of GNP" (namely, aggregate spending).[55]

The council's *Annual Report* for 1980, transmitted to Congress with what turned out to be Carter's valedictory *Report*, noted that the most important challenge to U.S. economic policy was indeed the persistence of inflation in the face of high unemployment and slack production. It then added that the costs imposed on society when demand restraint clashes with the downward insensitivity of wages and prices raised the following issues. How large were the costs that society was willing to bear in order to bring down inflation? And, could policies be designed that would reduce inflation faster and with smaller losses in output and employment? The main conclusion the council drew was that realistically the pace of nominal GNP growth (aggregate spending) "will undoubtedly need to fluctuate along a declining trend." The necessary restraint on the growth of aggregate demand will mean inevitably sustained slack in the economy and will result in a period of relatively slow growth in production and employment.[56] Jimmy Carter, who had come onto the presidential scene blaming Gerald Ford for having the "timid" goal of achieving only modest noninflationary economic growth, left the presidency urging noninflationary slow growth for years to come.

It was now the turn of the Republican candidate, Ronald Reagan, to confront Carter's "timidity" with a daring "Strategy for Economic Growth and Stability" in the 1980s. Reagan's strategy, put together by a group of prominent advisers (including Alan Greenspan and George Shultz, the future Secretary of State), blended in a somewhat unexpected mixture the approaches of the traditional conservative Republicans with those of the eclectic supply-side economists. It posited a smaller, decentralized government (in favor of the states), reduced federal spending and lower taxes, a stronger military along with the reduction of "waste" (welfare), control of money and credit, a balanced budget, regulatory relief, and confidence in a policy "that will not change from month to month." The mixture of higher spending for the military, lower taxes, and a promised balanced budget—characterized by George Bush, Reagan's competitor and eventual running mate, as "voodoo economics"—gained, however, wide public acceptance. President Reagan's Inaugural Address delivered on January 20, 1981, rang out the famous phrase: "In this present crisis, government is not the solution to our problem. Government is the problem"—a slogan tempered a little further down by the explanation that the president did not want "to do away with government" but only to make it "work with us, not over us."

On February 18, 1981, the new administration submitted its program to Congress in a document entitled "America's New Beginning: A Program for Economic Recovery." The program developed the principles presented during the presidential campaign. It stressed the need for spending control, while strengthening defense and "preserving" (actually setting the role and scope of) the "social safety nets" with a view to drastically cutting entitlements in order to eliminate "unintended" benefits. It emphasized the necessity of reducing the marginal tax rates for individuals across the board, 10 percent per year for the next 3 years, starting July 1, 1981, and of providing as investment incentives for business an accelerated cost recovery system for machines, equipment, and structures. It proposed to terminate certain regulatory agencies (for example, the Council on Wage and Price Stability created in 1974), to deregulate certain prices, postpone pending regulations, and institute various rules reforms (standard economic analyses of all significant regulations). Finally, it indicated that the growth of money and credit would be reduced from 1980 levels to one-half those levels by 1986, thus reducing the federal deficit financing and achieving "a balanced budget in 1984 and in the years that follow."[57]

Ever since, no matter what happened to his proposals in Congress, the president has not deviated either from his program or from its underlying assumptions. At first, the congressional Democrats, who were stymied by his large electoral victory, disoriented by their own defeat, and confused by the apparent intractability of Stagflation, left much of the president's program pass through Congress virtually unopposed. The president felt that the road to full victory was open. The cornerstone of his policy, the Economic Recovery Tax Act, was indeed signed into law in August 1981. The president saluted its passage as implying a fundamental reorientation of our taxes from a system "used to redistribute income" (read, as one conceived by the Democrats from Franklin D. Roosevelt on, to create the basis of the welfare state) to one restructured "to encourage people to work, save, and invest more."[58] Yet, already noticeable in May 1981, a widening split started to develop between the president's desires and inclinations and the opinions and constraints of an increasing number of congressmen. Typically, after having achieved its early victory in Congress and seen the passage of much of its spending cuts, the administration lost a decisive battle over its requested cuts in Social Security benefits (concerning reduction of benefits extended to early retirees and deferment of cost-of-living adjustments). In some respects, Congress's increasing resistance to the proposals of the administration not only brought to a halt the progress of some parts of its program but also accented various centrifugal tendencies within the president's own group of advisers. In December 1981 the director of the Office of Management and Budget, David A. Stockman, by that time viewed as the very embodiment of budget cuts and of budget "rationality," asserted publicly that the administration's budget cuts had been no more than a hastily improvised, haphazard set of proposals, often the result of miscalculations and of bluster, that had "everyone fooled for a while."

The president and his advisers swallowed hard Stockman's strange confession, and things seemed to go on as before. The official documents continued to stress the same ideas and principles to which the president was indeed faithful. But Democratic congressmen started to grope for alternatives, proposal by proposal, detail by detail, without, however, arriving at any overall conception clearly opposed to the administration's choices. In his "State of the Union" address on January 26, 1982, the president even felt that he could congratulate Congress for having joined him in cutting government spending, reducing and restructuring taxes, returning power and resources to the states, cutting regulations, restoring "military safety," and creating a federal strike force to cut out waste and fraud.[59] In the budget message delivered soon afterwards he asserted that he was "reordering [the country's] priorities" and that "where government had passively tolerated the swift, continuous growth of automatic entitlements and had actively shortchanged the national security, a long overdue reordering of priorities had begun, entitlement growth is being checked, and the restoration of our defenses is under way."[60] Actually, by that time the president had already lost much of his grip on Congress, and much of his program was in deep trouble, as we will see below.

The president's first *Economic Report*, transmitted to Congress in February 1982, was characterized by James Tobin as a "manifesto of counter-revolution" (counter to the neo-Keynesian economics of the past). Actually, the manifesto repeated the already familiar presidential theses that the growth of the federal government's spending, taxing, and "meddling" in the economy had been the source of all economic difficulties, that stagflation had been a consequence of mistaken theories and policies, and that the "foremost" task ahead was "reducing the role of the Federal Government in all its dimensions." The *Annual Report* of the Council of Economic Advisers—a council chaired by Murray L. Weidenbaum—added a blend of monetarist and supply-side theoretical underpinnings to all this. It stated notably that the major error of the past administrations (particularly of the late 1960s and early 1970s) had been to neglect "long-term effects" while emphasizing short-term "fine-tuning" from quarter to quarter; that because the rate of inflation was slow to adjust, the policymakers had acted as if "there was no reason to expect inflation to increase significantly until a high level of employment had been reached"; that successive administrations had failed to notice that wage and price controls and guideposts were inefficient; that they had moreover failed to take account of the effects of tax and income-transfer policies on unemployment and potential output; and that they had refused to see that a decrease in money growth was the necessary tool to end inflation. The *Report* finally rejected "paternalism" as a basis for policy, since government commands cannot do a better job than an individual can do in regard to his own welfare.[61] The budget proposal for fiscal year 1983 (to which we alluded before) drew attention to the increasing danger of the budget deficit. In planning the budget the president had indeed been faced by a rising deficit despite the unprecedented cuts in nondefense spending—a deficit due to the recession, the tax cuts, and the growing defense outlays. He rejected, however, the alternative of a tax increase perhaps because he believed as one of his adversaries conjectured (though there is no evidence for this) that "the economic damage to private incentives from the reversal of basic policy would be greater than the gain from reducing the deficit."[62]

The *Annual Report* of the Council of Economic Advisers—a council then chaired by Martin S. Feldstein—accompanying the second *Economic Report of the President*, transmitted to Congress in February 1983, asserted also that the budget deficit had henceforth become "a major problem for the American economy" and that without the newly proposed cuts—of virtually every domestic program—the U.S. would experience "a series of deficits that would consume more than 6 percent of GNP in each of the next 6 years." The *Report* then added that the high unemployment rate had a cyclical and a structural component, the first of which was certainly a major problem, but only a transitory one that would be corrected by the recovery process. The second required continuous improvements of the "functioning of the labor markets." In any case "it would be imprudent to use macroeconomic policies to reduce the unemployment rate below its inflation threshold level of 6 to 7 percent."[63] It may be interesting to recall here that by then, that is in the first year of economic recovery after the recession, unemployment still involved over 10 million people, some industrial branches were in deep distress (steel, auto, home building, exports) and the level of economic activity was about 5 percent higher than at the 1979 peak.

On the eve of the introduction of the budget for 1984, only some 60 percent of the president's dollar-saving proposals had been adopted in some form by Congress. He had obtained most of the cuts he had sought early in his first term, concerning food stamps, unemployment insurance, subsidies for non-needy students, abuses of Medicaid, aid to families with dependent children, cost-of-living adjustments for certain retirees, trade adjustment assistance benefits, but, as we have recalled, he had been rebuffed concerning Social Security. Moreover, Congress had appropriated more money than he had requested and had made more modest cuts than he had proposed. His success with Congress fell sharply from 1981 to 1982 and from then on. According to John William Ellwood of Dartmouth College, the president "got approximately 85 to 90 percent of the dollar savings he wanted in 1981, but he got no more than 30 percent of what he wanted in 1982."[64] The impetus of the "revolution" was largely spent by the turn of 1983. The divergence between the administration and Congress increased as Congress tried repeatedly to get the president to compromise on deficit reduction, on the 1982 tax increase, on defense-spending growth.

Yet the third *Economic Report* of the president could proclaim with self-congratulatory satisfaction: "Reducing the rate of inflation was my most immediate economic goal when I arrived in Washington. . . . The inflation rate has declined dramatically over the past three years. . . . Americans can again have confidence in the value of the dollar."[65] This was accompanied by a loose fiscal policy combined with high interest rates, a mix not tried previously for any length of time. The genesis of this policy lay in the administration's fiscal policies set in 1981 and in the new approaches to monetary policy adopted by the Federal Reserve Board under the Carter administration in October 1979. For the first two years of that program, fiscal policy was either outright restrictive or not stimulative; from 1983 on it became stimulative.[66] The Federal Reserve managed the anti-inflation recessions of 1980 through 1982 and brought in the 1983 recovery by putting on the monetary brakes and then relaxing them when the economy became sluggish. According to James Tobin, it was the Chairman of the Fed, Paul A. Volcker who "earned a place in history as the triumphant general of the war against inflation, but the victory will be tarnished if its legacy is permanent high unemployment."[67] Be that as it may, the general could not have won his war without the acquiescence of the commander-in-chief. In any case, politics being politics, the indicated *Report* blamed Congress for the continuously rising budget deficit and for its reluctance to accept a "downpayment reduction program" of this deficit, namely some $100 billion, that would restore public confidence in the ability of the political system to deal with the problem. By then, the priorities established by the president had been carried out at least in part: military spending had risen from less than 23 percent of the budget in 1981 to close to 27 percent in 1984, while spending on nonmilitary programs had fallen from over 67 percent to about 59 percent. The deficit, however, was also rising, with no end in sight.

In the fourth and last *Economic Report* of his first term—with which we conclude the analysis of the Reagan "revolution"—the president and his advisers drew their own balance sheet of the administration's four years in office. On one side of the ledger, they noted that inflation had declined from about 9.0 percent per year in 1981 to about 3.5 percent in 1984, that unemployment had declined during 1983–84, and that the rate of growth of the GNP had reached a higher level than before. Stating that the welfare of society did not depend solely on the "quantity of goods and services produced," the *Report* added that for healthy growth it was more important to pay attention to incentives rather than to the desires to "soften the shocks resulting to individuals" from the growth process itself. On the other side of the ledger, the president and his advisers deplored that federal expenditures had continued to grow— a fact which they characterized as "the most serious problem facing the American economy." On the same side of the ledger, the president also included the deficit, "which cannot grow indefinitely in relation to poten- tial receipts." And the *Annual Report* of the Council of Economic Advisers added that to constrain the growth in expenditures and to reduce federal borrowing, we had either to reduce the growth of noninterest expenditures, broaden the tax base to permit a future tax reduction, or simply, as a last resort, accept the unacceptable, namely "increase tax revenues if necessary to finance the level of government that is broadly supported." History would eventually decide if these past presidential years had been only a "volatile episode in which gains from improved policies were later lost" or whether they had constituted a period "fol- lowed by an era of substantially improved economic performance."[68] The essentials of the entire Reagan program had indeed been laid out and tested during these four years. They elicited then both the approvals and the criticisms to which we turn immediately below.

THE CONTROVERSY ABOUT "REAGANOMICS"

As we saw, at the heart of Reagan's philosophy was the idea that the most important cause of our economic problem was the government itself. In the words of "America's New Beginning: A Program for Economic Recovery," the federal government had "greatly contributed" to the persistence of inflation, had discouraged work, innovation, and incentives with its tax system, had contributed to the fall in productivity and the increase in economic inefficiency, and, finally, had engendered uncertainty and fluctuations with its erratic policies. The program promised accordingly to reduce the role of the government in all its dimensions, to limit federal spending and balance the budget, cut taxes, deregulate the economy, and assure a predictable and steady growth of money supply. It thus combined the objectives of the fiscal conservatives, the supply-side economists, the advocates of deregulation, and the monetarists, in a program positing shifts in national priorities and changes in the use of the fiscal and monetary instruments.

The posited shift in priorities involved the de-emphasis of government in favor of the free market, along with transfer of resources from the civilian sectors to defense, from the federal to the state and local authorities, from the beneficiaries of social programs to the taxpayers. The de-emphasis of government's role derived from Reagan's contention that the government was "pernicious" and that most individuals, except the truly needy, could fend for themselves in the free market. In opposition to these contentions, Richard A. Musgrave argued that the president was "dead wrong" in his view that "our problem will not be solved by government, the government is the problem." Freedom, added Musgrave, "cannot be seen apart from the broader concept of a just society, and government is a necessary partner in securing it."[69]

The administration stressed the need for a "safety net" for the economy's casualties but insisted that aid could come better from private helping networks. The administration simply ignored its traditional role of providing "purchasing power" in order to stabilize the economy. Moreover, the specific efforts to divest certain chunks of public responsibility in favor of the private sector and to redesign other blocks of responsibility did not yield either efficient or consistent solutions. Proposed cuts in various service programs, which allegedly could be better provided by the private sector (mostly by nonprofit organizations), were dumped on organizations that evidently were themselves dependent on federal support and that by then were affected by federal budget reductions. The "redesign"—really the reduction—of certain general and training programs (for example, the Comprehensive Employment and Training Act superseded by the Job Training Partnership Act) served ultimately fewer people and even less the disadvantaged. The "truly needy" were actually ignored. The administration's wide-ranging plan to substitute vouchers for more direct provision from the private market for certain populations (concerning food, jobs, education) encountered widespread opposition and finally expanded only in some areas (particularly in housing).[70] "The starting point," remarked Musgrave with respect to all these divestiture policies, "should not be a presumption—as suggested by President Reagan's demeaning references to the public sector—that public programs are useless while private uses of funds are productive. Rather, alternative uses of funds and resources should be weighted against each other at the margin."[71]

Control of federal outlays in order to give prominence to defense simultaneously was to be achieved with a tax cut said to offset eventually a potential increase in the deficit by built-in revenue gains as the economy returned to high employment. The scheduled large increases for a wide range of defense programs garnered as usual great support, both inside and outside Congress, while criticism was confined to specific strategy aspects and to the technical choices, which most of the public could not grasp. Some contended that the Reagan defense program was "well within the evolutionary boundaries of policy development in the late 1970s." Others asserted that the new administration had broken loose "from the past consensus concerning the scope and instrumentalities of conventional containment" and aimed not only "for ability to launch controlled nuclear counterattacks" but also to secure the "earliest termination of hostilities on terms favorable to the United States."[72] Whatever the truth might be in this regard, what ought to be noted here is that all this was predicated economically on what Paul A. Samuelson had called "a game of Russian roulette." If the revenue slashes (due to the tax cuts) were to induce commensurate slashes in nondefense welfare spending, the increase in military spending could be achieved without an increasing deficit.[73] But first, the cutbacks in nondefense programs proved infeasible on the scale proposed; second, additional outlays arose through rising interest rate and recession effects; and, finally, the expected built-in revenue increases turned into losses because of a deepening recession and then into large budget deficits.

In President Reagan's view the proper role of the government with respect to social programs was the provision of basic welfare benefits for those who cannot work, the maintenance of temporary benefits for the unemployed, and the allowance of basic health and retirement benefits to the aged. Moreover, the public sector's functions were assumed to be better performed not at the federal but at the state and local level. The devolution of responsibilities within the government was initially embodied in proposals to consolidate ninety categories of programs into four block grants, with a 25 percent reduction in federal funding. Congress accepted a less ambitious consolidation and a less drastic cut in funding. Attempts to carry out devolutions to the states via "swap and turnback programs," for example, devolution to the states of financial responsibility for food stamps and aid to families with dependent children in exchange for the federal government's taking over Medicaid, encountered the opposition of the states. In the end, the administration, "rebuffed in this grand vision of federalism . . . settled for a mixed bag of carrots and sticks that would encourage states to control expenditures more tightly under jointly funded entitlement programs."[74] The very concept of devolution was dismissed by Musgrave as anachronistic: "We do not form an idyllic society of small rural communities." We have large government but also large corporations, modern industries, banks, etc. Common policies and business cycles affect us all even though regional patterns may differ: "It is only fair . . . that the consequences of joint policies be borne jointly."[75]

The idea of federal social outlays spiraling out of control was put forward in order to justify draconian policy measures concerning welfare in favor of all the taxpayers. Actually, as pointed out by various studies, social spending had indeed increased from the mid-1960s through the mid-1970s but "at rates that could be explained in part by the gradual implementation of new social programs and in part by decisions made by Congress to shield beneficiaries under a number of programs from the accelerating pace of inflation." The rising costs could be attributed only to a limited extent to welfare in the conventional sense of the term: "means-tested social programs accounted for only about one out of ten dollars in federal outlays, and in real terms did not increase during the 1970s." The growth in spending had resulted from the rise in the purchasing power of the elderly, from benefits in kind such as housing assistance, food stamps, and Medicaid, and from experiments with new measures, notably those concerning education and training programs. The Reagan administration succeeded, however, in 1981 in selling "its own welfare reform position to Congress," though it was not able "to fully convince Congress to buy its proposed alternative—mandatory workforce."[76] The closely related thesis that the budget as a whole reflected a "runaway and hemorrhaging condition" was also debatable: actually the expansion of the budget had not been violent and had occurred at a declining rate. A number of economists pointed out in this regard that the adjustments needed as a kind of stabilization policy were more appropriately to be made on the revenue rather than on the expenditure side under condition of inflation, which required higher rather than lower tax rates.[77] This brings us to the heart of the controversy concerning Reagan's macroeconomic program.

The anti-Reaganites challenged the administration's thesis concerning the impact of "fiscal ease *cum* tight money" (actually *cum* low inflation), the policy of rapid dis-inflation, and its overall approaches to real economic growth. According to James Tobin, for instance, the administration's fiscal package of the early 1980s was actually neither stimulative nor contractive. Tobin added that the three years of Kemp-Roth "across the board" tax cuts was both unfortunate and improperly calibrated. Tobin would have preferred that the cuts had aimed at reducing payroll levies and had been accompanied by inducements for dis-inflationary wage and price behavior. Other economists, like Musgrave for instance, complained that the supply-siders' stressing the effects of tax cuts on incentives may have conflicted with the idea of progressive taxation and that the real problem was to use good judgment about the trade-offs between efficiency and equity. Be that as it may, paradoxically, the stimulation of demand with Republican-proposed tax cuts and planned deficits was attacked by the Democrats in Congress, who issued dire warnings against stimulating the economy with tax reductions—at a time when the employment rate was high and capital utilization was low![78] The irony of the situation did not escape either the Keynesians, like Tobin, or the supply-siders, like Paul Craig Roberts. Normally, as Roberts remarked with tongue in cheek, the Keynesians would have pointed out that the deficit could not come down until the employment rate did, making it fruitless to reduce the deficit with austerity measures. In the meantime it was the Republican administration itself that succeeded in making the deficit an issue on which its own fate depended while proving totally unable to do anything about this very deficit.[79]

The serious problem to which most Keynesian economists drew attention was the combination of fiscal ease with tight money. As Tobin put it, the administration had hitched the Paul A. Volcker and his Fed engine at one end of its train and the Stockman-Kemp locomotive at the other end, while telling us that "the economic train will carry us to full employment and dis-inflation at the same time." Actually, tight money was bound to offset the fiscal ease, slow down inflation, cut into jobs and output, raise interest rates, and discourage investment. The high interest rates brought about a huge inflow of foreign capital, pushed up the value of the dollar, engendered foreign trade deficits, and further aggravated the farm crisis and the distress of certain industries. Certain economists of Democratic persuasion—not the Democrats in Congress—clamored for temporary income tax surcharges or for a value-added tax along with further budget cuts, for instance in agricultural price supports, in order to bring down the federal deficit. But these proposals did not generate any responding political echoes.[80]

The great Reagan objective of shrinking the size and scope of the government increasingly eluded the president. Total federal spending continued to climb, reaching higher percentages of the GNP. Reagan did change the composition of the budget substantially, but he could not reduce the total share of the GNP taken by government spending: The president accomplished in this respect only as much as our uniquely dispersed political power permitted.

LEGACIES

Liberal and conservative economists alike agree that the Roosevelt and Reagan presidencies changed the course of the economic order as did no other presidencies in this century. Both Roosevelt's and Reagan's accession to power signified indeed the introduction of critical changes in economic policy. "It is possible that Ronald Reagan's landslide victory in 1980 will be reckoned by historians to be the most important American electoral triumph in the twentieth century—second only to Franklin Roosevelt's 1932 victory over Herbert Hoover that culminated in the New Deal and the welfare state," wrote Paul A. Samuelson.[81] "The election of Ronald Reagan in 1980 signified the end of an era in economic policy that had began almost fifty years earlier," echoed Herbert Stein.[82] The great contrasts between the two presidents have been examined and evaluated on many planes. Perhaps none of these differences was more readily popularized than the alleged supercontrast between Roosevelt, the Democratic champion of the underpriviliged, the advocate of income transfers and of massive state interventions in the economy, the compassionate creator of the welfare state, and Reagan, the Republican champion of business interests, embodiment of conservative economics, the enemy of income transfers (except to agriculture), the partisan of the "reduction of the government in all its dimensions" (excluding of course defense), the demolisher of the foundations of the welfare state and of its bureaucracies. Bold contrasts, however, tend easily to overlook both the conditions in which certain policies are formulated and certain philosophies are accepted by the electorate, as well as the ways in which circumstances and the shifting relationships of power—from one election to the next—between Congress and the presidency tend to bend and adjust policies in their implementation.

In the early 1930s a "threefold economic debacle" engulfed the economy: an apparently unstoppable decline in prices bearing down heavily on agriculture and on the general overload of debt; contracting business activity and a seemingly ever-expanding unemployment along with falling capital values; and a growing paralysis of banking, hampering its ability to play its traditional roles. Simultaneously, the international market was collapsing and each and every country was enacting inward-looking economic policies and strategies. At the time, President Hoover claimed that all our problems were attributable to exogenous shocks that would eventually wear out, while the Democrats pointed an accusing finger toward the Republican policies, and asserted that things could not be righted without the intervention in the economy of an activist government. Economists of various persuasions advocated monetary and banking changes, controls and reorganization of the economy's producing sectors, and various forms of planning. Once in power, Roosevelt groped toward increasing consumption via income transfers, agricultural price supports, wage increases, temporary or more permanent welfare measures, and social insurance. FDR perceived the depression as both an economic and a social issue. His measures did not overcome the depression, though it is generally and erroneously believed that they did. The crucial economic theory formulated at the time, Keynes's *General Theory*, whose stated objectives were to discover what determines actual employment and unemployment and which distinct factors shape consumption and investment, did not emerge from the American experience, though the latter must have played a part in its conception. Be that as it may, the cardinal preoccupations of how to activate the economy and how to avoid its drift toward massive wastage of human and material resources dominated the early postwar years here as well as abroad. Employment never ceased to preoccupy our policy makers. The Full Employment Act of 1946 made explicit the connection between government spending in its full Keynesian meaning and our national objective of full employment. For the next three decades, Keynesianism became an article of faith and its premises were largely accepted by both Democrats and Republicans. Eventually, under President Johnson, some of its implications were extended in new directions concerning welfare.

When the search for solutions "beyond Keynesianism" became imperative as the Great Stagflation unfolded, the Democrats, echoing Herbert Hoover's disclaimers of 1932, asserted that the phenomenon was not the consequence of "mistaken policy based on mistaken theory" but rather the result of "the unprecedented *sequence of shocks*—Vietnam, dollar devaluation, OPEC I in 1973–74, OPEC II in 1979–80." In particular, the two oil supply restrictions and energy price jumps were "the most serious stagflationary jolts of modern peacetime historical experience."[83] It was now the turn of the Republicans to point to mistaken policies rather than to exogenous shocks and to stress the impact of the over-tolerant attitude of the Democrats toward inflation and toward counter-cyclical stimulations and monetary accommodations. From the dawn of the Great Stagflation the political climate had turned against increased stop-and-go policies, against inflation, and against the expanded welfare bureaucracies. There was dissatisfaction with the federal government's "handouts," with its involvement in the economy, with inflation, with stagnation, with the country's apparent weakness in the world, with the seeming purposeless drift of the country. President Reagan acceded to power in conditions totally different from those of the early 1930s. His program, combining as we have seen a number of disparate tenets, had one popular thrust: reducing the government "in all its dimensions" and increasing private investment. While within Reagan's coalition the old-time conservatives looked down on the monetarists, who looked down on the supply-siders, who looked down on everybody else, the president held together his inconsistent coalition by changing policy emphases, shuffling advisers according to what seemed more expedient at the moment, and securing one thing they all desired, namely, the shifting of the country's priorities away from further income redistribution in favor of more business investment—even though the U.S. continued to have a higher inequality in income distribution than many other industrialized countries. The Reagan administration's lack of memory as to the social purposes and implications of FDR's (and of President Johnson's) economic policies was not accidental. It was due to differences in the assumptions behind the two great policy regime changes—FDR's and Reagan's—concerning the economy's activity, the causes and impact of various degrees of unemployment, the nature of and remedy for various social problems. The answers differed between the two presidents about what activates a stagnating economy—broader consumption or more private investment; about what levels of unemployment are actually acceptable (or "tolerable"); and about who, as between the government and various private mechanisms (personal savings and support by charitable private foundations), could provide the "safety nets" needed by the socially disadvantaged and by the old.

President Reagan did not achieve his basic goal, namely the reduction of the size and role of the government. He did not succeed in overcoming unemployment after inflation went down, in reducing welfare as much as he had set out to do, or in always fostering market solutions with regard to the economy's sectors and branches. As we indicated, the balance sheet is clear: the share of the government in GNP increased; unemployment still remained high and intractable as far as certain groups of the population were concerned; welfare strictures remained unchanged in the complex and ambiguous issue of Social Security; the government immersed itself even more deeply than before in subsidies, grants, and loans, not only with respect to agriculture but also in regard to banks and industries of all kinds, including the new high-tech industries, supposedly our cutting edge in the international market. Last but not least, surreptitiously, various forms of protectionism reappeared on the political scene under the new name of "competitiveness" and gained support among not only the "anti-Reaganites."

Yet the president succeeded in perhaps a deeper and subtler sense in what he had set out to do: he bent the course of American's policies; he deepened the already existing doubts about the ability of the government to provide simultaneously and at all times the "great trinity" of economic policy: stability, full employment, and steady growth. He convinced a large part of the body politic of the need for setting limits to government intervention, for considering more carefully the extension of such interventions, for reducing rather than expanding the multiplicity of such intrusion in the economy. Finally, he forced his adversaries to re-evaluate some of the assumptions on which their policies have been based for over a half-century (of "throwing more money at problems") and convinced a large part of the electorate for a time at least that the cumulative consequences of counter-cyclical stimuli may weigh heavily on the present as well as on the future. During his first term, when his program made its historical impact, his popularity remained unchallenged. Shortly afterwards, James Tobin complained that "Reagan had scared the Democrats out of talking about macroeconomic policy. They're basically just buying the Republican conservative allegations that those ideas that stabilized the economy are outmoded and counterproductive. That left the Democrats without any proposals."[84] The political pendulum swings back, yet one wonders whether all this will be entirely forgotten and whether the Democrat commitment to the "principles of the 1930s" has not been significantly weakened.

Contrary to the Great Depression, the Great Stagflation did not generate a widely accepted new theory of economic policy. The most outstanding new way of thinking about policies and the private agents they aim to affect was opened by the rational expectations school. It concerned not only the incorporation of the theory of dynamic games and probability elements into macroeconomics but also the verification of certain limits to what economic policies can and cannot accomplish.[85] As to supply-side theory, even according to prominent Republicans it fell into disrepute, though some of its emphases concerning the reduction of marginal tax rates and broadening the tax base bore fruit in the Tax Reform Act of 1986. (Attempts to reduce government subsidies and regulations, as well as rigidities in labor markets, continue to be made in various parts of the world in the name of supply-side economics.) Out of all these currents and counter-currents, "sophisticated" Keynesianism reemerged as "mainstream economics" but lost in the process the consistency, the elegance, and, above all, the inner confidence that was the hallmark of "simple" Keynesianism in its heyday.

CHAPTER
5

ECONOMIC ADVICE AND POLICY MAKING

LIMITS OF ECONOMICS AS A GUIDE TO PUBLIC POLICY

The role of the government has changed profoundly since the pre-Roosevelt era. The government has come to be held responsible by public opinion for the economy's performance. It has been forced to state what it thinks about whatever happens in the economy and to specify what it proposes to do about matters. The presidents have become the dominant decision makers in economic policy and have assumed an active role in its management, as power has flowed to them from the subordinate executive agencies, the Congress, and the Federal Reserve. Moreover, as Herbert Stein has pointed out, even the language of the government switched after World War II to the language of economics, and the demand for economists increased sharply in Washington. "It was almost as if someone had suddenly decreed that the language of government would be Latin. There would be a great demand for people who could speak Latin. So there was a great demand for people who could speak economics."[1]

Presidents became dependent on advice in economics, perhaps more so than in the other areas of their concern. The organization of presidential advice changed in various ways over time: some presidents tended to rely on advice from people outside the government, others on the advice of their cabinet ministers briefed by their staffs, still others on a combination of outsiders and insiders. The academic economists gained important advisory roles only after World War II. In the prewar years, until the 1930s, the absence of direct academic input in policy formulation was due, to a large extent, to a minimalist conception of the government's functions in the economy. It was also due to the insularity of most academic economists and to the limited prestige of economists

126

among the broad masses of the public. Soon after World War I, Irving Fisher stated that the American Economic Association from its very inception some thirty years earlier had been split between the senior economists influenced by the Manchester School, who thought it "beneath their dignity to engage at all in practical affairs except to cry 'Laissez faire,'" and the younger, enthusiastic economists fresh from their studies in Germany, who hated academic seclusion and who advocated the "practical application of their principles" in the service of the "state."[2] At the time of the Great Depression, however, the role of the economists inside the government was negligible. There were fewer than eight hundred positions in economics in the U.S. government, half of which were filled by economists working at low levels in research in agricultural and business statistics.[3] The New Dealers numbered probably no more than two hundred or three hundred people, mostly young and mostly lawyers and economists, with a scattering from other fields, and mostly in the second and third ranks of the governmental hierarchy.[4] The academic economists exercised influence on certain policy makers and on the top layers of the intellectual community, but they had no serious impact on broad public opinion. As Jacob Viner put it, "the economist . . . has little prestige with the American public, even on those subjects on which he alone has expert knowledge, and the public prefers to take its economics from newspaper editors, politicians, bankers, and men who in happier days were able to accumulate or inherit a million dollars or more."[5] Economic advice came to President Roosevelt from many sources but particularly from his "brain trust," his own top cabinet officers, while certain New Deal measures originated not with the executive directly, but rather with liberal congressmen faithful to the New Deal ideas. By 1939, however, when Lauchlin B. Currie became the first economist in the White House, the New Dealers became a larger group with influence in the higher levels of the administration. Through the war years, the academic economists' influence grew, especially in the planning components of the military services and the new agencies created at the time, particularly in those administering economic controls. Yet even then Congress had enacted a law (the so-called anti-professor amendment) "prohibiting persons from holding policy-making positions in the Office of Price Administration unless they had experience in business or politics" that is, those who "had met a payroll or carried a precinct."[6] Academic economists reached their highest advisory position in government only after World War II, when the Employment Act of 1946 created the president's Council of Economic Advisers (CEA). The act that created the CEA—a council that at times was the outpost of academic economics—simultaneously gave the law's qualified yet explicit support to the crucial Keynesian concept that both employment and output were responsive to policy decisions. This fundamental connection between the creation of the CEA and Keynesian theory largely influenced the destiny of the CEA and its advisory, analytical, and policy-making functions. As we shall see in the next section, the CEA's scope and influence changed appreciably under various presidents. In order to better understand these changes, let us point out briefly, first, the possible limits of economics as a guide to public policy and, second, the complex difficulties raised in the very process of policy advising.

Do economic teachings strongly influence policy making? In the *General Theory*, Keynes had asserted that "the ideas of economists and political philosophers, both when they are right and when they are wrong, are more powerful than is commonly understood." Indeed, he added, "the world is ruled by little else," and "practical men . . . are usually the slaves of some defunct economist."[7] Undoubtedly, the influence of economics has become increasingly pervasive; and as the volume, sophistication, diversity, and complexity of information have increased, the living economists, more numerous than ever, have a better chance to be heard if not always listened to. Of course, this does not mean that their influence always supersedes that of dead economists—particularly when the ideas of the latter were already embodied in certain institutions—or that they reach deeper in the broad strata of public opinion than do those who, as Viner put it, "were able to accumulate or inherit a million dollars or more." Yet, particularly at such critical times as recessions, inflations, growth accelerations, or stagflations, the theories of academic economists do establish the framework and the content of the debates on economic policy and impact in numerous ways on policy-making decisions. The theorists often clash, and the lines of action they suggest differ widely; that, however, is not a sign of weakness but of strength and of continuous search for appropriate answers. The economists exert an extensive influence on government through the "climate of thinking" created by the academic community, through publications, teaching, and the ascension of former students to the highest levels of government.

There are, of course, important areas of economic theory that do not have a direct bearing on policy. And those parts of economic theory that do not supply immediately useful answers to the business of government tend to receive little or no attention, while those that purport to throw light on practical issues tend to command attention and even respect. As Clair Wilcox remarked, there are economic policies that originate not in economics, but in military, political, or social necessities. There are also policies for which economic theories are lacking, and there are theories that may be obsolete when they come to fruition after the phenomena on which they were predicated have ended. Even when economic theory and public policy broadly coincide, certain theoretical views may be set aside by political pressures. Yet the academic economist feels bound to attempt continuously to expand the frontiers of his discipline and to equip it with new analytical tools that may also help in the formulation and evaluation of policies. But better tools and better analysis do not necessarily result in better policy. Governments, under political pressures, "may still follow a course that renders lower benefits at higher costs."[8] Though by their very existence analyses of alternatives do affect the choices that are made, a caveat must always be taken into account: namely that, on a balance of considerations, the economic factors may not turn out to be the most decisive ones.

As we pointed out above, since World War II the number of economists in government has greatly increased. The vast majority is engaged in work related primarily to administrative policies—data collection, processing and analysis in administrative agencies, bureaus, and departments. But, more importantly, the main development in the executive branch since the war has been the change in the *level* of economists. Starting with the CEA, we have had an increasing number of economists of cabinet or subcabinet rank.[9] The Economists are now close to the main centers of power in economic affairs and provide inside economic advice to the president and to his administration, to the Congress and to its committees, and to the Federal Reserve at its highest levels. (Some economists are on the Board of Governors of the Fed.) Outside the government, economic advice is furnished by prominent academic economists who either participated at a certain time in government, or never participated in it, and by certain recognized institutions such as the Brookings Institution, the American Enterprise Institute, the Rand Corporation, and Data Resources. Top policy advisers and top civil servants—Walter W. Heller, Gardner Ackley, Arthur M. Okun, Herbert Stein, George P. Shultz, Charles L. Schultze, and Alice M. Rivlin, for instance—have provided illuminating analyses of the scope and limitations of the inside economic adviser. While the role of the inside adviser in the executive office has varied greatly from president to president (as we shall see below in the detailed analysis of the vicissitudes of the CEA), it is important to keep in mind the key factors that necessarily determine the fundamental framework within which the process of economic advice unfolds. The first concerns the complex relations between adviser and advisee; the second refers to the role of the adviser as representative of the discipline within the government; the third pertains to the role of the adviser with regard to the public and the discipline.

Usually, the adviser and the policy maker approach any given issue from different angles and with a different language, different frames of reference, different objectives, and different considerations with regard to the decisions to be taken. While in principle the economist is concerned first of all with the possible economic alternatives and with their eventual economic consequences, the policy maker is concerned with the political angles of the given issue, the feasibility of the measures to be selected, the appropriate legislative strategy, administrative implementations, and political consequences. "When the adviser wishes to communicate with the lay decision maker he must *translate* from the technical jargon to the vernacular. . . . There is no escaping it: the economic adviser and the policymaker are in a complex human relation entangled in various uncertainties and communicating with each other through an inevitable haze of emotional reactions."[10] Alice M. Rivlin asserts, on the basis of experiences with the Congress, that "economists and political leaders not only miscommunicate, but each accuses the other of incompetence, obfuscation, self-serving motives, and anti-social behavior."[11] Arthur M. Okun, however, remarks on the basis of his experience as economic adviser of President Johnson that while "nobody comes out of graduate school with a Ph.D. in priority setting or applied political ideology," these are the "major tasks in executive's policy making."[12] But he adds that the adviser cannot be effective if he does not operate with "sensitivity and understanding" of the policy maker's values and objectives. Indeed, only when such a coming together exists or develops will the insider's advice be more readily accepted than any other, and the policy maker will find it convenient to examine all the options offered, debate the suggested alternatives, and decide, away from the limelight, on the final proposals.

The inside adviser is not the "messenger" of the *entire* profession in the government. Indeed, he cannot espouse and represent all the divisions that separate economists on macroeconomic issues. As Charles L. Schultze cogently remarked, the adviser in order to be effective cannot and must not be deterred in his work either by the huge uncertainties within which macropolicy operates or by the lack of unity that besets his discipline.[13] Economists differ indeed with respect to macroeconomic theories to the extent of the trade-off among different macro goals and the importance of each of these goals, as well as with respect to the analysis of certain variables and their interrelations. Nevertheless, the economist adviser inside the highest levels of government cannot be oblivious to the debates within his discipline. He operates under the watchful eyes of the entire economic profession. The criticism of these "outsiders" is always a factor that enriches his analysis—if it does not shake his confidence—and often adds depth and interest to the economic documents released by the administration.

The "politicized economists," as Herbert Stein called the most senior economists inside the government, enjoy great public exposure—a privilege that may at times be a source of embarrassment. Some chairmen of the CEA relished being deeply involved in the advocacy of the Presidents they advised. Others tried to preserve their professional integrity by keeping a low public profile. Arthur M. Okun, for instance, fully accepted the responsibility of going public in favor of the policies of

President Johnson; he stated that the adviser cannot "serve two masters"—his president and the economics profession—and that both "the society and the profession" had to recognize that it was in their own interest "to have economists who . . . can have the greatest influence on the inside [of government]."[14] Herbert Stein was less charitable with the advisers who are called forth to "inform" the public. He pointed out that many of these economists are not always "the most candid or best informed" so that one wonders whether their public appearances "are reducing what people don't know more than they are increasing what people know that isn't so."[15] In all fairness one needs to distinguish between ephemeral media appearances (for example, on television), where the "president's man" might be forced to "bite the bullet" and to defend specific policy measures, and the lasting, written documents where the advisers feel the need to weigh carefully all the alternatives and to take account of the divergent views of the profession.

The underlying logic of Keynesian macroeconomic activism was that the instabilities of the private economy could be remedied by government activities and that the adviser knew exactly what these remedies were. The alternative view, put forward in the 1930s and later stressed again by the monetarists and then by the rational expectationists, was that the operations of the private sector were stable and that economic disturbances were the results of government's activism. "Advice" was hence reduced either to the advocacy of submission to certain fixed rules (for example, concerning money supply) or to the expectancy that an optimal equilibrium would be restored automatically. Now, what happens if one assumes not only that the private economy acts efficiently but also that the government does things *sensibly*—or at least with calculation? What then of the economic adviser? Where does he come in? Robert J. Barro asserts that in this situation the answer concerning advice may be "nowhere, or at least not much." In any case, he adds, the prerequisite to useful advice would be to first examine and understand the rationale of an existing policy—for example, incompetence, structural distortions, or some other reason unknown to us. And he concludes: "In many cases the understanding of actual behavior will give us reasons not to advocate changes in that behavior."[16] This is not entirely convincing: obviously, the catchall "many cases" does not in fact fit *all* situations. "Many" means that there are *some* cases in which intervention is useful. Perhaps those are the most important situations.

VICISSITUDES AT THE CENTER OF ECONOMIC ADVICE

Since the Roosevelt era, the president has been increasingly perceived "as the dominant decision maker in economic policy, as the judge of economics and economists, and as the major figure attempting to set the psychological tone of the economy."[17] The president's ideology identifies him in the mind of the electorate with some "fundamental beliefs" concerning the economy, guides his choices of cabinet officers and advisers, allows him to sort the demands of party coalitions, congressional factors, and interest groups, and permits him to stress certain commitments and options and to put forward certain priorities. Yet, difficult economic situations may lead to astounding ideological reversals. Roosevelt ascended to the presidency stressing conservative views, but the depression turned him into a great institutional reformer. Nixon, a long-time foe of mandatory economic controls, imposed wage and price controls during his presidency, a cardinal sin for a Republican president and a cruel embarrassment for his economic advisers, Paul W. McCracken and Herbert Stein, who had previously denounced such controls as inefficient, inflationary, and counter-productive. In some other cases, presidential policies can indeed be unequivocally traced to firmly held ideological beliefs—as was more often than not the case, for instance, for Presidents Truman, Eisenhower, Kennedy, and Reagan. A comfortable situation ensues for the advisers, unless the chief executive decides to shift his emphases between various component elements of his beliefs, as when President Reagan abandoned en route at least parts of the supply-siders' credo.

Some chairmen of the CEA and some of its members played prominent roles in the profession both before and after their government service.[18] The first chairman of the CEA, Edwin G. Nourse, adopted the position of a detached expert-scholar. The second chairman, Leon H. Keyserling, chose the posture of an involved public advocate of his president. The third chairman of the CEA, Arthur F. Burns, tried to strike a balance between the two extremes. Burns wanted to be viewed as a "consultant to the president," defending the latter's positions within the administration but maintaining his own professional integrity outside by keeping a low profile vis-à-vis the public. Starting with Walter W. Heller, the fifth chairman of the CEA, many of the top managers of this center of economic advice knew how to defend their policies both inside and outside the administration without sacrificing their professional integrity. This was particularly easy in the early and mid-1960s when the economy was on the upswing, the position of chairman of the CEA commanded the highest prestige and influence, and when a broad consensus existed in the profession with respect to the underlying rationale of the policies adopted by the government. As the position of the chairman became less comfortable, the economy declined and the consensus on policies broke down, CEA chairmen become more defensive about their policies (for example, Arthur M. Okun and later Charles L. Schultze) and at times more embarrassed (for example, Herbert Stein).

An open conflict between the chairman of the CEA and the president's closest economic counselors took place under President Reagan. Martin S. Feldstein, a prominent scholar and the thirteenth chairman of the CEA, was attacked by Treasury Secretary Donald T. Regan, who suggested that the council's 1984 *Annual Economic Report* could be torn up. The distasteful public remarks of the treasury secretary against the CEA and its chairman marked the lowest point in the evolution of what was designed in 1946 to be the main source of economic advice for presidents.

In point of fact, the CEA and its chairmen have had from the beginning somewhat ambiguous and at times uncomfortable positions. The CEA was established to produce "advice," not policies, the latter being the responsibility of the president and of his cabinet. But advice cannot be entirely separated from policy formulation. The chief economic policy maker under each president is his secretary of the treasury, while monetary policy is more or less independently determined by the chairman of the Federal Reserve. Various cabinet combinations called forth to determine economic policies are necessarily centered around the treasury secretary and include various cabinet officers as well as the chairman of the Board of Governors of the Federal Reserve. In these combinations, the chairman of the CEA cannot play more than a subordinate role. His input can certainly be significant, but the decision making is not in his hands. Moreover, if he wishes his contribution to be counted, the economist, like all the other intellectuals in government, must continuously "steer between the Scylla of letting the bureaucracy prescribe what is relevant or useful and the Charybdis of defining these criteria too abstractly." If he inclines too much to the former, he turns into a technician; if he inclines too much to the latter, "he runs the risks of confusing dogmatism with morality and of courting martyrdom."[19]

During the entire postwar period under review, the council, usually composed of university professors on leave, was "an outpost of academic advice in the federal government." As James Tobin put it, it was "able to look at things from the standpoint of the economy as a whole, as against sectoral interests, to look for ultimate and remote consequences as well as immediate and superficial effects, to worry about the great mass of silent consumers as well as highly vocal and visible producers, to examine the mutual consistency of diverse policies, to appeal to statistics and history . . . and to seek alternative solutions which might reconcile conflicting objectives with less cost and inefficiency."[20] Its historical contributions are constituted by its methodical analyses, year in and year out, of all the data concerning the diverse aspects of the economy's functioning. The *Economic Report of the President* and the council's *Annual Report* are indeed extraordinarily detailed records of the formulation and implementation of the entire gamut of U.S. economic policies since 1946—starting with the goals of government and extending to the problems of employment and unemployment, stabilization and inflation, budgetary issues, income security and income distribution, sectoral policies, a variety of growth policies, and policies toward the international economy. Emphases, approaches, and depth of analysis have changed over time, depending on the year's preoccupation and the professional convictions and competence of the advisers. Yet the overall record amazes and instructs in its kaleidoscopic variety. The first CEA *Report* in December 1946 focused on the "economic philosophy" of sustained employment, and the 1949 *Report*, on the ways of achieving what was called at the time "balanced growth" (with consumption rising in step with total production). The Eisenhower *Reports* centered on a program of "Economic Growth with Price Stability" (1950), preventing inflation; on flexibility in credit and fiscal policies (1954); and on the role of the government in moderating economic fluctuations in general (1957 and 1960). The celebrated Kennedy *Reports* of 1962 focused on "maximum employment and production," and the 1963 *Report*, on tax reform and policies for faster growth. The Johnson *Reports* were concerned notably with the implications of poverty in America (1964), the approaches to full employment and the nature of policy experiences throughout twenty years of the Employment Act (1966), and finally with ways of expanding individual opportunity and of formulating policies for balanced expansion (1968, 1969). The Nixon *Reports* dealt primarily with stabilization policies (1970), the unemployment-inflation dilemma (1971), and the control of inflation under the Economic Stabilization Act (1972, 1973). The Ford *Reports* continued to be preoccupied with unemployment and inflation as well as with regulation reform (1975); and with productivity, growth, and resource utilization (1977). The Carter *Reports* debated crucial long-term policies in an inflationary environment (1978, 1979, 1980), and the need for deregulation and the prospects for growth and inflation in the 1980s (1981). The Reagan *Reports*, after critical rejections of the "legacies" of the 1960s and 1970s, focused notably on the "limited case" for government intervention (1982), on the consequences of inflation and the interplay of structural and cyclical unemployment (1983), and on the rejection of centralized industrialization policies (1984).

At the peak of the influence of the CEA in 1967, Walter W. Heller stated confidently that the "age of the economist" had arrived. Pointing with pride to a list of economists in high places—directors of the Budget Bureau, key policy makers in the White House and the Pentagon, undersecretaries of state—he added that even though the economists had never met a payroll or carried a precinct, they knew how to meet a crisis and help carry on an economic expansion and therefore they were "worth their salt."[21] Since then the unfolding of stagflation, the unraveling of consensus within the discipline, and, last but not least, the progressive loss of influence of the CEA, have generated a chorus of laments by a wide variety of economists about the "failure" of economics as a science or policy, the devious ways of the discipline to conceal facts and mask scales of value, the "poverty of formal economics," and its absence of relevance with respect to "observable reality."

CORE AND TECHNIQUES OF ECONOMICS AND THE GOALS OF POLICY

The chorus of laments coming in particular from the institutionalist, liberal, and "radical" schools complained about the discipline's assumptions, relevance, and capacity to deal with policy problems. These laments were accompanied by detailed indictments of the *core* concepts of neoclassical and Keynesian economics, of the theories and models based on this core, and of the course of action recommended by mainstream economists. Of course, laments and indictments of economics have often been heard before. But the new attacks raised a number of issues that are still with us. To understand better the thrust and implications of this critique, it may be useful to think of neoclassical, mainstream economics in terms of the so-called Kuhn-Lakatos model or "paradigm" as interpreted by either Roy Weintraub or Mark Blaug.

Following Weintraub, we may view mainstream economics as having at its core the "Walrasian Research Program." The program's propositions refer to interactions among economic agents in interrelated markets, interactions whose observable outcomes are coordinated. The consistency of the core's program is established by a model—the Arrow-Debreu-McKenzie (ADM) model—in which a competitive equilibrium exits. The refinement and reinterpretations of the core (its "hardening") evolve over time. The ADM model may need to be further extended to the future to take into account uncertainty and intertemporal linkages: macroeconomics deals in effect with coordination failures induced by uncertainty and time. The core functions in relation to the discipline like the axioms in relation to geometry. As the geometer sets out to prove theorems derived from the axioms, so the economists engage in the development of theories and models concerning changes in equilibrium states. These theories, say demand theory, marginal productivity theory, monetarism, Keynesianism (with the indicated proviso), share the common "hard core" but differ from one another in the auxiliary hypotheses they use. The theories, not the axioms, are subject to testing, verification, and rejection.[22]

Alternatively, with Mark Blaug, we may distinguish at the heart of economics a "disciplinary matrix" comprised of the entire constellation of beliefs, values, and techniques shared by economists and based on the concept of economic equilibrium via the market mechanism. Related to the investigative logic of the discipline are the theories and programs that economists have developed about economic processes, theories that are testable and, as the case may be, refutable.[23] We may then consider the critiques as they address themselves (a) to the core concepts, in the restrictive sense of Weintraub or in the more extensive interpretation of Blaug; (b) to the theories and to the discipline's investigative methods; and (c) to the courses of action that result from either (a) or (b) or from both.

a. **Attacks against the Core**. Criticism of the core concepts have involved a gamut of issues concerning the nature of the economists' beliefs and of their implicit values with respect to the modeling of their theories, the discipline's oversight of past and current changes in the institutional environment and of its likely changes in the future, and the detachment manifested in professional empirical analyses in regard to power relations in the economy and to their implications.[24]

The late Gunnar Myrdal, a Nobel Laureate, alleged that the concepts of economics were permeated with the eighteenth- and nineteenth-century maxims of natural law and utilitarianism, implying abstract assumptions totally removed from reality. Steeped in these defunct philosophical tenets, the economists conceal so deeply the evaluations that underlie their analytical structures "that they can happily remain unaware of them in their researches and trust that the latter are merely factual." With "welfare theory," they have "provided themselves with a vast and elaborate cover for their escape from the responsibility to state simply and straightforwardly, their value premises in concrete forms." The illogical division they have made between production and distribution has been used "as a means to escape" from the problem of the latter while concentrating on those of the former. Now the distribution issue must be brought to the fore, and in its analysis must be included "all the 'non-economic' factors—political, social, and economic structure, institutions and attitudes, indeed all interpersonal relations."[25]

Professor Robert Lekachman, whose liberal orientation is akin to Myrdal's, asserted that the "vision" of neoclassical or Keynesian economics, which once may have been congruent with the realities of capitalism, has now become "outmoded by changes in behavior, economic institutions, and power relations within domestic boundaries and among nations. . . . Shorn of morality and history, economics is reduced to techniques" no better as guides to social policy than the "ruminations of accountants, lawyers, advertisers and public relations people." The profession's "gravest failures of institutional understanding" are the economists' long-standing reluctance to "struggle with giant corporations," the ignorance of the trade unions, and their "naivete" when dealing with the consequences for analysis "of the close ties between political institutions and private interest groups."[26]

Marxists have always dismissed the entire corpus of "bourgeois economics," except for some tenets of Smith and Ricardo concerning the labor theory of value. They contended that "academic economics" was predicated on the wrong assumption that the history of society was the history of interactions among selfish individuals viewed in isolation from their social matrix, instead of perceiving that history was the expression of "class warfare" and that capitalism was the acme of exploitation of all the have-nots. The modern American radical economists find their roots both in Thorstein Veblen's institutionalism and in a kind of freewheeling interpretation of Marx.[27] The radicals dismiss economic beliefs of the "conservative" and the "liberal" economists alike, because the first assert that "private ownership of resources under capitalism assures economic and political freedom for individuals in that society," and because the second accept the "structure of the capitalist economic system and its basic institutions of private property and markets." The radicals argue that the capitalist system is hopelessly infected with the incurable diseases of inequality, alienation, consumerism, militarism, racism, sexism, imperialism, and environmental pollution. That system cannot tolerate the amount of redistribution needed to eliminate poverty; only a radical restructuring of the institutions and of the economic system could eliminate its incidence.[28]

b. **Indictments of Theories and Models**. Let us consider closely the "list of indictments" concerning the techniques of analysis. Indictments against theories and models have come from certain partisans of various forms of empirical research and planning; from a number of economists allergic to and distrustful of mathematics; and, finally, from the institutionalists, liberals, and radicals, for these same reasons as well as because of the alleged "irrelevance" of these theories and models with regard to the problems that they view as crucial and as being in need of solution.

Wassily Leontief, formerly of Harvard, has been especially critical of the modern economists' "continued preoccupation with imaginary, hypothetical, rather than with observable reality" and has quoted with approval the statement of a president of the Econometric Society who asserted that there was "something scandalous in the spectacle of so many people refining the analysis of economic states which they give no reason to suppose will ever, or have ever, come about. . . . It is an unsatisfactory and slightly dishonest state of affairs."[29] In the same vein, Robert Aaron Gordon noted in his 1975 presidential address to the American Economic Association that in both micro- and macroeconomics, "efforts are sometimes made to extract a drop or two of relevance from exercises in analytical rigor" but much of this literature rests on assumptions that "fly in the face of the facts."[30]

Leontief stated further that traditional economic theory does indeed explain how the operation of competitive price mechanism automatically brings about equality between supply and demand. But, added Leontief, given the lack of reliable information, many business leaders have come to realize that this "trial and error game, instead of bringing about a desired state of stable equilibrium, results in misallocation of resources, underutilization of resources, and periodic unemployment." Sketchy descriptions and analyses of the economic system in the aggregate are not more successful in compensating for "the lack of systemic foresight." Hence the need of a "comprehensive" internally consistent National Economic Plan.[31]

The attacks against the use of mathematics in modern economics are legion. Among the new critics, Melville J. Ulmer of the University of Michigan, for instance, asserted that the diversion of economics from the "productive historical and dynamic approach" had started in 1947 with Paul A. Samuelson's *Foundations of Economic Analysis*. Directly or indirectly this "unhappy" change reinforced and generalized the three major flaws of contemporary economics: "nearly exclusive reliance on deductive reasoning; preoccupation with the static concept of equilibrium; and the oversimplification required to match actual data with mathematical abstractions."[32] It may be interesting to note that the philosopher Alexander Rosenberg argued not only that the economists were henceforth "not really much interested in questions of empirical applicability at all" but also that they had simply abandoned the aim of developing an "empirical science of human behavior": they had transformed their discipline into a "branch of mathematics." The latter is devoted only to "examining the formal properties of a set of assumptions about the transitivity of abstract relations." In short, economic theory shifted to formalism, insulated itself from empirical assessment, and became interested only in proving formal and abstract possibilities.[33]

The "relevance" of economic theory and models has been questioned particularly because economics lacks a "unifying theory of social change" or, more bluntly, because the walls of economic theory have not been broken down to let in the other social sciences. Other causes of "irrelevance" are allegedly due to the incapacity of "conservative" economics to "control or predict" economic phenomena. According to Robert L. Heilbroner of the New School for Social Research, "the restricted scope of economic vision serves to limit the relevance of economic theory," and, by way of consequence, the results produced by the application of conventional economics "too often have no usefulness." Heilbroner concludes that economics appears not as a "genuinely objective science" but rather as "a kind of high level apologetics that tends to illuminate only those issues for which economics has an 'answer,'" overlooking those for which it has none.[34]

All this is supposed to be hidden by mathematical symbols perplexing to the laity. Moreover, in their conversion to a mathematical way of talking and writing, theoretical economists supposedly "adopted a crusading faith, a set of philosophical doctrines that makes them now prone to fanaticism and intolerance."[35] As a consequence, puffery, braggadocio, and similar vices have spread in the profession. The mathematical language and the deductive method have tended to give the economists a certitude that theirs—and theirs alone—is a "hard social science."[36]

c. **Courses of Policy Action**. The key policy goals pursued by the Keynesians, full employment and economic growth—truly humane goals—are denounced by the institutionalist, liberal, and radical economists alike as the most devious ways of propping up capitalism and of avoiding tackling the "real" problems of society, namely the maldistribution of power that is the root cause of the maldistribution of income, and the misuse of resources. According to Daniel R. Fusfeld of the University of Michigan, the goals of full employment and growth were no less than "the keystones of the understanding between those who held and exercised power and those who did not." Full employment and growth were but part of a *quid pro quo*: in exchange for letting power in the hands of big business and big government, the great middle-income majority was given the benefits resulting from economic expansion. Now the "sacrosanct" goal of growth has finally been compromised, and the time has come to move "toward greater concern for human values."[37]

The question of the *distribution of power* in society was hailed as a new and illuminating approach to the workings of the economy, with or without due references to the old and forgotten theses of Marx and Veblen or to the more "modern" tomes of John Kenneth Galbraith. The distribution of goods and services, stressed the institutionalist Robert Aaron Gordon, depended on much more than the "operation of market forces": it involved the power to influence commodity and factor markets, the distribution of wealth, and the network of rules and taxes emerging from the political process.[38] Instead of concentrating on the growth of the gross national product, added the liberal Lekachman, economists should better concentrate "on the distribution of that product among rich, middling and poor."[39] Yet all this still seemed to the radicals to miss the true solution. Redistribution of income within capitalism was still perhaps only a new way of saving capitalism. Even state planning, *à la* Leontief, would amount to not more, in a period of capitalist decline, than balancing "the reduction of business profits against our own standards of living." The true culprit was private property and the profit system based on it: "As long as profits remain private, the profit addicts will still pursue their prosperity trips, pushing us feverishly toward recurrent instability." This rejuvenated Marxian thesis, rewritten by David Gordon of the New School for Social Research in the language applied to drug addicts, was supposed to "embolden" the radicals "to struggle for socialist America." The latter would of course be "a society promoting both rational planning and democratic control of our working and political lives."[40]

The chorus of institutionalist, liberal, and radical laments, aimed thus at more than denouncing the shortcomings of mainstream economics or its misuse of techniques: it aimed at both formulating proposals for restructuring the entire discipline and redirecting its macroeconomic goals. As far as the restructuring is concerned, these critics have drawn attention to certain legitimate social problems, which, as we shall see immediately below, have never been dismissed either as unimportant or as uninteresting, or as not amenable to analysis with the standard tools of economics. As far as policy redirection is concerned, besides the stress on redistribution of income, little emerged from the chorus except some pious socialist wishes. What the public may have perceived as a clash of economic concepts was indeed "a clash of ideologies and values," cutting sharper and deeper than the conflicts between the Keynesians, the monetarists, and the neoclassics with which we have been dealing.[41]

ANSWER TO THE CRITICS: NEITHER BLISSFUL CANDIDES NOR DOGMATIC RADICALS

John Maynard Keynes rejected the popular conceptions of the economist as either an optimistic Candide who believed that "all is for the best in the best of all possible worlds," or as a dogmatic radical, who pushes the economy toward being engulfed by state socialism. He distanced himself from the Candides of his time who accepted Say's law for the macroeconomy and who believed that there was a natural tendency in the society toward the optimum employment of resources, provided that we neglect to notice the drag on prosperity exercised by an insufficiency of effective demand. And he distanced himself from the radicals who asserted that the ownership of the instruments of production was more important or more necessary than the search, by the public authority, for compromises with the private initiative in order to secure the investment needed for approximating full employment.[42] He taught us to view economics as "a science of thinking in terms of models joined to the art of choosing models which are relevant to the contemporary world."[43] It is these views that have served most of the profession as canons in the approach to contemporary policy problems.

Until the Great Stagflation, the profession was dominated by the thought and actions of the exponents of the neoclassical synthesis. Until then, most members of the profession (including the most prominent ones) displayed increasing confidence in the teaching and techniques of the discipline's approach to macroeconomics. This confident, optimistic outlook—not in regard to the "natural tendency" of the economy to function according to the classical postulates but in regard to the profession's ability to map the necessary paths in that direction—was often viewed by its critics as a kind of Keynesian hubris. Actually, other economic schools have not been immune to this same "sin." Long before the triumph of Keynesianism, the old institutionalists—whose teachings form much of the substance of the new institutionalists—were just as confident in the validity of their views. Wesley Clair Mitchell, for instance, wrote in 1924 that the prospect of making progress in economics was "bright," that we were "entering upon a period of rapid theoretical development and of constructive application" and that in this development economics "will focus its attention upon the cumulative change of institutions," thus becoming "less the science of wealth and more the science of welfare."[44] The new institutionalists still believe that the discipline will indeed focus upon the "change of institutions," and more on "welfare" (in the Veblen or Marx's sense). Be that as it may, mainstream economics chastised by stagflation has tried for its part to absorb, as we already noted, various elements of the monetarist and neoclassical critiques and has also tried to examine analytically and dispassionately at least some of the social issues emphasized by the contemporary institutionalist-liberal-radical schools.

Certainly, many mainstream economists confine their work to purely scientific-technical mathematical issues. But this is indispensable for both "hardening" the discipline's core and for expanding the discipline's frontiers. Further, many models and hypotheses generated in theoretical works can and are often applied: the modeler (or the user of these models) must, in the process, correct his judgment "by intimate and messy acquaintance with the facts to which his model has to be applied."[45] The alleged separation between the conception of models and the resort to "observable reality" may often be less clear-cut than Leontief, for instance, seemed to assume. On the other hand, economics *qua* discipline—not excluding microeconomics—could not avoid being a social science, concerned with social issues and interested in a variety of society's activities and in its government's policies. The mainstream economists have systematically emphasized that it was possible to have more of every good thing simultaneously: they have devised for the purpose both theoretical models of economic growth and prescriptions for achieving economic growth. What should be recalled here in connection with certain criticisms concerning income inequality is that economic growth, that is, the increase of output per person, may be "the only way we are likely to achieve a more equitable distribution of income in society" (under capitalism and, incidentally, under socialism as well). Indeed, as Professor Robert M. Solow rightly pointed out, even a given relative distribution of income—supposing it cannot for any reason be made more clearly equal—may be "less unattractive if the absolute standard of living at the bottom is fairly high than it is if the absolute standard at the bottom is very low. From this point of view, even if economic growth does not lead to more equity in distribution, it makes the inequity we've got more tolerable."[46] Mainstream economists have in fact examined many other implications of the question of inequality in their analyses of a host of questions related to labor markets, labor supply, rewards for alternative occupations, education, cost in individual allocative decisions, obsolescence of acquired human skills, and the complex problems of poverty.[47]

While most young radicals may view all technical solutions concerning fiscal and monetary policies as "shabby and mean" or simply as stopgaps for supporting money and wealth, other critics, like Robert L. Heilbroner, do not deny "the power of economic reasoning in action" and cannot but be impressed by the clarifications that economics "in its conventional use" can bring to "tangled social problems."[48] However, what is apparently not always clear even to these critics is that this "power of economic reasoning" and the insights the economists have about economic processes are predicated on the disciplinary matrix constituted by the general equilibrium "research program." Economics, as a coherent and systematic investigative logic, has even been able to extend its scope beyond the frontiers of the discipline to help clarify crucial issues in politics, sociology, ethnology, law, biology, and psychology. While some members of these disciplines have berated this alleged "imperialism," many social scientists have recognized that the application of the investigative methods of economics has yielded new and important results in the study, explanation, and prediction of the behavior of living systems in general, of groups and associations, and of organizations in the environment.[49]

We have examined in this work the ways in which certain economic theories have impacted economic policies. It is beyond doubt that mainstream economics has made striking contributions both in the explanation of short-term fluctuations—notwithstanding somewhat myopic approaches to the danger of inflation and unavoidable predictive errors—and in the analyses of long-term trends. It is also certain that it has helped orient systematic policy efforts toward the issues of employment and investment. At the peak of its success, Walter W. Heller stated with pride that "interwoven with the growing presidential reliance on economists has been a growing political and popular belief that modern economics can, after all, deliver the goods."[50] But, as inflation started to grow and as the public disenchantment with economics and economist-advisers began to gain in breadth and depth, Milton Friedman remarked that the economists themselves had been responsible for the public's disappointment because they (he generously included the monetarists) had tended to claim more than they could deliver and because they had encouraged politicians "to make extravagant promises, inculcate unrealistic expectations in the public at large, and promote discontent with reasonably satisfactory results because they fall short of the economists' promised land."[51] Later in the game, in 1976—that is, after the onrush of stagflation—Heller addressed the following caveat to a reproachful public: "We never promised you a rose garden without thorns." And he added for good measure that the New Economics had promised "no money-back guarantees against occasional slowdowns or even recessions."[52] But by then it was too late to regain a modicum of public favor: as usual, the public is rapidly oblivious of success and tenacious in remembering failure.

CONCLUDING COMMENTS

Notwithstanding legitimate criticisms and unavoidable changes in public moods, the historical record of economic policies from the Great Depression to the end of stagflation that we have presented in these pages shows the enormously creative, imaginative, and versatile contribution of economic theory. The most eminent economic theoreticians took part in the debates posed by the economy's problems. Irving Fisher, Jacob Viner, Sumner H. Slichter, John Maynard Keynes, and Alvin H. Hansen were involved in the fight against the depression. Gottfried Haberler, Friedrich von Hayek, Abba P. Lerner, William Fellner, Harry G. Johnson, Paul A. Samuelson, and many others participated in the discussions concerned with economic stability in post–World War II years. Again Paul A. Samuelson, Robert M. Solow, James Tobin, Kenneth Arrow, and Milton Friedman, in particular, debated the issues of economic growth and inflation. Robert E. Lucas, Thomas J. Sargent, Martin S. Feldstein, and William J. Baumol joined the debate on stagflation, with Paul A. Samuelson and the others mentioned above. Along with the "pure" theoreticians, prominent members of the profession demonstrated not only the ability to apply the discipline's investigative logic and its tools to everyday policies but also the capacity to synthesize their own experience in outstanding studies of economic policy. Arthur F. Burns, Walter W. Heller, Gardner Ackley, Arthur M. Okun, Herbert Stein, Charles L. Schultze, and Martin S. Feldstein not only occupied the high position of chairman of the Council of Economic Advisers but also contributed to enriching in innumerable ways the profession's understanding of policy making, to presenting alternative choices to presidents, and to educating the public at large.

Economists do not "produce" policies. They produce theories, formulate hypotheses, and at times propose and, as the case may be, offer advice on policy measures. Scholars and teachers outside the government, and economic practitioners and advisers inside the government, contribute to the broad matrix in which the policy decisions must ultimately take shape. The fundamental tenets of the Keynesians remain as valid as they were during the postwar decades. As Alan S. Blinder put it, "The private economy is not a giant auction hall, and will not regulate itself smoothly and reliably; recessions are economic maladies, not vacations; the government has tools that can limit recession or fight inflation, but it cannot do both at once, and neither constantly growing money supply nor constantly shrinking tax rates will cure all our ills."[53] In the din of criticism and in the search for solutions "beyond Keynesianism," these basic tenets may seem obsolete. In fact, they have not lost their cogency; they will, I feel, reassert their significance in the post-stagflation years. Under the impact of endogenous or exogenous changes, the economic system will of course bring to the fore some of the old problems as well as new ones. But we cannot predict these turns in advance, no matter how certain we are that we will face them sometime down the road.

There is no "stable equilibrium" reachable in the relation between the economics adviser—even at the highest level in the CEA—and the chief policy maker. The "chief economist," the president, is bound to try to have as much "advice" from as many sources as possible, from both inside and outside the government, and to see his task as that of molding this diversity into some kind of consensus. Given the differences between the president, the leaders of his administration's economic policy headed by the secretary of the treasury, and the special role of the chairman of the Federal Reserve, it is unavoidable that numerous points of view should clash on important issues. In this process, the biggest strength of the profession's influence may at times still come from the *outside*, that is, from the entire community of scholars and researchers, rather than directly from the academic outpost, the CEA.[54]

The profession is perceived by the public and by many politicians as being continuously torn by its own uncertainties and dissensions. Actually, as far as microeconomics is concerned, the profession has always displayed a broad mainstream consensus. As for macroeconomics, the ongoing discussions are not "an endless carrousel," an incessant repetition resulting in stalemate. The discussions, and the divergences they bring to the fore, are a necessary means for better focusing on the appropriate issues and for increasing the profession's ability to tackle given problems. The debates are in many respects an expression of the profession's involvement in the country's policy problems and the outward manifestation of its vitality and dynamism.

Notes

CHAPTER 1. ANTIDEPRESSION POLICIES

1. *Commercial and Financial Chronicle*, 1 November 1929.

2. Walter E. Spahr, "Bank Failures in the United States," *American Economic Review* (hereafter *AER*) 22, Supplement (March 1932): 215 ff; E. A. Goldenweiser, *Monetary Management* (New York: McGraw-Hill, 1949), pp. 56–57.

3. Data in this and the following paragraphs of this section are based on *Historical Statistics of the United States*, vol. 1: *Colonial Times to 1970* (Washington, D.C.: Government Printing Office, 1975), *passim*; and the statistical tables of *The National Income and Product Accounts of the United States, 1929–1976* (Washington, D.C.: U.S. Department of Commerce, Bureau of Economic Analysis, September 1981), *passim*.

4. *Commercial and Financial Chronicle*, 2 January 1932.

5. Jacob Viner, *Balanced Deflation, Inflation, or More Depression* (Minneapolis: University of Minnesota Press, 1933), 9.

6. See "Annual Message to Congress on the State of the Union, December 3, 1929," in *Public Papers of the Presidents of the United States: Herbert Hoover, 1929* (Washington, D.C.: Government Printing Office, 1974), 404ff. See also Sumner Slichter, "Economic Planning in Recent Literature," *Harvard Business Review* 14 (1936): 507; and Herbert Stein, *The Fiscal Revolution in America* (Chicago: University of Chicago Press, 1969), 9–10, 16–17.

7. Viner, *Balanced Deflation*, 11ff.

8. See Irving Fisher, *Booms and Depression: Some First Principles* (New York: Adelphia Co., 1932), 13, 23, 29, and Appendix VI.

9. J. H. Rogers, "Federal Reserve Policy in World Monetary Chaos," *AER*. 23, Supplement (March 1933): 119ff.

10. Cf. in particular Walter E. Spahr's critique of George F. Warren and Frank A. Pearson's book, *Prices* (1933), and implicitly of Irving Fisher: "Warren assumes that the amount of money in circulation determines business activity and that a government can force money into circulation as it pleases and thus determine the price level as it desires. . . . The amount of money in circulation is determined primarily by . . . business activity and does not cause it." Walter E. Spahr, *The Monetary Theories of Warren and Pearson* (New York: Farrar & Rinehart, 1934), 2.

11. Arthur B. Adams, *Our Economic Revolution: Solving Our Depression Problems through Public Control of Industry* (Norman: University of Oklahoma Press, 1934), 62, 65.

12. Viner, *Balanced Deflation*, 18, 24ff. In a more general statement, Viner had noted in 1931 that "when business activity is declining or is stagnant at a low level, increased expenditures, reduced taxation, and budget deficits are, from the points of view of the national economy as a whole, sound policy rather than unsound." The Institute of Politics (Williams College), *Report of the Round Tables and General Conferences at the Eleventh Session*, ed. Arthur Holland Buffington (Williamstown, Mass.: n.p., 1931), 182.

13. Milton Friedman has asserted that "Simons and Keynes emphasized the state of business expectations and the desire for liquidity" and that accordingly both turned to fiscal policy as the primary tool for promoting economic stability. See Milton Friedman, "The Monetary Theory and Policy of Henry Simons," *Journal of Law & Economics*, October 1967, pp. 1ff. These remarks were quoted

approvingly by J. Ronnie Davis in "Chicago Economists, Deficit Budgets, and the Early 1930s," *AER* 58 (June 1968), Part 1: 476. See also Friedman, "Comments on the Critics," in *Milton Friedman's Monetary Framework*, ed. Robert J. Gordon (Chicago: University of Chicago Press, 1974), 162ff. Such "rapprochements" between the Chicago economists and Keynes, however, glide somewhat equivocally over the different rationales of Viner, Simons, or Keynes concerning the root causes of the depression and, above all, over the differences between them and the conceptual framework to which the name of Keynes has been finally attached and which he developed subsequently in his *General Theory of Employment, Interest and Money* (New York: Harcourt, Brace & Co., 1936).

14. Sumner Slichter, "The Economics of Public Works," *AER* 24, Supplement (March 1934): 175.

15. John Maynard Keynes, *Treatise on Money* (New York: Harcourt, Brace & Co., 1930), 2:194, 196.

16. Herbert Stein, who quotes this letter of 31 December 1933 published by the *New York Times*, rightly points out its deficiencies with respect to Keynes's thoughts about fiscal policy at that time and in subsequent years. As Stein reminds us, many of the people around President Roosevelt—Senators Wagner, La Follette, and Costigan, as well as Frances Perkins, Rexford Tugwell, Harold Ickes, and Hugh Johnson—were in support of a spending program, but their arguments did not rest on a "pump-priming" idea (that is, on spending up to reaching full employment) or on the "multiplier" notion. Stein, *Fiscal Revolution in America*, 51, 149–50, 152ff. Cf. also Keynes, *General Theory*, 113ff, 248–54.

17. Keynes, *General Theory*, 249.

18. See Alvin H. Hansen, *Full Recovery or Stagnation* (New York: W. W. Norton, 1938), 314ff; Hansen, "Economic Progress and Declining Population Growth," *AER* 29 (March 1939), Part 1: 1–15; Alvin H. Hansen, Statement at the Hearings before the Temporary National Economic Committee (TNEC), *Investigation of Concentration of Economic Power*, 77th Cong., 1st sess., 16 May 1940, (Washington, D.C.: Government Printing Office, 1940), Part 9, pp. 3501ff; Alvin H. Hansen, *Fiscal Policy and Business Cycles* (New York: W. W. Norton, 1941), 33, 42ff.

19. Thorstein Veblen, *The Engineers and the Price System* (New York: B. W. Heubsch, 1921), pp. 7ff, 42ff, and *passim*.

20. See John D. Black, *Agricultural Reform in the United States* (New York: McGraw-Hill, 1929), 271–89; and William D. Rowley, *M. L. Wilson and the Campaign for the Domestic Allotment* (Lincoln: University of Nebraska Press, 1970), 44, 47ff. See also Raymond Moley, *After Seven Years* (Lincoln: University of Nebraska Press, 1939), 41ff.

21. See Statement of 26 October 1931 of Henry I. Harriman at Hearings before a Subcommittee of the Committee on Manufactures, 72d Cong., 1st sess., October 22–December, 1931, *Establishment of a National Economic Council* (Washington, D.C.: Government Printing Office, 1932), 161ff, 182ff. See also Henry I. Harriman, "The Stabilization of Business and Employment," *AER* 22, Supplement (March 1932): 66–67.

22. "Each trade association should hold itself responsible for the coordination of production and consumption to stabilize its industry, with the consequent benefits to the employees and to society." See Statement of Gerard Swope in Subcommittee of the Committee on Manufactures, *Establishment of a National Economic Council*, 300ff, 308, 313.

23. Ibid., *passim*. See also Paul T. Homan, "Economic Planning: The Proposals and the Literature," *Quarterly Journal of Economics* 47 (November 1935): 111.

24. Arthur Robert Burns, *The Decline of Competition: A Study of the Evolution of American Industry* (New York: McGraw-Hill, 1936), 146ff.

25. Arthur B. Adams, "The Business Depression of Nineteen Hundred Thirty—Discussion," *AER* 21, Supplement (March 1931): 183ff. For the second thesis, see Adams, *Our Economic Revolution*, 40–41, 50.

26. Alvin H. Hansen, *Economic Stabilization in an Unbalanced World* (New York: Harcourt, Brace & Co., 1932), 317ff.

27. Wesley C. Mitchell, "The Social Sciences and National Planning," in *Planned Society: Yesterday, Today, Tomorrow: A Symposium*, ed. Findlay Mackenzie (New York: Prentice-Hall, 1937), 108–27.

28. Statement of John Maurice Clark in Subcommittee of the Committee on Manufactures, *Establishment of a National Economic Council*, 211, 213; "Long Range Planning for the Reorganization of Industry," signed by Clark, in ibid., 737–52.

29. Rexford G. Tugwell, "The Principle of Planning and the Institution of Laissez Faire," *AER* 22, Supplement (March 1932): 76ff; and Tugwell, *The Industrial Discipline and the Governmental Acts* (New York: Columbia University Press, 1933), 211ff.

30. See notably Frank H. Knight, "Barbara Wootton on Economic Planning," *Journal of Political Economy* 43 (December 1935): 809–14; Slichter, "Economic Planning in Recent Literature," 502–08; Homan, "Economic Planning," 102–22; Allan G. Gruchy, "The Concept of National Planning in Institutional Economics," *Southern Economic Journal* 6 (October 1939): 121–44.

31. Veblen, *Engineers*, 52.

32. See Caroline F. Ware and Gardiner C. Means, *The Modern Economy in Action* (New York: Harcourt, Brace & Co., 1936), 26–36; and "Basic Characteristics," in *The Structure of the American Economy*, a report prepared by the Industrial Section under the direction of Gardiner C. Means for the National Resources Committee (Washington, D.C.: Government Printing Office, June 1939), 170ff.

33. Arthur M. Schlesinger, Jr., "The Hundred Days of F.D.R.," *New York Times*, 10 April 1983.

34. Albert U. Romasco, *The Politics of Recovery: Roosevelt's New Deal* (New York: Oxford University Press, 1983), 5.

35. Ibid.

36. Alexander Sachs (Chief and Organizer of Economic Research and Planning, National Recovery Administration), "National Recovery Administration Policies and the Problem of Economic Planning," in *America's Recovery Program*, by A. A. Berle, Jr., et al., edited by Clair Wilcox et al. (Oxford: Oxford University Press, 1934), 124.

37. See the detailed explanatory note to the "Presidential Proclamation Fixing the Weight of the Gold Dollar, January 31, 1934," concerning the entire sweep of the monetary program, in *The Public Papers and Addresses of Franklin D. Roosevelt*, vol. 3: *The Advance of Recovery and Reform, 1934*, ed. Samuel I. Rosenman (New York: Random House, 1938), 70ff.

38. Ibid., vol. 2: *The Year of Crisis, 1933*, 177.

39. See the "Presidential Statement on Signing the Agricultural Adjustment Act of 1938," in ibid., vol. 7: *The Continuing Struggle for Liberalism, 1938*, ed. Samuel I. Rosenman (New York: Macmillan, 1941), 86–97. See also Edwin G. Nourse, Joseph S. Davis, and John D. Black, *Three Years of the Agricultural Adjustment Administration* (Washington, D.C.: The Brookings Institution, 1937), 23,

469, 512, *passim*; and Harold G. Halcrow, *Agricultural Policy Analysis* (New York: McGraw-Hill, 1984), 95.

40. "The Goal of the National Industrial Recovery Act," in ibid., vol. 2: *The Year of Crisis, 1933,* 246.

41. "Presidential Statement on N.I.R.A.," in ibid., 252. This same idea is repeated over and over throughout the 1930s. Isador Lubin, Commissioner of Labor Statistics, Department of Labor, was explaining on 1 December 1938 at a hearing of the Temporary National Economic Committee (TNEC) that American industry, which is geared to large-scale production, cannot profitably maintain itself from proceeds of sales to the 2.7 percent of the total families of the nation with incomes of more than $5,000. Nor could it maintain itself on the sales to the income group that receives $2,500 or more, comprising 13 percent of all families. However, industry touches only half of the families with $1,250 or more, accounting for approximately 46 percent of all families. If, added Lubin, "there were moderate increases in the incomes of all families receiving less than $2,500, you could reasonably expect that most of our surplus capacity in the United States would disappear, and in many industries our present capacity would run far short of the demands by the population of this country." Testimony before TNEC, *Investigation of Concentration of Economic Power,* 75th Cong., 3d sess., Part I, *Economic Prologue* (Washington, D.C: Government Printing Office, 1938), 74–77.

42. Arthur M. Schlesinger, Jr., *The Age of Roosevelt,* vol. 2: *The Coming of the New Deal* (Boston: Houghton Mifflin, 1957), 87ff; also Ellis W. Hawley, *The New Deal and the Problem of Monopoly: A Study in Economic Ambivalence* (Princeton, N.J.: Princeton University Press, 1966), 25, *passim*; Henry Steele Commager, ed., *Documents of American History,* 6th ed. (New York: Appleton-Century-Crofts, 1958), 451ff.

43. Charles C. Chapman, *The Development of American Business and Banking through 1913–1936* (New York: Longmans, 1936), 134ff.

44. See Clair Wilcox, *Public Policies toward Business,* 3d ed. (Homewood, Ill.: Richard Irwin, 1966), 686–87.

45. "Three Essentials for Unemployment Relief" and "The President Signs the Unemployment Relief Bill," in Rosenman, ed., *Year of Crisis, 1933,* 80ff, 183ff; and "A Greater Future Economic Security of the American People," statement on "Report from the President's Committee on Economic Security," and "Presidential Statement upon Signing the Social Security Act," in *The Public Papers and Addresses of Franklin D. Roosevelt,* vol. 4: *The Court Disapproves, 1935,* ed. Samuel I. Rosenman (New York: Random House, 1938), 43ff, 49ff, 324ff. See also The American Assembly, *Economic Security for Americans* (New York: Graduate School of Business, Columbia University, November 1953).

46. See Means, *Structure of the American Economy,* Part I, and Part II, "Toward Full Use of Resources."

47. Edward S. Mason, "Controlling Industry," in *The Economics of the Recovery Program,* by Douglass V. Brown et al. (New York: McGraw-Hill, 1934), 56ff.

48. See, for instance, James P. Warburg, *The Money Muddle* (New York: Alfred A. Knopf, 1934), 155ff, 211ff. See also Spahr, *Monetary Theories.*

49. Cf. Statement of Bernard M. Baruch, 13 February 1933, in *Investigation of Economic Problems,* Hearings before the Committee on Finance, United States Senate, 72d Congress, Part I, February 13–14, 1933 (Washington, D.C.: Government Printing Office, 1933), 15.

50. Berle et al., *America's Recovery Program,* Introduction, pp. 7–19 (emphasis supplied).

51. J. M. Clark, "Economics and the National Recovery Administration," *AER* 24 (March 1934): 23.

52. See Moley, *After Seven Years*, 23; and Schlesinger, *Coming of the New Deal*, 184ff.

53. Roland S. Vaile, "Marketing under Recovery Legislation," Papers and Proceeding of the Forty-sixth Annual Meeting of the American Economic Association, December 1933, *AER* 24, Supplement (March 1934): 72.

54. Cf. John Dickinson, "Economics of the Recovery Act," ibid., 84ff.

55. *National Income and Product Accounts of the United States*, 6, 375.

56. Rosenman, ed., *Continuing Struggle for Liberalism, 1938*, 230, 246 (emphasis supplied).

57. Ibid., 221ff, 227–28.

58. Arthur Smithies, "The American Economy in the Thirties," *AER* 36 (May 1946): 16 (emphasis supplied).

59. See Gardiner C. Means, discussion of Smithies, "American Economy in the Thirties," ibid., 32ff.

60. Hansen, *Fiscal Policy*, 84.

61. Stein, *Fiscal Revolution*, 116. See also E. Cary Brown, "Fiscal Policies in the Thirties: A Reappraisal," *AER* 46 (December 1956): 863–66. Brown remarks after a detached examination that "The trend of the direct effects of fiscal policy on aggregate full-employment demand is definitely downward through the 'thirties. . . . Fiscal policy, then, seems to have been an unsuccessful recovery device in the 'thirties—not because it did not work, but because it was not tried."

62. Rosenman, ed., *Continuing Struggle for Liberalism, 1938*, 230, 234, 240.

63. President Hoover, "Address at Madison Square Garden in New York City, October 31, 1932," in *Public Papers of the Presidents of the United States, Herbert Hoover, January 1, 1932 to March 4, 1933* (Washington, D.C.: Government Printing Office, 1977), 56ff.

64. Veblen, *Engineers*, 141–42.

65. James Burnham, *The Managerial Revolution* (Bloomington: Indiana University Press, 1960), vii, 80.

66. Means, *Structure of the American Economy*, 97, 107, 158.

67. John Kenneth Galbraith, *The New Industrial State* (London: Hamish Hamilton, 1967), 2ff, 392ff. For a more detailed discussion, see chapter 3.

68. See Nicolas Spulber, "On Some Issues in the Theory of the Socialist Economy," *Kyklos* 25 (1972), Fase. 4, pp. 715–35.

69. See Leo Rogin, "The Significance of Marxian Economics for Current Trends of Government Policy," Papers and Proceedings of the Fiftieth Annual Meeting of the American Economic Association, December 1937, *AER* 28, Supplement (March 1938): 10ff.

CHAPTER 2. COUNTER-CYCLICAL POLICIES

1. National Resources Planning Board, *National Resources Development: Report for 1942* (Washington, D.C.: Government Printing Office, January 1942), Introduction.

2. Stephen Kemp Bailey, *Congress Makes a Law: The Story behind the Employment Act of 1946* (New York: Columbia University Press, 1950), 9–10.

3. Herbert Stein, *The Fiscal Revolution in America* (Chicago: University of Chicago Press, 1969), 171.

4. See Paul T. Homan, "Economics in the War Period," *American Economic Review*, (hereafter *AER*) 36 (December 1946): 855–71.

5. Everett E. Hagen and Nora Boddy Kirkpatrick, "The National Output at Full Employment in 1950," *AER* 34 (September 1944): 494.

6. Julius Hirsch, "Facts and Fantasies concerning Full Employment," *AER* 34, Supplement (March 1944), Part 2: 118ff.

150 / Notes to Pages 25–33

7. Hagen and Kirkpatrick, "National Output," 494–95.

8. Council of Economic Advisers, *First Annual Report to the President* (Washington, D.C.: Government Printing Office, December 1946), 2–3.

9. James Tobin, *The New Economics One Decade Older* (Princeton, N.J.: Princeton University Press, 1974), 8–9.

10. Bert G. Hickman, *Growth and Stability of the Postwar Economy* (Washington, D.C.: The Brookings Institution, 1960), 44.

11. For these and the following data, see the *Historical Statistics of the United States*, vol. 1: *Colonial Times to 1970* (Washington, D.C.: Government Printing Office, 1975), *passim*; and the statistical tables of *The National Income and Product Accounts of the United States, 1929–1976*, (Washington, D.C.: U.S. Department of Commerce, Bureau of Economic Analysis, September 1981), *passim*; Edward F. Denison, *Trends in American Economic Growth, 1929–1982* (Washington, D.C.: The Brookings Institution, 1985), 76ff; Herbert Stein, *Presidential Economics: The Making of Economic Policy from Roosevelt to Reagan and Beyond* (New York: Simon and Schuster, 1984), 379ff; and "Statistical Tables Relating to Income, Employment and Production," in *Economic Report of the President, transmitted to Congress February 1986* (Washington, D.C.: Government Printing Office, 1986), *passim*.

12. John Maynard Keynes, *The General Theory of Employment, Interest and Money* (New York: Harcourt, Brace & Co., 1936), 168–85.

13. Ibid., 249–54.

14. David McCord Wright, "The Future of Keynesian Economics," *AER* 35 (June 1945): 305.

15. Walter A. Morton, discussion on "American Economic Stabilization," Papers and Proceedings of the Sixty-third Annual Meeting of the American Economic Association, December 1950, *AER* 41 (May 1951): 199.

16. Dudley Dillard, "The Influence of Keynesian Economics on Contemporary Thought," Papers and Proceedings of the Sixty-ninth Annual Meeting of the American Economic Association, December 1956, *AER* 47 (May 1957): 84.

17. See Evsey D. Domar, "Expansion and Employment," *AER* 37 (March 1947): 54

18. Paul A. Samuelson, *Economics: An Introductory Analysis*, 1st ed., (New York: McGraw-Hill, 1948), 15.

19. Paul A. Samuelson, "Linear Programming and Economic Theory," in *The Collected Scientific Papers of Paul A. Samuelson*, ed. Joseph E. Stiglitz, 5 vols. (Cambridge, Mass.: MIT Press, 1966–86), 1:494. Originally published as part of the *Proceedings of the Second Symposium in Linear Programming* of the National Bureau of Standards and the United States Air Force, January 27–29, 1955.

20. Paul A. Samuelson, "Principles and Rules in Modern Fiscal Policy: A Neoclassical Reformulation," in *Collected Scientific Papers*, 2:1271–90. See also John Hicks, "IS-LM Explanation," in John Hicks, *Money, Interest and Wages: Collected Essays in Economic Theory* (Cambridge, Mass.: Harvard University Press, 1982), 2:318–31. For Hicks, a change in policy ensures that an economy in disequilibrium in the labor market will eventually settle into what may be regarded as a new equilibrium. For Samuelson, such a policy change may or may not be appropriate.

21. Keynes, *General Theory*, 322.

22. Cf. Abba P. Lerner, "The Economic Steering Wheel: The Story of the People's New Clothes," *University Review*, June 1941, pp. 2–8; and Abba P. Lerner, "Functional Finance and the Federal Debt," *Social Research* 10 (February 1943): 38–51. For a discussion on postwar fiscal plans, see Stein, *Fiscal Revolution*, 197ff, esp. 233ff.

23. Statement of Sixteen Economists: "Federal Expenditure and Revenue Policy for Economic Stability," *AER* 39 (December 1949): 1263–68. Along the same lines of thought, see the Report of a Subcommittee of the Committee on Public Issues of the American Economic Association, *AER* 40 (June 1950): 503–38. For a critique of the then dominant themes of built-in flexibility and automatic policy in economic stabilization, for policy decisions instead of rules, and for fiscal rather than for monetary instruments, see Walter W. Heller, "CED's Stabilizing Budget Policy after Ten Years," *AER* 47 (September 1957): 634ff.

24. Paul J. Strayer, "Public Expenditure Policy," *AER* 39 (March 1949): 383ff.

25. Paul A. Samuelson and Robert M. Solow, "Problems of Achieving and Maintaining a Stable Price Level," *AER* 50 (May 1960): 177.

26. Paul J. Strayer, "An Appraisal of Current Fiscal Theory," Proceedings of the Sixty-fourth Annual Meeting of the American Economic Association, December 1951, *AER* 42 (May 1952): 141, 144.

27. Cf. Harry G. Johnson, "The General Theory after Twenty-Five Years," *AER* 51 (May 1961): 14ff.

28. William Fellner, "Keynesian Economics after Twenty Years," Papers and Proceedings of the Sixty-ninth Annual Meeting of the American Economic Association, December 1956, *AER* 47 (May 1957): 68–69.

29. William Fellner, *Monetary Policies and Full Employment* (Berkeley: University of California Press, 1946), 3.

30. Friedrich von Hayek, "Full Employment, Planning and Inflation," *Institute of Public Affairs Review*, 4 (1950) and reprinted in his *Studies in Philosophy, Politics and Economics* (New York: Simon and Schuster, 1967), 270ff. See also Edwin G. Nourse, "Ideal and Working Concepts of Full Employment," Papers and Proceedings of the Sixty-ninth Annual Meeting of the American Economic Association, December 1956, *AER* 47 (May 1957): 98–99.

31. Friedrich von Hayek, "Inflation Resulting from the Downward Inflexibility of Wages," reprinted from Committee for Economic Development, *Problems of United States Economic Development* (1958) in von Hayek, *Studies in Philosophy, Politics and Economics*, 297.

32. Henry C. Wallich, "United Nations Report on Full Employment," *AER* 40 (December 1950), Part 1: 881.

33. Nourse, "Concepts of Full Employment," 99ff.

34. Samuelson and Solow, "Problems of Achieving and Maintaining," 189ff.

35. Gottfried Haberler, contribution to *Problems of United States Economic Development* (New York: Committee for Economic Development, January 1958), 1: 137ff. See also William Fellner, "Problem of Achieving and Maintaining a High Rate of Economic Growth," Papers and Proceedings of the Seventy-second Annual Meeting of the American Economic Association, December 1959, *AER* 50 (May 1960): 95–96.

36. See Keynes, *General Theory*, 257ff.

37. Von Hayek, "Downward Inflexibility of Wages," 295ff.

38. Fellner, "Keynesian Economics after Twenty Years," 73ff.

39. See Calvin B. Hoover, "Economic Growth I. Statement of the Problem of Keeping the United States' Economy Moving Forward, but Steadily," Papers and Proceedings of the Sixty-eighth Annual Meeting of the American Economic Assocation, December 1955, *AER* 46 (May 1956): 1ff.

40. Arthur F. Burns, "Some Reflections on the Employment Act," *Political Science Quarterly* 77 (December 1962): 481ff; and Arthur F. Burns, "Economics and Our Public Policy of Full Employment," in *The Nation's Economic Objectives*,

ed. Edgar O. Edwards (Chicago: University of Chicago Press, for William Marsh, Rice University, 1966), 55ff.

41. *Economic Report of the President to the Congress, January 8, 1947* (Washington, D.C.: Government Printing Office, 1947), 1–2, 18, 20ff.

42. *Economic Report of the President to the Congress, January 14, 1948*, together with the *Annual Report* of the Council of Economic Advisers (Washington, D.C.: Government Printing Office, 1948), 5–7, 46ff.

43. Council of Economic Advisers, *Third Annual Report to the President* (Washington, D.C.: Government Printing Office, 1948), 31–32.

44. *Economic Report of the President to the Congress, January 1949*, together with a *Report to the President* by the Council of Economic Advisers (Washington, D.C.: Government Printing Office, 1949), 2–3, 52, 61.

45. *Midyear Economic Report of the President to the Congress, July 11, 1949*, together with a Report by the Council of Economic Advisers, *The Economic Situation at Midyear* (Washington, D.C.: Government Printing Office, 1949), 1–2.

46. *Economic Report of the President, transmitted to the Congress January 6, 1950*, together with a Report to the President by the Council of Economic Advisers, *The Annual Economic Review* (Washington, D.C.: Government Printing Office, 1950), 12ff, 80, 85.

47. *Midyear Economic Report of the President, transmitted to the Congress, July 23, 1951*, together with a Report to the President by the Council of Economic Advisers, *The Economic Situation at Midyear 1951* (Washington, D.C.: Government Printing Office, 1951), 40–49.

48. *Economic Report of the President, transmitted to the Congress, January 16, 1952*, together with a Report to the President by the Council of Economic Advisers, *The Annual Economic Review* (Washington, D.C.: Government Printing Office, 1952), 25.

49. *Midyear Economic Report of the President to the Congress, July 19, 1952*, together with a Report to the President by the Council of Economic Advisers, *The Midyear 1952 Economic Report* (Washington, D.C.: Government Printing Office, July 1952), 12ff.

50. *Economic Report of the President, January 14, 1953*, (Washington, D.C.: Government Printing Office, 1953), 16ff.

51. *Economic Report of the President, January 28, 1954*, (Washington, D.C.: Government Printing Office, 1954), 52, 54ff, 81–82, 112ff.

52. *Economic Report of the President, January 20, 1955*, (Washington, D.C.: Government Printing Office, 1955), v–vi, 2ff, 18ff, 64ff, 69–71.

53. *Economic Report of the President, January 24, 1956*, (Washington, D.C.: Government Printing Office, 1956), 10–11, 28–29.

54. *Economic Report of the President, January 23, 1957*, (Washington, D.C.: Government Printing Office, 1957), 40.

55. *Economic Report of the President, January 20, 1958*, (Washington, D.C.: Government Printing Office, 1958), 1ff, 8.

56. *Economic Report of the President, January 20, 1959*, (Washington, D.C.: Government Printing Office, 1959), 1–5, 48ff..

57. *Economic Report of the President, January 28, 1954*, 52.

58. *Economic Report of the President, January 18, 1961*, (Washington, D.C.: Government Printing Office, 1961), 46–47.

59. *Economic Report of the President, January 6, 1950*, 80.

60. Alvin H. Hansen, *The American Economy* (New York: McGraw-Hill, 1957), 38–39.

61. *Economic Report of the President, January 20, 1958*, 1; *Economic Report of the President, January 18, 1961*, 49.

62. M. B. Schnapper, ed., *The Truman Program: Addresses and Messages by President Harry S Truman* (Washington, D.C.: Public Affairs Press, 1949), 100.

63. Adlai E. Stevenson, *Major Campaign Speeches, 1952* (New York: Random House, 1953), 169, 231.

64. Paul J. Strayer, "The Council of Economic Advisers: Political Economy on Trial," Papers and Proceedings of the Sixty-second Annual Meeting of the American Economic Association, December 1949, *AER* 40 (May 1950): 146–48.

65. Gottfried Haberler, Contribution to *Problems of United States Economic Development*, 1:140–41.

66. Schnapper, *Truman Program*, 100, 101. Also Stevenson, *Major Campaign Speeches*, 65.

67. J. K. Galbraith, "Economic Preconceptions and the Farm Policy," *AER* 44 (March 1954): 40ff.

68. Hansen, *American Economy*, 21.

69. Dwight D. Eisenhower, *The White House Years, Mandate for Change, 1953–1956* (Garden City, N.Y.: Doubleday & Co., 1963), 488.

70. Henry C. Wallich, "Postwar United States Monetary Policy Appraised," in The American Assembly, *United States Monetary Policy* (New York: Columbia University, December 1958), 100.

71. Arthur S. Burns, "Monetary Policy and the Threat of Inflation: An Address to the 14th American Assembly," in ibid., 210.

72. Ezra Taft Benson, *Crossfire: The Eight Years with Eisenhower* (Garden City, N.Y.: Doubleday & Co., 1962), 429.

73. Nathaniel Goldfinger, in "The Economics of Eisenhower: A Symposium," *Review of Economics and Statistics* 37 (November 1956): 383.

74. See Edward S. Shaw, in ibid., 376.

75. Seymour E. Harris, *The Economics of the Political Parties* (New York: Macmillan, 1962), 19, 48–49.

76. See Arnold C. Harberger, in "The Economics of Eisenhower: A Symposium," 381; and Harold M. Groves, in ibid., 378.

77. For an extensive critique of the Eisenhower administration on this and other points, see *Staff Report on Employment, Growth and Price Levels*, prepared for consideration by the Joint Economic Committee of the 86th Cong., 1st sess., 24 December 1959 (Washington, D.C.: Government Printing Office 1960), xxx, *passim*, pp. xxi–xxxvii.

78. Compare data in the *Historical Statistics of the United States*, Tables E 135–160 and D 689–717, pp. 163, 210.

79. Burns, "Monetary Policy," 212.

80. *Staff Report on Employment*, xxvii.

81. Schnapper, *Truman Program*, 80.

82. See Tobin, *New Economics*, 7.

83. Gottfried Haberler, "The Place of *The General Theory of Employment, Interest and Money* in the History of Economic Thought," *Review of Economics and Statistics* 28 (November 1946): 187ff.

84. Keynes, *General Theory*, 372–73.

85. For all the authors mentioned in this paragraph, see *John Maynard Keynes, Critical Assessments*, ed. John Cunningham Wood (London: Croom Helm, 1983), 4 vols.

86. Keynes, *General Theory*, 323–24.

CHAPTER 3. GROWTH-ORIENTED POLICIES

1. See, for instance, President Nixon's "Address to the Nation on Economic Policy and Productivity," 17 June 1970, in *Public Papers of the Presidents of the United States: Richard M. Nixon, 1970* (Washington, D.C.: Government Printing Office, 1971), 502ff.

2. Arthur M. Okun, *The Political Economy of Prosperity* (New York: W. W. Norton, 1969), 37.

3. For these and the following data, see the *Historical Statistics of the United States*, vol. 1: *Colonial Times to 1970* (Washington, D.C.: Government Printing Office, 1975), *passim*; and the statistical tables of *The National Income and Product Accounts of the United States, 1929–1976*, (Washington, D.C.: U.S. Department of Commerce, Bureau of Economic Analysis, September 1981), *passim*; Edward F. Denison, *Trends in American Economic Growth, 1929–1982* (Washington, D.C.: The Brookings Institution, 1985), 76ff; Herbert Stein, *Presidential Economics: The Making of Economic Policy from Roosevelt to Reagan and Beyond* (New York: Simon and Schuster, 1984), 379ff; and "Statistical Tables Relating to Income, Employment and Production," in *Economic Report of the President, transmitted to the Congress, February 1986* (Washington, D.C.: Government Printing Office, 1986), *passim*.

4. For the United States, see *Statistical Abstract of the United States* for 1976 and 1986 (Washington, D.C.: U.S. Department of Commerce, 1976 and 1986), 395 and 434, respectively; for the OECD and the Soviet Union, see *USSR: Measures of Economic Growth and Development, 1950–1980*, Studies prepared for the use of the Joint Economic Committee, Congress of the United States, 97th Cong., 2d sess., 8 December 1982 (Washington, D.C.: Government Printing Office, 1982), 20.

5. Michael Kalecki, "Econometric Models and Historical Materialism," in *On Political Economy and Econometrics, Essays in Honor of Oskar Lange*, edited by a Collective of Scholars (Warsaw: PWN, Polish Scientific Publishers, and London: Pergamon Press, 1965), 233ff. See also Adolph Lowe, "The Classical Theory of Economic Growth," *Social Research* 21 (July 1954): 145.

6. Nicolas Spulber, *Soviet Strategy for Economic Growth* (Bloomington: Indiana University Press, 1964), 38ff.

7. Charles P. Kindleberger and Bruce Herrick, *Economics Department*, 3d ed. (New York: McGraw-Hill, 1977), 3 (emphasis supplied).

8. Gerald M. Meier and Robert E. Baldwin, *Economic Development: Theory, History, Policy* (New York: John Wiley & Sons, 1961), 19ff. See also Bert F. Hoselitz, "Theories of Stages of Economic Growth," in *Theories of Economic Growth*, by Bert F. Hoselitz et al. (Glencoe, Ill.: Free Press, 1960), 193ff.

9. Walter W. Rostow, *The Stages of Economic Growth, A Non-Communist Manifesto* (Cambridge: Cambridge University Press, 1960), 4ff; John C. H. Fei and Gustav Ranis, "Agrarianism, Dualism and Economic Development," in *The Theory and Design of Economic Development*, ed. Irma Adelman and Erik Thorbecke (Baltimore: Johns Hopkins University Press, 1966), 3ff.

10. Lloyd G. Reynolds, "Is 'Development Economics' a Subject?" in *Industrial Organization and Economic Development, in Honor of E.S. Mason*, ed. Jesse W. Markham and Gustav F. Papanek (New York: Houghton Mifflin, 1978), 322–23.

11. Gerald M. Meier, *Leading Issues in Economic Development* (New York: Oxford University Press, 1984), 707.

12. Ibid., 358.

13. Kenneth J. Arrow and Mordecai Kurz, *Public Investments, the Rate of Return, and Optimal Fiscal Policy* (Baltimore: Johns Hopkins University Press, for Resources for the Future, 1970), 14ff.

14. See notably Robert M. Solow, "A Contribution to the Theory of Economic

Growth," *Quarterly Journal of Economics* 70 (February 1956): 65–94. See also Robert M. Solow, "Technical Change and the Aggregate Production Function," *Review of Economics and Statistics* 39 (August 1957): 312–20; and F. H. Hahn and R. C. O. Matthews, "The Theory of Economic Growth: A Survey," in *Surveys of Economic Theory, Growth and Development*, vol. 2, prepared for the American Economic Association and the Royal Economic Society (London: Macmillan, and New York: St. Martin's Press, 1965), 5ff.

15. Sukhamoy Chakravarty, *Capital and Development Planning* (Cambridge, Mass.: MIT Press, 1969), 2, 19ff, 185ff; Tjalling C. Koopmans, "Objectives, Constraints and Outcomes in Optimal Growth Models," *Econometrica* 35 (1967): 1ff. See also Y. Murakami, K. Tokoyama, and J. Tsukui, "Efficient Paths of Accumulation and the Turnpike of the Japanese economy," in *Application of Input-Output Analysis*, ed. A. P. Carter and A. Brody (Amsterdam: North Holland, 1970), 24ff.

16. Arrow and Kurz, *Public Investments*, xv, 128.

17. Paul A. Samuelson, "Public Responsibility for Growth and Stability," originally published in 1956 as "The New Look in Tax and Fiscal Policy," reprinted in Edmund S. Phelps, *The Goal of Economic Growth* (New York: W. W. Norton, 1962), p. 41. Also Paul A. Samuelson, *Stability and Growth in the American Economy*, Wicksell Lectures, 1962 (Stockholm: Almquist & Wicksell, 1963), pp. 27ff.

18. James Tobin, "Economic Growth as an Objective of Government Policy," Papers and Proceedings of the Seventy-sixth Annual Meeting of the American Economic Association, December 1963, *American Economic Review* (hereafter *AER*), 54 (May 1964): 10–13.

19. James Tobin, *The New Economics One Decade Older* (Princeton, N.J.: Princeton University Press, 1974), 15.

20. Herbert Stein, discussion of Tobin, "Economic Growth," 25.

21. Harry G. Johnson, ibid.

22. Okun, *Political Economy*, 134–35.

23. See Herbert Stein, "Changes in Macroeconomic Conditions," in *The American Economy in Transition*, ed. Martin Feldstein (Chicago: University of Chicago Press, 1980), 171. See also Tobin, *New Economics*, 16–17.

24. James W. Knowles, with Charles B. Warden, Jr., *The Potential Economic Growth in the United States*, Materials for the Study of Employment, Growth, and Price Levels, for the Joint Economic Committee, Congress of the United States, 86th Cong., 1st sess., Study Paper No. 20, 30 January 1960 (Washington, D.C.: Government Printing Office, 1960); Edward F. Denison, *The Sources of Economic Growth in the United States and the Alternatives Before Us*, Supplementary Paper No. 13 (New York: Committee for Economic Development, 1962).

25. Otto Eckstein, "The Economics of the 1960s: A Backward Look," *Public Interest* 19 (Spring 1970): 87; Robert M. Solow, "Economic Growth and Residential Housing," in Proceedings of the *Conference on Savings and Residential Financing* (Chicago: United States Savings and Loan League, 1962), p. 129.

26. See Milton Friedman and Walter W. Heller, *Monetary vs. Fiscal Policy: A Dialogue* (New York: W. W. Norton, 1969), *passim*.

27. Sidney Kraus, ed., *The Great Debates: Background, Perspective, Effects* (Bloomington: Indiana University Press, 1962), 352.

28. *Public Papers of the Presidents: John F. Kennedy, 1961* (Washington, D.C.: Government Printing Office, 1962), 20.

29. Arthur F. Burns and Paul A. Samuelson, *Full Employment, Guideposts and Economic Stability*, Rational Debate Seminars, (Washington, D.C.: American Enterprise Institute, 1967), 96.

30. "Economic Frontiers," first published as "Prospects and Policies for the 1961 American Economy: Report to President-elect Kennedy by a Task Force, 6

January 1961," reprinted in *The Collected Scientific Papers of Paul A. Samuelson*, ed. Joseph E. Stiglitz, 5 vols. (Cambridge, Mass.: MIT Press, 1966), 2: *passim.* See also Seymour E. Harris, *Economics of the Kennedy Years and a Look Ahead* (New York: Harper and Row, 1964), 59.

31. *Public Papers: Kennedy, 1961*, 41ff; *Economic Report of the President, transmitted to the Congress, January 1962*, together with *The Annual Report* of the Council of Economic Advisers (Washington, D.C.: Government Printing Office, 1962), 4, 7, 86.

32. Ibid., 4, 8, 16–17. See also *Public Papers of the Presidents: Kennedy, 1962* (Washington, D.C.: Government Printing Office, 1963), 457.

33. Ibid., 877–78.

34. Ibid., 470ff; Harris, *Economics of the Kennedy Years*, 23, 60, 66ff; Herbert Stein, *The Fiscal Revolution in America* (Chicago: University of Chicago Press, 1969), 374ff; Walter W. Heller, *New Dimensions of Political Economy* (New York: W. W. Norton, 1967), 37.

35. *Economic Report of the President, transmitted to the Congress, January 1963*, together with *The Annual Report* of the Council of Economic Advisers (Washington, D.C.: Government Printing Office, 1963), p. 5.

36. *Public Papers of the Presidents: John F. Kennedy, 1963* (Washington, D.C.: Government Printing Office, 1964), 73.

37. *Economic Report of the President, January 1963*, 37, 52.

38. *Public Papers: Kennedy, 1963*, 75, 77 (emphasis supplied).

39. Stein, *Fiscal Revolution*, 185–86; *Economic Report of the President, January 1962*, 78ff.

40. James L. Sundquist, *Politics and Policy: The Eisenhower, Kennedy and Johnson Years* (Washington, D.C.: The Brookings Institution, 1968), 42ff.

41. Harris, *Economics of the Kennedy Years*, 71, 73.

42. *Two Top Priority Programs to Reduce Unemployment* (Washington, D.C.: Conference on Economic Progress, December 1963), 3ff.

43. Harris, *Economics of the Kennedy Years*, 66; Eckstein, "Economics of the 1960s," 112.

44. Ibid.

45. Paul A. Samuelson, "Fiscal and Financial Policies for Growth," in *Economic Growth, An American Problem*, ed. Peter M. Gutman (Englewood Cliffs, N.J.: Prentice Hall, 1964), 162.

46. Tobin, "Economic Growth," 5 (emphasis supplied).

47. *Economic Report of the President, transmitted to the Congress, January 1964*, together with *The Annual Report* of the Council of Economic Advisers (Washington, D.C.: Government Printing Office, 1964), 41–42.

48. Stein, *Fiscal Revolution*, 372. See also his *Presidential Economics*, 107.

49. Tobin, *New Economics*, 34.

50. *Economic Report of the President, transmitted to the Congress, January 1966*, together with *The Annual Report* of the Council of Economic Advisers (Washington, D.C.: Government Printing Office, 1966), 4, 12, 20, 182.

51. Okun, *Political Economy*, 70ff.

52. James Tobin, "Inflation and Unemployment," *AER* 42 (March 1972): 17, *passim.*

53. Heller, *New Dimensions*, 42ff.

54. George P. Shultz and Robert Z. Aliber, eds. *Guidelines, Informal Controls and the Market Place* (Chicago: University of Chicago Press, 1966), 37, 64–65.

55. *The 1967 Economic Report of the President*, Hearings before the Joint Economic Committee, Congress of the United States, 90th Cong., 1st sess., February 15–17, 1967 (Washington, D.C.: Government Printing Office, 1967), Part 3, pp. 498, 614, 655ff.

56. *Economic Report of the President, transmitted to the Congress, February 1968*, together with *The Annual Report* of the Council of Economic Advisers, (Washington, D.C.: Government Printing Office, 1968), 9, 10, 19.

57. Ibid., 73, 75, 78, and *passim.*

58. Cf. Stein, *Presidential Economics*, 144–45.

59. *Public Papers of the Presidents of the United States: Richard M. Nixon, 1969* (Washington, D.C.: Government Printing Office, 1970), esp. 376, 755, 958. See also "Address to the Nation on Economic Policy and Productivity," 17 June 1970, in *Public Papers of the Presidents of the United States: Richard Nixon, 1970* (Washington, D.C.: Government Printing Office, 1971), 502.

60. *Public Papers: Nixon, 1970,*12; and *Economic Report of the President, transmitted to the Congress, February 1970*, together with *The Annual Report* of the Council of Economic Advisers (Washington, D.C.: Government Printing Office, 1970), 3.

61. See notably "Dr. McCracken on Price-Wage Controls," *Economic Education Bulletin* 12 (January 1972): 1–2; and John K. Galbraith, *Economics, Peace and Laughter* (New York: New American Library, 1971), 88–99.

62. *Economic Report of the President, transmitted to the Congress, February 1971*, together with *The Annual Report* of the Council of Economic Advisers (Washington, D.C.: Government Printing Office, 1971), 85.

63. "The 1971 Report of the President's Council of Economic Advisers" (particularly the articles by Abba P. Lerner and Robert Eisner), *AER* 41 (September 1971): 524, 527.

64. *Economic Report of the President, transmitted to the Congress, February 1974*, together with *The Annual Report* of the Council of Economic Advisers (Washington, D.C.: Government Printing Office, 1974), 4–7, 99.

65. *The Conference on Inflation*, Held at the request of President Gerald R. Ford and the Congress of the United States, September 27–28, 1974 (Washington, D.C.: Government Printing Office, 1974).

66. Ibid., 255–56, 257, 259, 271, 279.

67. *Economic Report of the President, transmitted to the Congress, February 1975* (Washington, D.C.: Government Printing Office, 1975), 137.

68. John Maynard Keynes, *The General Theory of Employment Interest and Money* (New York: Harcourt, Brace & Co., 1936), 249, 313, 320 (emphasis supplied).

69. *Economic Report of the President, January 1962*, 70–72.

70. Walter W. Heller, "Adjusting the 'New Economics' to High-Pressure Prosperity," in *Managing a Full Employment Economy*, a CED Symposium on Problems of Maintaining Prosperity without Inflation, Held in Los Angeles, May 1966 (New York: Committee for Economic Development), 9; Heller, *New Dimensions*, 69; Friedman and Heller, *Monetary vs. Fiscal Policy*, 41.

71. Karl Brunner, "Issues of Post-Keynesian Monetary Analysis," in *The Structure of Monetarism*, by Thomas Mayer et al. (New York: W. W. Norton, 1978), 74.

72. Friedman and Heller, *Monetary vs. Fiscal Policy*, 52, 53.

73. *The 1967 Economic Report of the President*, Hearings before the Joint Economic Committee, 661ff.

74. Keynes, *General Theory*, 301, 303.

75. Okun, *Political Economy*, 40.

76. John Hicks, *The Crisis in Keynesian Economics*, Yrjö Jahnsson Lectures (Oxford: Basil Blackwell, 1974), 62–63.

77. Tobin, "Inflation and Unemployment," 2, 9.

78. Allan Meltzer, "Monetarist, Keynesian and Quantity Theories," in *Structure of Monetarism*, 173.

79. Milton Friedman, "Comments" in *Guidelines, Informal Controls and the Market Place*, 59–60; Milton Friedman, "The Role of Monetary Policy," *AER* 58 (March 1968): 8–9.

80. Tobin, "Inflation and Unemployment," 9.

81. Heller, *New Dimensions,* 71–72.

82. Friedman and Heller, *Monetary vs. Fiscal Policy,* 28–32.

83. Robert J. Gordon, "What Can Stabilization Achieve?" Papers and Proceedings of the Ninetieth Annual Meeting of the American Economic Association, December 1977, *AER* 68 (May 1978): 336.

84. E. J. Mishan, *The Economic Growth Debate: An Assessment* (London: Allen and Unwin, 1977), *passim.*

85. See William Nordhaus and James Tobin, "Is Growth Obsolete?" in *Economic Growth,* Fiftieth Anniversary Colloquium V (New York: National Bureau of Economic Research, 1972), 4ff, 82–83. For a critical examination of the measure of economic welfare (MEW), see Henry M. Peskin, "National Income Accounts and the Environment," in *Environmental Regulation and the Economy,* ed. Henry M. Peskin et al. (Baltimore: Johns Hopkins University Press, for Resources for the Future, 1981), 80–81.

86. See the cogent book of Depak Lal, *The Poverty of "Development Economics"* (Cambridge, Mass.: Harvard University Press, 1985), 5ff.

87. J. E. Meade, "Is 'The New Industrial State' Inevitable?" *Economic Journal* 78 (June 1968): 372ff. See also Nicolas Spulber and Ira Horowitz, *Quantitative Economic Policy and Planning* (New York: W. W. Norton, 1976), 371ff.

88. Johannes van den Doel, *Konvergentie en Evolutie* (Assen, Holland: Van Gorcum, 1971), *passim.*

89. Spulber and Horowitz, *Quantitative Economic Policy,* 374.

90. Meade, "New Industrial State," 391; George N. Halin, "Will Market Economies and Planned Economies Converge?" in *Roads to Freedom, Essays in Honor of Friedrich A. von Hayek,* ed. Erick Streissler et al. (New York: Augustus M. Kelly, 1970), 76, *passim.*

91. Nordhaus and Tobin, "Is Growth Obsolete?" 1.

92. Robert M. Solow, "Where Have All the Flowers Gone? Economic Growth in the 1960s," in *Economics in the Public Service, Papers in Honor of Walter W. Heller,* ed. Joseph A. Pechman and N. J. Simler (New York: W. W. Norton, 1982), 46ff.

93. C. J. Bliss, *Capital Theory and the Distribution of Income* (Amsterdam and New York: North Holland and Elsevier, 1975), 5, 10ff.

94. Paul A. Samuelson, "Comment (Post-Camelot Dilemmas)," in *Economics in the Public Service,* 40ff.

95. Erik Lundberg, "The Contributions of the Economics of Growth to Economic Policy," in *Towards an Explanation of Economic Growth, Symposium 1980,* ed. Herbert Giersch (Tübingen: J.C.B. Mohr, 1980), 447ff.

CHAPTER 4. ANTISTAGFLATION POLICIES

1. See "The Great Recession of 1974–75: Monitoring Econometric Forecasts," in *Business Fluctuations, Forecasting Techniques and Applications,* by Dale G. Bails and Larry C. Peppers (Englewood Cliffs, N.J.: Prentice Hall, 1982), 66ff. One may sadly recall that the forecasts made some forty-three years earlier, before the onset of the Great Depression, had been equally optimistic and also totally off the mark.

2. Gottfried Haberler, *The Problem of Stagflation: Reflections on the Microfoundation of Macroeconomic Theory and Policy* (Washington, D.C.: American Enterprise Institute, 1985), 9.

3. Ibid., Chap. 2, n. 86. The passage from Keynes's *General Theory* quoted in the latter is a basic illustration of the idea of the "exhaustion" of investment opportunities. For the 1930s, see Alvin H. Hansen's statement in *Investigation of Concentration of Economic Power,* Hearings before the Temporary National Eco-

nomic Council, Part 9: Savings and Investment, May 16–26, 1939 (Washington, D.C.: Government Printing Office, 1940), 3495ff.

4. For these and the following data, see the *Historical Statistics of the United States*, vol. 1: *Colonial Times to 1970* (Washington, D.C.: Government Printing Office, 1975), *passim;* and the statistical tables of *The National Income and Product Accounts of the United States, 1929–1976,* (Washington, D.C.: U.S. Department of Commerce, Bureau of Economic Analysis, September 1981), *passim;* Edward F. Denison, *Trends in American Economic Growth, 1929–1982* (Washington, D.C.: The Brookings Institution, 1985), 76ff; Herbert Stein, *Presidential Economics: The Making of Economic Policy from Roosevelt to Reagan and Beyond* (New York: Simon and Schuster, 1984), 379ff; and "Statistical Tables Relating to Income, Employment and Production," in *Economic Report of the President, transmitted to the Congress February 1986* (Washington, D.C.: Government Printing Office, 1986), *passim.*

5. Paul A. Samuelson, "Worldwide Stagflation," *The Morgan Guaranty Survey,* June 1974, reprinted in *The Collected Scientific Papers of Paul A. Samuelson,* ed. Hiroaki Nagatani and Kate Crowley, (Cambridge, Mass.: MIT Press, 1977), 4: 802–3.

6. See Paul A. Samuelson, "The House that Keynes Built," *New York Times,* 29 May 1983, pp. 6F-7F.

7. Robert J. Barro (discussant), "Reflections on the Current State of Macroeconomic Theory," Papers and Proceedings of the Ninety-sixth Annual Meeting of the American Economic Association, December 1983, *American Economic Review* (hereafter *AER*), 74 (May 1984): 417.

8. Friedrich von Hayek, "The Keynes Centenary: The Austrian Critique," *The Economist,* 11 June 1983, pp. 39ff.

9. Robert E. Lucas, Jr., and Thomas J. Sargent, "After Keynesian Macroeconomics," in *Rational Expectations and Econometric Practice,* ed. Robert E. Lucas, Jr., and Thomas J. Sargent (Minneapolis: University of Minnesota Press, 1981), 295–319. See also Herschel I. Grossman, "The Natural Rate Hypothesis and the Remarkable Survival of Non-Market Clearing Assumptions," in *Variability in Employment, Prices and Money,* ed. Karl Brunner and Allan H. Meltzer, Carnegie-Rochester Conference on Public Policy, vol. 19 (Autumn 1983), 225ff.

10. Lucas and Sargent, "After Keynesian Macroeconomics," 296.

11. See, for instance, Bails and Peppers, *Business Fluctuations,* 73ff.

12. Lucas and Sargent, "After Keynesian Macroeconomics," 316–17. See also Thomas J. Sargent, *Dynamic Macroeconomic Theory* (Cambridge, Mass.: Harvard University Press, 1987), 2.

13. Thomas J. Sargent and Neil Wallace, "Rational Expectations and the Theory of Economic Policy," in *Rational Expectations and Econometric Practice,* 213.

14. See Martin Feldstein, "Supply-Side Economics: Old Truths and New Claims," Papers and Proceedings of the Ninety-eighth Annual Meeting of the American Economic Association, December 1985, *AER* 76 (May 1986), 26ff; and Paul Craig Roberts, *The Supply-Side Revolution: An Insider's Account of Policymaking in Washington* (Cambridge, Mass.: Harvard University Press, 1984), 5–6.

15. Paul A. Samuelson, "Comment (Post-Camelot Dilemmas)," in *Economics in the Public Service: Papers in Honor of Walter W. Heller,* ed. Joseph A. Pechman and N. J. Simler (New York: W. W. Norton, 1982), 40ff.

16. See Paul A. Samuelson and William D. Nordhaus, *Economics,* 12th ed. (New York: McGraw-Hill, 1985), 327–43, *passim.* See also William D. Nordhaus, "Macroconfusion: The Dilemmas of Economic Policy," in *Macroeconomics, Prices and Quantities, Essays in Memory of Arthur M. Okun,* ed. James Tobin (Washington, D.C.: The Brookings Institution, 1983), 251, 253–54, 256–58.

17. Craufurd D. Goodwin, "Changing Ideas of Planning in the United States," in *National Economic Planning*, Six papers presented at a Conference in Washington, D.C., 12 November 1975, by Craufurd D. Goodwin et al. (Washington, D.C.: The Chamber of Commerce of the United States, 1976), 25.

18. G. J. Santoni, "The Employment Act of 1946: Some History Notes," The Federal Reserve Bank of St. Louis *Review* 68 (November 1986): 15.

19. See, for instance, Barry Bluestone and Bennett Harrison, *The Deindustrialization of America* (New York: Basic Books, 1982), 27ff, *passim*.

20. Charles L. Schultze, "Industrial Policy: A Dissent," *The Brookings Review*, Fall 1983, pp. 3ff. See also Richard E. Caves, Walter B. Wriston, and James R. Schlesinger, "The Structure of Industry," in *The American Economy in Transition*, ed. Martin Feldstein (Chicago: University of Chicago Press, 1980), 501ff.

21. Caves, Wriston, and Schlesinger, "Structure of Industry," 502.

22. Statement of Arnold A. Saltzman, Chairman, Advisory Committee on National Growth Policy Processes, at the Hearings before the Joint Economic Committee of Congress, 94th Cong., 2d sess., 19 November 1976, on *Long-Term Economic Growth* (Washington, D.C.: Government Printing Office, 1977) p. 252, *passim*.

23. Cf., for instance, John W. Kendrick, "International Comparisons of Recent Productivity Trends," in *Essays in Contemporary Economic Problems: Demand, Productivity and Population*, William Fellner, Project Director (Washington, D.C.: American Enterprise Institute, 1981), 125–70. See also *Productivity Growth: A Better Life for America*, White House Conference on Productivity: A Report to the President of the United States, Springfield, Va., April 1984, (Washington, D.C.: Department of Commerce, National Technical Information Service, 1984), 37ff.

24. William J. Baumol, "Productivity Growth, Convergence and Welfare: What the Long-Run Data Show," *AER* 76 (December 1986): 1072ff; William J. Baumol, "America's Productivity 'Crisis': A Modest Decline Isn't All That Bad," *New York Times*, 15 February 1987. A study by Michael R. Darby, "The U.S. Productivity Slowdown: A Case of Statistical Myopia," *AER* 74 (June 1984): 301ff, focused on the period 1900–79 and asserted that the evidence did not support the view that there had been a significant decline in U.S. productivity growth since 1965, especially since 1973. Darby started with an aggregate production function and tried to measure labor in a new way, taking into account the number of workers, their age, sex, education, and immigration as determinants of both quality of the labor force and average number of hours worked.

25. Edwin Mansfield, "Economic Growth or Stagnation: The Role of Technology," in *Economic Growth or Stagnation: The Future of the U.S. Economy*, ed. Jules Backman (Indianapolis: Bobbs-Merrill, 1978), 35ff; Edwin Mansfield, "Technology and Productivity in the United States," in *The American Economy in Transition*, 563ff.

26. Caves, Wriston, and Schlesinger, "Structure of Industry," 539.

27. *Global Competition, the New Reality: Report of the President's Commission on Industrial Competitiveness* (Washington, D.C.: Government Printing Office, January 1985), 2: 17. With regard to high technology exports, compare p. 14 of this source with Schultze, "Industrial Policy," which presents conflicting data.

28. Robert Eisner, "Capital Shortage: Myth and Reality," Papers and Proceedings of the Eighty-ninth Annual Meeting of the American Economic Association, September 1976, *AER* 67 (February 1977): 110ff.

29. Martin Feldstein, "Does the United States Save Too Little?" ibid., 116ff.

30. See, for instance, Herbert Stein, *Economic Planning and the Improvement of Economic Policy* (Washington, D.C.: American Enterprise Institute, 1975), 7ff.

31. See in particular *Full Employment and Balanced Growth Act of 1976*, Hearings before the Committee on Banking, Housing and Urban Affairs, U.S. Senate, 94th Cong., 2d sess., May 20, 21 and 25, 1976, (Washington, D.C.: Government Printing Office, 1976)—with an array of depositions by economists for or against the Act; Wassily Leontief and Herbert Stein, *The Economic System in an Age of Discontinuity: Long-Range Planning or Market Reliance?* (New York: New York University Press, 1976); and Goodwin et al., *National Economic Planning*.

32. Jacob K. Javits, "The Need for National Planning," *Wall Street Journal*, 8 July 1975, p. 14.

33. "The Political Realities of Industrial Policy," with the participation of George C. Eads, Arthur Levitt, J. Thomas K. McCraw, Robert G. Reich, and Lester C. Thurow, edited by Allan M. Kantorow, *Harvard Business Review* 5 (September-October 1983): 76ff. See also Lester C. Thurow, "The Zero-Sum Society," *New York Times*, 28 August 1983; and Thurow, *The Zero-Sum Society* (New York: Basic Books, 1980).

34. Amitai Ezioni, *An Immodest Agenda: Rebuilding America before the Twenty-First Century* (New York: New Press, 1983).

35. Robert B. Reich, "Making Industrial Policy," *Foreign Affairs* (Spring 1982): 876ff. Also Reich in "Political Realities of Industrial Policy," 81, 86; Robert B. Reich, "Industrial Policy: Ten Concrete, Practical Steps to Building a Dynamic, Growing and Fair American Economy," *New Republic*, 31 March 1982, pp. 28–31; and Robert B. Reich, *The Next American Frontier* (New York: Penguin Books, 1983).

36. Robert M. Solow, "Wheeling and Dealing for the Common Good," review of *The Twenty-Year Century*, by Felix G. Rohatyn, *New York Times Book Review*, 5 February 1984, p. 11.

37. "Industrial Policy–Industrial Politics," *New York Times*, 23 January 1984, p. 16.

38. Schultze, "Industrial Policy," 7, 8, 11.

39. Roger G. Noll and Bruce M. Owen, *The Political Economy of Deregulation, Interest Groups in the Regulatory Process* (Washington, D.C.: American Enterprise Institute, 1983), 3. See also *Case Studies in Regulation, Revolution and Reform*, ed. Leonard W. Weiss and Michael W. Klass (Boston: Little, Brown, 1981), 1ff.

40. Jules Backman, ed., *Regulation and Deregulation* (Indianapolis: Bobbs-Merrill, 1981), 1–33.

41. *Global Competition, The New Reality*, , xii.

42. Alan M. Webber, " 'Competitiveness,' Not Industrial Policy," *New York Times*, 26 January 1987 (emphasis supplied).

43. *Global Competition, the New Reality*, xi–xii.

44. Henry Owen and Charles L. Schultze, eds., *Setting National Priorities, The Next Ten Years* (Washington, D.C.: The Brookings Institution, 1976), 7.

45. *Economic Report of the President, transmitted to the Congress, February 1975*, together with the *Annual Report* of the Council of Economic Advisers (Washington, D.C.: Government Printing Office, 1975), 7.

46. Annual Budget Message to the Congress, Fiscal Year 1976, 3 February 1975, in *The Public Papers of the Presidents of the United States: Gerald R. Ford, 1975* (Washington, D.C.: Government Printing Office, 1975), 1:146ff.

47. *Economic Report of the President, transmitted to the Congress, January 1976*, together with the *Annual Report* of the Council of Economic Advisers (Washington, D.C.: Government Printing Office, 1976), 5–6.

48. *Economic Report of the President, transmitted to the Congress, January 1977*,

together with the *Annual Report* of the Council of Economic Advisers (Washington, D.C.: Government Printing Office, 1977), 4–5.

49. Ibid., 52–53; *Economic Report of the President, transmitted to the Congress, January 1978*, together with the *Annual Report* of the Council of Economic Advisers (Washington, D.C.: Government Printing Office, 1978), 83; *Economic Report of the President, transmitted to the Congress, January 1979*, together with the *Annual Report* of the Council of Economic Advisers (Washington, D.C: Government Printing Office, 1979), 72, which states that "The level of potential output is less meaningful than its *rate of growth*. The latter gives the best estimate of how much the economy can actually grow over the next few years without putting additional pressure on labor or product markets."

50. Stephen Woolcock, "The Economic Policies of the Carter Administration," in *The Carter Years*, ed. M. Glenn Abernathy, Dills M. Hill, and Phil Williams (London: Frances Pinter, 1984), 37–38.

51. *Economic Report of the President, January 1978*, 4–6.

52. *Economic Report of the President, January 1979*, 76–81.

53. Ibid., 77, 78.

54. Woolcock, "Economic Policies of the Carter Administration," 44.

55. *Economic Report of the President, transmitted to the Congress, January 1980*, together with the *Annual Report* of the Council of Economic Advisers (Washington, D.C.: Government Printing Office, 1980), 90–95, 102.

56. *Economic Report of the President, transmitted to the Congress, January 1981*, together with the *Annual Report* of the Council of Economic Advisers (Washington, D.C.: Government Printing Office, 1981), 46–47

57. Ronald Reagan, *America's New Beginning: A Program for Economic Recovery*, speech presented to Congress, 18 February 1981 (Washington, D.C.: The White House Office of Press Secretary, 1981), 10, 14, 15–16, 19, 22.

58. *Economic Report of the President, transmitted to the Congress, February 1982*, together with the *Annual Report* of the Council of Economic Advisers (Washington, D.C.: Government Printing Office, 1982), 7.

59. President Reagan's "State of the Union Address," *Congressional Quarterly*, 30 January 1982, p. 176.

60. "Budget Message of the President," presented to Congress, 8 February 1982, *Congressional Quarterly*, 13 February 1982, pp. 283–89.

61. *Economic Report of the President, February 1982*, 4, 52, *passim.*

62. See Charles L. Schultze, "Long-Term Budget Strategies," in *Setting National Priorities, The 1983 Budget*, ed. Joseph A. Pechman (Washington, D.C.: The Brookings Institution, 1982), 189.

63. *Economic Report of the President, transmitted to the Congress, February 1983*, together with the *Annual Report* of the Council of Economic Advisers (Washington, D.C.: Government Printing Office, 1983), *passim.*

64. Robert Pear, "The Reagan Revolution: The Plans, The Progress," *New York Times*, 31 January 1983, 48–49.

65. *Economic Report of the President, transmitted to the Congress, February 1984*, together with the *Annual Report* of the Council of Economic Advisers (Washington, D.C.: Government Printing Office, 1984), 4.

66. Andrew F. Brimmer and Allen Sinai, "The Monetary-Fiscal Policy Mix: Implications for the Short Run," Papers and Proceedings of the Ninety-eighth Annual Meeting of the American Economic Association, December 1985, *AER* 76 (May 1986): 203–04

67. James Tobin, "Why Lower Rates Wouldn't Hurt," *New York Times*, 14 September 1986.

68. *Economic Report of the President, transmitted to the Congress, February 1985,* together with the *Annual Report* of the Council of Economic Advisers (Washington, D.C.: Government Printing Office, 1985), *passim.*

69. See Richard A. Musgrave, "The Reagan Administration's Fiscal Policy: A Critique," in *Reaganomics: A Midterm Report,* ed. William Craig Stubblebine and Thomas D. Willett (San Francisco: ICS Press, Institute for Contemporary Studies, 1983), 115ff.

70. D. Lee Bowden and John L. Palmer, "Social Policy: Challenging the Welfare State," in *The Reagan Record, An Assessment of America's Changing Domestic Priorities,* ed. John L. Palmer and Isabel V. Sawhill (Cambridge, Mass.: Ballinger Publishing Co., 1984), 211–12.

71. Musgrave, "Reagan Administration's Fiscal Policy," 123.

72. See James K. Oliver and James A. Nathan, "The Reagan Defense Program: Concepts, Continuity and Change," in *The Reagan Defense Program: An Interim Assessment,* ed. Stephen J. Cimbala (Wilmington, Del.: Scholarly Resources, 1986), 6, 13.

73. Paul A. Samuelson, "Evaluating Reaganomics," *Challenge* 27 (December 1984): 7.

74. Bowden and Palmer, "Social Policy," 209–10. See also J. Meyer, "Perspectives on the Reagan Years," in *Perspectives on the Reagan Years,* ed. John L. Palmer (Washington, D.C.: Urban Institute Press, 1986), 67.

75. Musgrave, "Reagan Administration's Fiscal Policy," 130.

76. See Meyer, "Perspectives," 68–70. See also David E. Rosenbaum, "In Four Years, Reagan Changed Basis of the Debate on Domestic Programs," *New York Times,* 25 October 1984, p. Y15.

77. Musgrave, "Reagan Administration's Fiscal Policy," 121.

78. James Tobin, "The Reagan Economic Plan: Supply-Side, Budget and Inflation," in *Supply-Side Economics, A Critical Appraisal,* ed. Richard H. Fink (Frederick, Md.: University Publications of America, 1982), 332ff. See also Musgrave, "Reagan Administration's Fiscal Policy," 128.

79. Paul Craig Roberts, "Where Did All the Keynesians Go?" *New York Times,* 21 December 1982.

80. See Meryl Gordon, "A Keynesian Who Refuses to Quit," *New York Times,* 13 October 1985, p. 28f.

81. Samuelson, "Evaluating Reaganomics," 4.

82. Stein, *Presidential Economics,* 15ff.

83. James Tobin, "The 1982 Economic Report of the President: The Annual Report of the Council of Economic Advisers: Comment" *Journal of Monetary Economics,* November 1982 10 (3), p. 301.

84. James Tobin quoted in Gordon, "Keynesian Who Refuses to Quit."

85. See Robert E. Lucas, Jr., *Models of Business Cycles,* Yrjö Jahnsson Lectures (London: Basil Blackwell, 1987), 103ff.

CHAPTER 5. ECONOMIC ADVICE AND POLICY MAKING

1. Herbert Stein, "The Washington Economics Industry," Papers and Proceedings of the Ninety-eighth Annual Meeting of the American Economic Association, December 1985, *American Economic Review* (hereafter *AER*),76 (May 1986): 5.

2. Irving Fisher, "Economists in Public Service," Presidential Address, Thirty-first Annual Meeting of the American Economic Association, December 1918, *AER* 9, Supplement (March 1919): 5.

3. Leonard D. White, "New Opportunities for Economists and Statisticians in Federal Employment," Papers and Proceedings of the Forty-ninth Annual Meeting of the American Economic Association, December 1936, *AER* 27, Supplement (March 1937): 210.

4. Lauchlin B. Currie (discussant), "The Keynesian Revolution and Its Pioneers," Papers and Proceedings of the Eighty-fourth Annual Meeting of the American Economic Association, December 1971, *AER* 62 (May 1972): 139.

5. Jacob Viner, *Balanced Deflation, Inflation, or More Depression* (Minneapolis: University of Minnesota Press, 1933), 5.

6. Gardner Ackley, "The Role of the Economist as Policy Adviser in the United States," in *Essays in Honour of Guiseppe Ugo Papi* (Padua, Italy: CEDAM, 1971), vol. 2, p. 9.

7. John Maynard Keynes, *The General Theory of Employment Interest and Money* (New York: Harcourt, Brace & Co., 1936), 383.

8. Clair Wilcox, "From Economic Theory to Public Policy," Papers and Proceedings of the Seventy-second Annual Meeting of the American Economic Association, December 1959, *AER* 50 (May 1960): 27ff. See also Sir Alec Cairncross, "Economics in Theory and Practice," Papers and Proceedings of the Ninety-seventh Annual Meeting of the American Economics Association, December 1984, *AER* 75 (May 1985): 5ff.

9. Stein, "Washington Economics Industry," 6.

10. R. G. Lipsey quoted in Gardner Ackley, "Providing Economic Advice to Government," in *Economics in the Public Service: Papers in Honor of Walter W. Heller*, ed. Joseph A. Pechman and N. J. Simler (New York: W. W. Norton, 1982), p. 209.

11. Alice M. Rivlin, "Economics and the Political Process," *AER* 77 (March 1987): 1.

12. Arthur M. Okun, "The Economist and Presidential Leadership," in *Economics for Policymaking, Selected Essays of Arthur M. Okun*, ed. Joseph A. Pechman (Cambridge, Mass.: MIT Press, 1983), 597.

13. Charles L. Schultze, "The Role and Responsibilities of the Economist in Government," Papers and Proceedings of the Ninety-fifth Annual Meeting of the American Economic Association, December 1981, *AER* 72 (May 1982): 62ff.

14. Okun, "Economist and Presidential Leadership," 580.

15. Stein, "Washington Economics Industry," 8.

16. Robert J. Barro (discussant), "Reflections on the Current State of Macroeconomic Theory," Papers and Proceedings of the Ninety-sixth Annual Meeting of the American Economic Association, December 1983, *AER* 74 (May 1984): 416.

17. Herbert Stein, "The Chief Executive as Chief Economist," in *Essays in Contemporary Economic Problems*, William Fellner, Project Director (Washington, D.C.: American Enterprise Institute, 1981), 57.

18. See, for instance, E. Ray Canterbury, *The President's Council of Economic Advisers* (New York: Exposition Press, 1961), *passim;* James Tobin, *National Economic Policy*, (New Haven, Conn.: Yale University Press, 1966), 201ff; Hugh S. Norton, *The Quest for Economic Stability, Roosevelt to Reagan* (Columbia: University of South Carolina Press, 1977) 269ff; and George P. Shultz and Kenneth W. Dam, *Economic Policy beyond the Headlines* (New York: W. W. Norton, 1978), 174ff.

19. Henry A. Kissinger, "The Policymaker and the Intellectual," in *The Presidential Advisory System*, ed. Thomas E. Cronin and Sanford D. Greenberg (New York: Harper and Row, 1969), 165.

20. Tobin, *National Economic Policy*, 203.

21. Walter W. Heller, *New Dimensions of Political Economy* (New York: W. W. Norton, 1967), 2–3.

22. E. Roy Weintraub, *General Equilibrium Analysis, Studies in Appraisal* (Cambridge: Cambridge University Press, 1985), 108ff, 134, 140ff; E. Roy Weintraub, *Microfoundations, The Compatibility of Microeconomics and Macroeconomics* (Cambridge: Cambridge University Press, 1979), 89ff.

23. Mark Blaug, "Paradigms versus Research Programmes in the History of Economics," in *The Philosophy of Economics*, ed. Daniel M. Hausman (Cambridge: Cambridge University Press, 1984), 363, 366ff.

24. See notably Robert Aaron Gordon, "Rigor and Relevance in a Changing Institutional Setting," *AER* 66 (March 1976): 1ff.

25. Gunnar Myrdal, *Against the Stream: Critical Essays in Economics* (New York: Pantheon, 1972), 10, 54, 62, 149. The same thesis is taken over by Robert Kuttner, "The Poverty of Economics," *Atlantic Monthly*, February 1985, p. 76.

26. Robert Lekachman, *Economist at Bay: Why the Experts Will Never Solve Your Problems* (New York: McGraw-Hill, 1976), 207, 266.

27. See Mark Blaug, "A Methodological Appraisal of Radical Economics," in *Methodological Controversy in Economics: Historical Essays in Honor of T. W. Hutchinson*, ed. A. W. Coats, vol. 2 of *Political Economy and Public Policy*, ed. William Briet and Kenneth G. Elzinga (Greenwich, Conn.: Jai Press, 1983), 213.

28. Ibid. See also Tom Riddell, Jean Shackelford, and Steve Stamos, *Economics: A Tool for Understanding Society*, 3d ed. (Reading, Mass.: Addison Wesley, 1987), 40–43.

29. Wassily Leontief, Presidential Address delivered at the Eighty-third Annual Meeting of the American Economic Association, December 1970, *AER* 61 (March 1971): 1ff.

30. Gordon, "Rigor and Relevance," 5.

31. Wassily Leontief, "National Economic Planning," in *The Economic System in an Age of Discontinuity* (New York: New York University Press, 1976), 29, 31.

32. Melville J. Ulmer, "Economics in Decline," *Commentary* 78 (November 1984): 44.

33. Quoted by Weintraub, *General Equilibrium Analysis*, 52.

34. Robert L. Heilbroner, "Introduction," in *Economic Relevance: A Second Look*, ed. Robert L. Heilbroner and Arthur Ford (Pacific Palisades, Calif.: Goodyear Publishing Co., 1976), vii, viii, xii.

35. Donald N. McCloskey, *The Rhetoric of Economics* (Madison: University of Wisconsin Press, 1985), 4.

36. See Ulmer, "Economics in Decline," 42; and Kuttner, "Poverty of Economics," 79. Incidentally, many of these indictments, including the charge that "current economics is unintelligible to the plain man," were circulating in the 1930s. See Barbara Wootton, *Lament for Economics* (London: Allen and Unwin, 1938), 16, 17, 19, 31, 33, and *passim*.

37. Daniel R. Fusfeld, "Post-Post-Keynes: The Shattered Synthesis," in *Economic Relevance*, 44–45.

38. Gordon, "Rigor and Relevance," 10, 11.

39. Lekachman, *Economist at Bay*, 57.

40. David Gordon, "Recession Is Capitalism as Usual," in *Economic Relevance*, 166–67.

41. Walter W. Heller, *The Economy: Old Myths and New Realities* (New York: W. W. Norton, 1976), 174.

42. Keynes, *General Theory*, 32, 378.

43. John Maynard Keynes to R. F. Harrod, 4 July 1938, in *Collected Writings of*

John Maynard Keynes, vol. 14, *The General Theory and After*, ed. Donald Moggridge (London: Macmillan, 1973), Part II, "Defense and Development."

44. Wesley Clair Mitchell, "The Prospects of Economics," in *The Trend of Economics*, ed. Rexford G. Tugwell (New York: Alfred A. Knopf, 1924), 33.

45. The expression is that of Keynes in a letter to R. F. Harrod, 16 July 1938, in *Collected Writings of John Maynard Keynes*, vol. 14.

46. Robert M. Solow, "Is the End of the World at Hand?" in *Economic Relevance*, 115.

47. See notably Harry G. Johnson, "The Economic Approach to Social Questions," *Economica* 35 (February 1968): 1–21.

48. See Charles L. Schultze, "Is Economics Obsolete? No, Underemployed," *Saturday Review*, 22 January 1972, pp. 50ff; and Heilbroner, "Introduction" in *Economic Relevance*, ix.

49. See Gerard Radmitzky and Peter Bernholz, eds., *Economic Imperialism: The Economic Approach Applied outside the Field of Economics* (New York: Paragon House, 1987), vii–ix, 1–18, *passim*.

50. Heller, *New Dimensions of Political Economy*, 3.

51. Milton Friedman, "Have Monetary Policies Failed?" Papers and Proceedings of the Eighty-fourth Annual Meeting of the American Economic Association, December 1971, *AER* 62 (May 1972): 17–18.

52. Heller, *Economy*, 194, 196.

53. Alan S. Blinder, "Keynes Returns after the Others Fail," *New York Times*, 19 February 1984.

54. See Okun, "The Formulation of National Economic Policy," *Economics for Policymaking*, 586–87.

Index

167

LINCOLN CHRISTIAN COLLEGE AND SEMINARY